Contents

Preface

For this edition *Communication in Business* has been revised throughout. Sweeping changes of plan and content have been avoided but there has been considerable modification of detail, partly in response to feedback from students. Some new material has been added. A number of the original exercises have been discarded and fresh ones substituted. All examples have been brought up to date and the effects of postal coding, decimalisation of money, and metrication taken into account.

Communication in Business is not intended to be a comprehensive survey of business communication in all media. It was written for the young man or woman training for entry to the ranks of management in commerce or the nationalised industries and for the young local government officer or civil servant. It concentrates on the aspect of communication most relevant to such a reader – the effective use of language for conveying factual information.

That business efficiency depends upon good communication is now generally accepted; but more than efficiency is involved. In any firm, or organisation, the sense of belonging, of unity with a team, also depends upon communication; and this is something affecting the happiness of everybody working there. The aspects of communication that affect happiness concern management attitudes – willingness to share knowledge possessed; awareness that subordinates need to know more about the job than just how to do it; recognition that communication is two-way and that it is part of the function of management to listen for and respond to suggestions, doubts, criticisms, coming from lower in the chain of command. These are important matters falling outside the scope of this book; but certainly every aspect of communication demands competence in employing the instruments of communication.

The English language is the principal instrument of communication of the English business man, civil servant, and local government officer. The author's aim is that the young man who uses this book will afterwards be able to speak, write, and read his own language with sufficient accuracy and ease to ensure that he is an effective communicator at least in everything to do with his work.

Part I of *Communication in Business* considers the basic principles of good communication by means of language; Part II deals with written applications of these principles in the business world; Part III with oral applications. Part IV consists of a group of passages (on themes relevant either to communication or to business studies) to provide practice in the accurate reception of written communication, together with four statistical tables to provide practice in receiving non-verbal communication and interpreting this verbally.

Two assumptions are made about those using this book. These are:

1. That they are young adults, either employed already in offices and seeking qualifications that will eventually lead to managerial positions, or undertaking a full-time course of instruction at a technical college with a view to a business career.

2. That they have a reasonable command of the English language (to approximately the standard of 'O' level).

It might be thought that another assumption is made – that all readers of this book are of the same sex – but it is for convenience only that the author alludes always to the business *man* and uses masculine pronouns throughout when referring to the reader.

Although the primary intention in preparing this book has been that it should be used in conjunction with an English course at a technical college, the possibility that it may also be used by students working on their own, or even by those already in managerial positions who wish to improve their command of language for communication purposes, has not been overlooked; all the exposition, and nearly all the exercises, will prove adaptable to private study.

The author has sought to make this a practical book that will be of value to the young man employed in an office whenever his daily work requires him to communicate. At the same time he recognises that most of those using it will have as an examination target a paper called 'English' not 'Communication'. The requirements of examining bodies at the post 'O' level stage of English have therefore also been borne in mind. *Communication in Business* provides an adequate preparation for the following examinations, the syllabuses and past papers for which have been consulted:

Ordinary National Certificate in Business Studies Year II, English

Ordinary National Diploma in Business Studies Year II, English

Ordinary National Certificate in Public Administration Year I, English

The London Chamber of Commerce, Private Secretary's Certificate/ Diploma, English

National Distribution Certificate, Communication

Royal Society of Arts, English Language Stage III and similar examinations of the regional examining boards

Intermediate professional examinations such as those of the Institute of Bankers, the Chartered Institute of Secretaries, the Corporation of Secretaries, the Institute of Transport.

With supplementary material, it can also be used as a preparation for the 'Use of English' examinations of the Local Government Training Board (Clerical and Intermediate) and for 'Communication' for the Higher Certificate in Office Studies.

The names and addresses of individuals, firms and organisations used in examples and exercises in this book are fictitious. Any resemblance to the name and address of an existing individual, firm or organisation is coincidental.

These fictitious addresses have been arbitrarily allocated postcodes which may in fact be the postcodes of existing areas or even specific addresses but which for the purpose of this book refer only to the fictitious addresses.

Acknowledgements

The author and his publishers are indebted to the following for permission to quote copyright material:

George Allen & Unwin Ltd for material from *Theory of Leisure Class* by T. Veblen; Edward Arnold (Publishers) Ltd for material from *The Science of Wealth* by C. P. Carter; the *Association of Teachers in Technical Institutions* for an extract from an Association document; Chatto and Windus Ltd for material from *The Long Revolution* by Raymond Williams; the author and The Guardian for an article by Judith Cook published in *The Guardian* 28 October 1963; The Daily Telegraph for part of an article by Norman Selwyn published in *The Daily Telegraph* 25 October 1968 and part of an article by Patrick Davies and a graph published 26 February 1969; *Encounter* for an extract from a questionnaire; Heinemann Educational Books Ltd for material from *Exploration in Management* by Wilfred Brown; the Controller of H.M.S.O. for material from *Monthly Digest of Statistics* and '*15–18*' *Report of the Central Advisory Council of Education (England)*; Hodder & Stoughton Ltd for material from *The Story of My Life* by Helen Keller; the *Journal of the Institute of the Motor Industry* for an extract from an article by Donald Lockyer from Vol. 5 No. 1, January 1969; *Journal of the Royal Society of Arts* for a statistical table, originally derived from the Bureau International d'Education, Geneva; the author and the Society of Industrial Artists and Designers for an article by L. J. Lickorish published in the *Journal* of the Society of Industrial Artists and Designers; the Editor of *The Manager* for an article published in *The Manager*; John Murray (Publishers) Ltd and Houghton Mifflin Company for material from *Inlaws and Outlaws* by C. Northcote Parkinson; the author and Granada TV for material from *Man to Man* by Eric Nixon; the author for material from an article by F. S. Northedge published in *The Listener*; The Observer Ltd for an extract from an article by Professor Colin Buchanan, published in *The Observer*; Penguin Books Ltd for material from *Language in the Modern World* by Simeon Potter; Sir Isaac Pitman & Sons Ltd for material from *Some Reflections on Genius* by Lord Russell Brain; Routledge & Kegan Paul Ltd and McGraw-Hill Book Co. Inc., for an extract from *Understanding Media* by Marshall McLuhan, Copyright © by Marshall McLuhan; and the following examining bodies for extracts from examination papers – the Corporation of Secretaries, the London Chamber of Commerce, the Royal Society of Arts, the Local Government Training Board.

Part I

Chapter 1

Introduction

1. THE MEANING OF 'COMMUNICATION'

Communication is a chameleon of a word, changing the colour of its meaning with the speaker or the listener more than most. The historian thinks of an army's 'lines of communication'; the civil engineer thinks of roads and railway lines, but the electronic engineer thinks of telegrams and telephone lines; the sociologist thinks of newspapers and broadcasting. For many English business men it is still probably most familiar in the obsolescent context: 'Your communication of the 15th inst. has been received', where it is Edwardian jargon for a letter or, more broadly, a message.

There is a common element in the various meanings, the idea of connection between people (communication between animals also exists, of course, but is a subject for specialised study outside the scope of this book), and – originally at least – connection with the purpose of passing on information, a message. The word can refer to the message itself, the channel along which the message is passed, or the act of message-passing.

The postwar period has seen a striking revival in the use of *communication* to refer particularly to the act of message-passing or, more precisely, *the process by which information is passed between individuals or organisations by means of previously agreed symbols*. It is in this sense that the word is used throughout this book.

There are many systems of such symbols in use apart from verbal languages (for example mathematics, mime, and such devices as international road signs) but it is obvious that for most people words, in the form of the mother tongue, constitute by far the most frequently employed system. There is much more to communication than the language in which it is expressed, but the most effective use of language (the English language since it is intended for Englishmen) is the limited target of this book. To quote the earliest use of the word in this sense that the compilers of the *Oxford Dictionary* discovered (Locke 1690), the intention is 'to make words serviceable to the end of good Communication'.

II. COMMUNICATION PATTERNS IN FIRMS

Every firm, or similar organisation, depends for its daily functioning upon an intricate communication network which has grown up during the years and has proved itself indispensable. The bigger the firm is, the more elaborate the system must be, and the greater the likelihood of expensive and time-wasting mistakes caused through misunderstandings. The precise form of the network will vary from firm to firm, but something of its complexity in a fairly large firm can be appreciated from the following diagrams; and it must be remembered that every practical network will be very much more complicated than it appears in a simplified diagram.

A. Vertical internal communication

The instructions of management moving downwards through a firm and reports passing upwards to management will both follow the authority line of the firm. Fig. 1 shows in broadest outline, a structure applicable to most firms and similar organisations. Only the largest require the intermediate levels of middle management and first line supervision.

Fig. 1

It is important to realise that the titles given to employees do not necessarily reveal their level on the line of authority. Some firms may have an Office Manager who is considered equal to other departmental managers but other firms will consider this rank equivalent only to a supervisor's. The Sales Manager may be either equal in level with, or superior to, the Office Manager in the same firm. The Works Manager may be equal to either, or superior to both in the type of firm where this is the title of the principal executive (who is most commonly called Managing Director).

Each department will have an authority and communication chain of its own; as many as a dozen such chains may come together at the departmental manager's level. An Office Manager with departmental manager ranking may have beneath him a chain like that shown in Fig. 2.

Fig. 2

This is, of course, a simplified diagram – only the costing section's network is shown in any detail – but considered with Fig. 1 it will give some impression of the complexity of the vertical communication channels that follow the line of authority.

Running parallel with these channels is another communication line provided by the existence within the firm of a staff association or branches of professional associations and trade unions. The representatives from these usually constitute the only intermediate stage between management and rank-and-file on this line. Part of a firm's total communication will pass up and down this line also. Deciding what communication material is more appropriate to the authority line, what to that of the staff representatives, and what should preferably be passed down both lines, is a major problem for management; but similar decisions have also to be made by a clerk or operative wishing to pass upwards through his firm a comment, a suggestion, a complaint.

It will be seen then that the total vertical communication network within a large firm will be exceedingly complex.

B. *Horizontal internal communication*

There will also be interdepartmental exchanges of information at several
levels of the vertical system. These will take the form of conversations,
both direct and by telephone, together with internal memos and reports.
A factory may have a horizontal organisation rather like that shown in
Fig. 3.

Fig. 3

C. *External communication*

Thus we may picture a firm as, at all times of the working day, pulsing
with messages transmitted vertically, both up and down, and horizontally
across the organisation. But this is only the internal situation; every firm
will also be linked with the outside world – customers, suppliers, government departments, branches, subsidiaries etc. A diagram of this communication pattern would look rather like a child's drawing of the sun,
with channels of communication radiating out from, and converging upon,
the firm, like spokes of a wheel.

III. THE ACT OF COMMUNICATION

These then are the principal patterns of a firm's communication channels.
When a message is sent along the channel there will be somebody to send
it and somebody to receive it. It is convenient to borrow from electronics
the terms *Tx* (Transmitter) and *Rx* (Receiver) to represent as broadly as
possible these two essential components of the act of communication. A
channel exists when access to the Rx is provided for the Tx. When the
channel is used, the message has to be transmitted by some *medium*.

The medium, if a verbal language medium, may be spoken or written.
If spoken, it may be direct face-to-face conversation, or a talk given to a
group, or indirect equivalents through electronic devices such as the tele-

Fig. 4

phone, a loudspeaker system, or a dictating machine. If written, it may take the form of a printed, typed, or handwritten document, or an electronically generated document such as a telegram or Telex message. Written documents range from scribbled notes pinned on to a man's desk in his absence – through internal memos, letters, minutes, abstracts, reports – to printed publicity, user handbooks, and technical manuals.

To be fully effective, communication must be two-way. To borrow another term from electronics, *feedback* must be provided from Rx to Tx (i.e. there must be some way in which the response of the Rx can be perceived by the Tx and the latter's message modified to suit this response). It will be seen that one of the principal advantages of spoken communication over written is speed of feedback – the Rx can ask questions of the Tx to clarify the message further and can also often immediately make the response that the Tx requires when the Tx is asking for information instead of passing it on.

In such a case the roles of Tx and Rx interchange as the conversation continues. Similarly the roles interchange when a message is passed down or up a vertical internal communication channel. The man who receives a message from above is an Rx then, but becomes a Tx as soon as he passes the information on to his subordinate.

IV. COMMUNICATION DIFFICULTIES IN FIRMS

Undoubtedly the most important distortions and misunderstandings occur in vertical communication, especially where messages shift between the oral and the written. Policy changes arising from a decision of the Board may well be transmitted to his departmental managers by the Managing Director orally. They in turn will probably pass down to their supervisors relevant parts of this information in the form of written instructions. These in turn will be passed on orally to the men actually doing the job. There is very likely to be a distortion of the message at each of these stages unless all concerned are proficient communicators. Middle management and/or first line supervision levels mean additional stages at which distortion may occur.

The man halfway up the ladder of management spends the best part of his working day alternating between Rx and Tx roles, receiving messages from both above and below, and frequently changing these from oral to written and vice versa. He has to be a very good communicator indeed. This man is quite likely in the future to be you.

The outstanding criticism that can be directed at the horizontal communication of most firms and organisations is simply that there is not enough of it. Departments tend to work in watertight compartments and do not make sufficient effort to let each other know what they are doing. Even at departmental management level there is often inadequate discussion of common problems and interchange of ideas; at lower levels very little horizontal communication exists at all. Where horizontal communication does take place it is much less liable to distortion and misunderstanding than is vertical communication. Much of it is by face-to-face discussion or telephone conversations, and these have the advantage of immediate feedback if there is misunderstanding. There is no difference in rank between Rx and Tx, and this makes for ease and confidence in exchanges of information.

External communication presents the special difficulty that the person at the other end of the communication channel is often somebody you know very little about and whose communication methods you have no control over. Much of it is carried on by letter, with delayed feedback (waiting for the Rx's reply), and misunderstandings can take a long time to clear up. A considerable demand is therefore made on communication skills in external communication; it is more difficult than the average business man often realises to express yourself clearly and unambiguously to a distant correspondent while at the same time making him feel that you are friendly and cooperative in your attitude (as you must do when your letter is the link between your firm and a customer or supplier, for example). Being at the receiving end of external communication is not easy either; much of the material you will have to read is difficult to understand either by virtue of the complexity of its subject matter or – more often – because of the communication weaknesses of your correspondent. The good communicator, when he is the Rx, does his best to make up for inadequacies in his Tx.

V. LANGUAGE AND COMMUNICATION

It will be seen from the preceding sections that communication in business is complex and difficult. The tendency all the time is toward larger business units; size brings economies and greater efficiency in some directions, but it accentuates the communication problem. The bigger the firm, the bigger the problem. Every manager and potential manager today needs to give extremely serious thought to how he can improve his efficiency as a communicator.

So far as the use of language is concerned you can study to improve your abilities as a communicator in four ways:

1. as an Rx of speech
2. as an Rx of writing
3. as a Tx of speech
4. as a Tx of writing.

1. You must be able to *listen*. Listening is active not passive. The spoken words must receive the concentrated attention; distractions in the room, personal discomfort, noise, etc., must be overcome by an act of will. Few people can listen for more than a few minutes without loss of concentration. You should remember that when you are a Tx. When you are the Rx you must fight to maintain your receptivity. Never merely wait till the other man stops talking so that you can say your piece. Try to sort out and systematise what he says as he speaks. If he is speaking for a long time and the material is complex, make notes; this will not only provide a record for future reference but help you to keep concentrating.

2. Your efficiency as an Rx of writing depends upon your general command of language, but especially upon your width of vocabulary and your capacity to pick out the essential from what you read and to summarise and classify it as you read. Your reading speed is also relevant. Reading speeds can vary between as slow as fewer than 200 words a minute and as fast as 800 words a minute, though the average performance is much nearer the lower level. Clearly the faster you can read, and still absorb the subject matter, the more efficient you are as an Rx. Increasing reading speed falls outside this book; but précis work and close study of difficult passages of prose will improve your skills as an Rx of writing.

3. When you are transmitting by the use of spoken language, a clear strong voice is necessary. An accent that makes it difficult to understand what you say or that annoys the Rx by emphasising class or regional differences is a handicap. The ability to think on your feet and form accurate sentences while you are speaking is essential – not only for public speaking but also for such everyday matters as dictating letters. Hesitations reduce the speed at which you are effectively communicating and irritate the Rx, with resultant loss of concentration. Chapter 13 of this book is intended to help you with these points.

4. As a Tx of writing the demand on you is greatest of all. The first

task is to think clearly so that you really know what you want to say; much muddled communication arises not from a failure of expression at all but from an original uncertainty in the mind of the communicator. Next you will need to arrange the material logically and express it clearly and unambiguously in accurate English, choosing your words to suit the probable vocabulary level of your Rx and a tone to suit the subject matter. Sentence length, and even paragraph length, may also have to be modified to suit the intelligence and educational standard of your Rx. *Know your Rx and suit your expression to him* is a basic tenet of communication and applies to speaking as well as writing. This means a rethinking of your use of English. The kind of English required is different from that which you employ in examination essays, for example, because your aims are different. Your aims in business are not literary; you are not trying to show how beautifully you can write, how wide your vocabulary, how varied your sentence structure – you are adapting your language to the capacity of the Rx and your intention is first to make sure he understands you and second to make him feel cooperative towards you.

The first four stages in communication when you are the Tx, for both writing and speaking, might be summed up as:

1. Think clearly
2. Arrange logically
3. Express clearly
4. Use appropriate language.

To these should be added:

5. Express concisely.

Conciseness is most desirable but should never be obtained at the cost of clarity or appropriateness; you should think of these five points in fact as in descending order of importance. They are returned to in detail in the next five chapters.

'Correctness' has not been mentioned. For communication purposes, formal correctness of grammar is of subordinate importance. Some constructions which have been considered incorrect in the past do not confuse meaning and are so widely established by usage that it is doubtful if they can any longer be classed as incorrect. Nevertheless, many errors of syntax[1] are direct causes of vague or ambiguous meanings. Even where meaning is not affected, faults of this kind may distract, or even antagonise, the Rx who is aware that they are faults. Sound syntax is therefore an

---

[1] *Syntax*: that part of grammar that deals with the construction of sentences and the arrangement of words within the sentence.

important aim of the conscientious communicator, and he will also wish to avoid handling his words in such a way that he offends against educated usage (see Chapter 4).

'Good style' has also not been mentioned. There will be very few occasions in business where conscious attention to style will be of any advantage to the communicator. Nevertheless, the writer who at all times has as his target clarity of expression in the minimum number of words will inevitably over the years develop a crisp and economical style, suited to its purpose and therefore 'good'.

Chapter 2

First Thinking

I. INTRODUCTION

The first step towards clear communication is to have the material to be communicated clear in your own mind; until you are sure that you know what you want to say there is no point in starting to say it. This would seem obvious enough; yet failure to act upon this truism is probably the commonest cause of communication breakdown.

The second step is to find a method of organisation for your material that will enable you to present it to your Rx in a coherent and logical form, according to a predetermined plan.

In spoken communication we are often called upon to speak under circumstances that do not permit more than the most hasty examination and organisation of our ideas on the subject, but when we write we always have time for *preparation* and *planning*, and this is an advantage that should not be wasted. In the pages that follow, preparation and planning are considered from the point of view of the writing Tx. Similar principles apply, wherever circumstances permit, to the speaking Tx.

II. PREPARATION

Preparation may involve the gathering of material from other documents, from personal interviews and telephone conversations, from our own existing knowledge of the subject, and from tests and experiments that we devise, together with the evaluation and interpretation of this material; or it may be merely a matter of sitting for a moment trying to sharpen the focus of what is in one's mind. This sharpening stage must never be omitted because if we start with a woolly idea we shall communicate only a woolly idea. An outstanding aid to clear thinking about your material is awareness of *purpose*. In a work context every document will have a purpose; this may be (1) to supply or request information, (2) to produce action or reaction, or (3) to persuade; or it may be a combination of these.

It is as well to state the purpose to yourself – 'I am writing this letter so that this customer will not develop a lasting grudge against the firm' or 'I am preparing this report so that Mr Thompson can explain exactly what my section has been working on when he attends the Sales Conference next week.' If purpose is brought into the open in this specific way there is much less chance of your producing in the first situation a pompous piece of face-saving that disgusts the customer, or in the second an inflated piece of empire-building that infuriates Thompson by its irrelevancies and unnecessary length.

At the preparation stage you should also try to *know your Rx*. The more you can bring to life the man who is going to read what you write, the better you will communicate. Often you will, of course, already know him quite well, as he is a member of your organisation, or you have had previous dealings with him, but much more frequently you will have to create your knowledge of him, by the use of imagination working upon such clues as a letter he has sent, or how he sounded over the telephone, or your previous experience of the kind of man to whom you have to send this particular type of document. Ideally you will need to know, or estimate, these things about the Rx:

1. His/her sex
2. His/her rank in his/her organisation compared with yours (if relevant)
3. His/her educational standard
4. His/her intelligence level
5. His/her knowledge of the subject you are writing about
6. How your document will affect him/her.

The degree of simplification which you apply to your subject matter, the kind of vocabulary you will employ, even your length of sentence – all will be controlled by the picture you form at this stage.

By combining purpose with your picture of the Rx, you are now in a position to apply to your material the *test for relevance*. This consists in asking for each piece of your material: 'Is this essential to the document, bearing in mind the document's purpose and the kind of man who is going to read it?' Only where the answer is a confident 'Yes' should the material be included. This is a severe test, but it is easy to lose all sense of what is relevant if you do not apply it strictly. Testing for relevance is not easy and probably you will make errors of judgment from time to time. It is better that these should take the form of omitting subject matter that later turns out to have been relevant after all than that you should give the benefit of the doubt to every borderline piece of material.

The sense of relevance can be developed by practice. You will find précis-writing a valuable aid and you should practice further by checking the relevance of everything you write, and – as often as you can remember

to – what you read as well. The smaller news items in newspapers frequently include irrelevant facts; picking these out can be good sport and
excellent training.

III. PLANNING

Planning is necessary with every piece of communication of any length or
complexity, if it is to appear coherent and logical to the Rx. Planning
consists of two stages:
1. devising a system of organisation for the material
2. deciding the most effective order of presentation.
The plan is not always written down, but all successful communication of
material of any complexity has careful planning behind it. The experienced
communicator can often carry the plan in his head, but you are advised to
get down on paper at least your principal section divisions and proposed
order of presentation.

A. The principle of unity

Organisation of written communication depends upon breaking up the
total material into logical divisions so that the material can be supplied
to the reader by instalments. These divisions may be indicated by chapters,
in a book, or section headings, in a report, or, in shorter work, by change
of paragraph. Clearly in longer work there will be subdivisions as well
as the principal divisions.

The reader thus has breathing space between sections, in which to
assimilate what he has received and prepare for the next stage. But he will
gain full advantage from the breathing space only if he can feel that he has
at that point reached the end of something which is complete in itself.
Thus every division of a piece of writing, whether as long as a chapter or as
short as a paragraph, should possess *unity*. In fact the principle of unity
must be observed throughout the document, because on the one hand the
entire piece of writing must be felt by the reader as a unity, as one thing
not a mixture, and on the other, each sentence must have unity.

The principle of unity is closely connected with testing for relevance,
and practice in the latter will make you unlikely to offend against the
former. It is not sufficient for two matters to be closely connected for
unity to be achieved; they must also be of the same kind. In the sentence
frequently used by schoolmasters to demonstrate breach of unity:
Cromwell was a great general and had warts on his nose, both statements
are about Cromwell but they are so dissimilar in kind that we instinctively
feel they are ridiculous together.

Breaches of unity in whole sections of a document are not so obvious as those in single sentences. We guard against them most successfully by dividing our work up according to a system, and letting the reader see what our system is. We reveal our system by:

1. an introduction explaining the method to be used; or
2. headings to the sections; or
3. topic sentences to the paragraphs; or
4. a combination of these methods.

The most useful basis for such a system of division, for factual material of the kind that is most frequently handled in business communication, is derived from either *classification* or *analysis*, or a combination of these.

B. Classification and analysis

When we classify material we organise it into groups according to a governing principle, or criterion. Thus a book on wild flowers may classify the flowers by colour and have one section on yellow flowers, another on white flowers, and so on. Or the flowers may be classified as perennials, annuals, biennials, etc., the criterion here being the plant's life cycle. Or they may be classified according to their method of reproduction. More scientifically, they could be classified according to their botanical families – compositae, rosaceae, leguminosae, umbelliferae, cruciferae, etc.

Again, various criteria could be applied in classifying the students of a technical college – sex, department, nationality, etc. – but only one criterion can be applied at one time. A valid classification of these students could be based on whether they are full-time or part-time students, in which case a subdivision of the latter group between day and evening would probably also be made. Written out in the form most useful when planning a document this would appear as:

College students
1. Full-time
2. Part-time: *a* Day; *b* Evening.

An alternative organisation of the same material, equally sound, would be:

College students
1. Full-time
2. Part-time day
3. Part-time evening.

When material is divided into classes all the material should be used up. Similarly when a class is subdivided, the subsection should use up all the material in the class.

If A is divided into B, C, Ɖ and E, then B + C + D + E must equal A. Thus the arrangement:

College students
1. Full-time
2. Evening

is unsound because it overlooks part-time day students and the parts do not add up to the whole.

The opposite fault occurs in the arrangement:

College students
1. Full-time
2. Part-time
3. Overseas

where the introduction of a second criterion of classification (i.e. whether British or overseas in origin) results in the parts adding up to more than the whole since overseas students will already have been included in the previous two categories.

The value of classification to the communicator is that it enables him to make logical divisions of his material by the application of criteria relevant to his purpose. The resultant groupings become chapters, sections, or paragraphs, according to the scale of the piece of communication. Subdivisions of the main groups are made, and further subdivisions as necessary, so that the same technique of organisation is applied to smaller and smaller units of the final work.

Although only one basis of classification can be employed at a time, there are occasions when it is desirable to classify material according to a succession of criteria. Thus at the beginning of Chapter 9 of this book reports are classified first by content, then as routine or special, then by length, and finally by form.

The method can be applied only to material which is multiple by nature (wild flowers, students, reports). Material which is single by nature (the smaller-flowered goat's-beard, J. J. Smith's academic ability, a report on the new comptometer) must be divided by analysis, i.e. splitting it up into those parts that together make up the whole.

Thus in the description of an appliance we divide it into component parts; in writing the account of a transaction we divide into stages; in explaining a process we break it down into steps. Again we must take care to check that the total of the parts is equal to the whole and that nothing has been left out inadvertently. Sometimes, for the sake of simplification or for lack of space, some minor parts of the material analysed are deliberately omitted but on such occasions the introductory wording should be modified to include such a phrase as : *The principal component parts are . . .*, or *The most important stages of this transaction can be listed as . . .*

Having decided on the principal divisions and subdivisions of the material for communication you should make a note of these in the form of headings and subheadings and then apply yourself to deciding the best *order of presentation* both for the main divisions and for the secondary material within those divisions.

C. Order of presentation

Most business communication material starts with an introduction and ends with a conclusion, though these may be very brief. The main body between is what presents the greatest difficulty in deciding in what order to present the material now arranged into logical groups.

1. The INTRODUCTION establishes what the Rx is to hear about and provides necessary background information – in short, *what? who? where? when?* In more formal documents, such as reports, it also makes clear the principle upon which the body of the work is arranged. The preface to this book illustrates this use of an introduction.

2. The CONCLUSION sums up what has gone before or makes a final appeal to the reader. In short informal communication some friendly message is sometimes used to round off the note or memo.

A conclusion is not indispensable. The kind of report, for instance, that provides a summary of findings at the beginning needs no conclusion.

3. The MAIN BODY of the material frequently reveals itself wholly or partially as a succession of steps or stages of a kind that inevitably lead to each other – the reader must understand A before he can grasp B, and C will make no sense unless he knows about B; therefore the order must be: A, B, C. A natural sequence of this kind must take precedence over any other.

However, only a proportion of communication material reveals a natural order of this kind, and it is not common for it to be applicable to every part of our material. In reporting on apprentice unrest in a factory it is natural to detail the extent of the unrest before listing the causes and the causes before the recommendations for their correction. But in what order are the causes to be presented?

Five main methods are used for deciding the order of presentation of material lacking a natural logical sequence :

a. Chronological order
b. Spatial order

    c. Descending order of importance
    d. Ascending order of importance
    e. Ascending order of complexity

or a combination of these five may be employed.

    a. CHRONOLOGICAL ORDER refers to the order in which events took place or in which they were observed. Its simplicity commends it, but unfortunately only a limited amount of communication material in business has a clear time sequence; even then it is only where the happenings to be narrated or the observations to be recorded are of approximately equal importance also that this is the best order of arrangement. Where there is an element of repetition in the material (e.g. what is observed at 18.00 hours is the same as was previously observed at 16.00 and 14.00), it is an unsatisfactory method.

    b. SPATIAL ORDER refers to the organisation of material on such a basis as north to south, or outside to inside, or front to back, or left to right. Again, where all material is of approximately the same importance (as, for example, a trading report on a company whose area is divided into geographical sectors which have all had very similar results that year) it is a useful method. Repetition material tends to be annoying with this system too.

    c. DESCENDING ORDER OF IMPORTANCE is probably the most useful device, though it will often need to be combined with methods *a* or *b*. This would be the method for deciding the order for the causes of apprentice unrest in the report mentioned above – the most important cause would be dealt with first, and the least important last.

    d. ASCENDING ORDER OF IMPORTANCE is principally a literary device to build up suspense and a sense of climax. It is valuable in planning essays, but is inappropriate for letters and reports, where the aim is certainly not to create suspense. It is also very important to use this method in presenting a succession of arguments. We expect in argument or oratory to be led up to a climax. If our expectation is disappointed we experience anticlimax, and the communicator's efforts have been wasted.

    e. ASCENDING ORDER OF COMPLEXITY is a particularly suitable order for explication (i.e. communication where the Tx's principal purpose is to explain something with which the Rx is unfamiliar). It is a method frequently used in this book. It is commonsense to arrange to put the simplest aspect of the subject matter in front of the Rx before proceeding to the more complex. A variant on this method is to proceed from the familiar to the unfamiliar. By starting with what the Rx knows best, you start with what he will find simplest.

The order of presentation will be finally selected on a basis of the considerations enumerated above, but will also be influenced by the purpose of the piece of communication and the qualities of the Rx, especially his previous knowledge of the subject.

Your previous note of the principal divisions and subdivisions of your subject matter should now be written out again in the form of an *outline plan* in the order you have decided upon, with indications to yourself of how you intend to start and finish. The following example illustrates how the principles discussed can be employed in the preparation of an office document.

IV. EXAMPLE

Outline plan for a directive on office organisation

A. Introduction
1. The need to improve office organisation.
2. Subject to be treated under three main heads - communications, filing, duplicating.

B. Communications
1. Letters in.
2. Letters out.
3. Telephones
4. Messenger service
5. Public address system.

C. Filing
1. Effects of change to centralised filing.
2. Redeployment of filing equipment.
3. Improvement of classification methods.
4. Agreed storage periods.
5. Security.

D. Duplicating
1. Spirit duplicating.
2. Stencils.
3. Photocopying.

E. Conclusion
1. Appeal to all staff to cooperate in improving office efficiency.
2. Stress the importance of the individual in making the reorganisation work.

V. EXERCISES

Exercise A

You are attempting to explain cricket to an American who has never seen the game played. What would be the best order for the following topics: the object of the batting side; how the result of the match is decided; the toss; how a batsman is out; the pitch; the object of the bowling side; the number of players; equipment required; how runs are scored?

Exercise B

By what criteria can the following be classified? Try to find as many different bases of classification as possible for each: cricketers; photographic films; books; typewriters; newspapers.

Exercise C

Analyse the following, and arrange the parts in logical order: a cricket bat; a book (physical components); a newspaper (content); driving out of a garage; opening a current account.

Exercise D

The following points were noted when Site 12 on Ridge Trading Estate was inspected with a view to building a new factory there for Adpress Engineering of Bandham.

  a. Rearrange them in sections under section headings.
  b. Indicate the order in which you would put these sections in a report.
  c. Indicate the order in which you would put the points in each section.

As the points are numbered there is no need to write them out.

  1. Working population (male), 30 km radius Ridge, 24 600
  2. Site 12 well drained, gravel sub soil
  3. Ridge Estate 30 km from port of Seamouth
  4. Skilled operatives would have to be brought from Bandham
  5. Electricity to site
  6. A111 passes through Ridge. Bandham 140 km
  7. Estate in development area, so government grant possible
  8. Site 150 m from A111, cinder road connecting
  9. Plentiful supply of unskilled female labour locally
  10. Three local building firms of adequate size for factory building, so local tenders possible
  11. Housing shortage in area
  12. Map reference, Ridge Estate, O.S. 163: SS 4943
  13. Station, Ridge, goods only

14. B road – Ridge/Seamouth
15. Water mains and sewers to site
16. Rail – Ridge/Seamouth
17. Unemployment figure (male) for area 6 per cent, mostly unskilled or semi-skilled
18. Hostel necessary for accommodation of workers from Bandham
19. Site slopes 1 in 14, north to south
20. Railway siding to site, connecting with line, Ridge/Seamouth
21. Site 12 one of three sites still unoccupied on estate, and only one suitable in size for our purposes
22. Suitable site for hostel available 0·8 km north-east of Site 12
23. Ridge Estate 1·2 km south-east of Ridge on A111.

Exercise E

Here is a letter about central heating systems. You will find it difficult to follow because the writer has no plan; he moves from topic to topic just as the points come into his head. Read it through several times and then prepare the outline plan that the author should have used.

Dear Harry,

You asked me to let you have an outline of what sort of choice there is in central heating systems today. One of the more unusual ideas is underfloor heating by electricity. This is convenient, but expensive to install and electricity is an expensive fuel.

Gas-fired boilers are popular, especially with ducted warm air systems, although gas is more expensive than electricity. Of course, you can have conventional hot water radiators from a gas boiler as well, or a ducted warm air system from a solid fuel boiler or oil-burning boiler. These oil-fired boilers are popular as they do not need stoking or raking and the fuel is easily delivered. The same advantage applies to the gas-fired boiler. A large storage tank is required for the oil and this can be difficult to find room for, or unsightly. At the same time it must be remembered that considerable storage space is necessary for solid fuels too, if you are not to be left without fuel during that part of the winter when demand is very heavy. This is the advantage of electricity and gas – no storage problem. However, both these supplies have been subject to cuts in very severe weather, and solid fuel has the further advantage of being comparatively cheap. Oil is also a much cheaper fuel than gas or electricity, though oil-fired boilers are dearer than gas or solid fuel boilers. The total installation cost will depend largely upon whether hot water radiators or warm air ducting is selected.

The cheapest installation of all is to put electric oil-filled radiators in every room of the house. Electricity is expensive, however; although you would have the opportunity to switch the appliance off quickly when not required which is not possible with boilers. However, boilers should not be very wasteful of fuel as they are thermostatically controlled. One method of reducing the running costs of electricity is to employ storage heaters that use off-peak electricity at a lower cost to supply heat when you require it next day. They are much dearer than ordinary electric radiators but do not require piping or air ducts as boiler systems do. Modern small bore piping systems with a pump to improve circulation are efficient and unobtrusive, but some people prefer warm air ducting. Such systems tend to be a little noisy as they are fan-forced. Electricity has the advantage of complete silence and cleanliness. Hot water systems are subject to noise in the piping if not installed with very great care.

Some solid fuel boilers have automatic hoppers thus reducing their previous disadvantages while raising the cost of the boiler to about the same as a gas boiler. A gas boiler has the advantage of cleanliness and freedom from daily maintenance problems, as has the oil-fired boiler.

Some gas boilers have a very efficient automatic device which prevents use of the boiler at times when heating is not required.

I think this covers the principal methods. I hope you have sufficient information now to enable you to come to a decision.

Yours sincerely,
JACK

Exercise F

In each of the following rearrange the sentences (or sections of sentences) so that they seem to you to be in logical order and explain your reasons for the order you select. As the sentences are lettered there is no need to write them out.

1.

a. Someone was drawing water and my teacher placed my hand under the spout.

b. I knew then that 'w-a-t-e-r' meant the wonderful cool something that was flowing over my hand.

c. There were barriers still, it is true, but barriers that could in time be swept away!

d. That living word awakened my soul, gave it light, hope, joy, set it free!

e. Suddenly I felt a misty consciousness as of something forgotten – a thrill of returning thought; and somehow the mystery of language was revealed to me.

f. We walked down the path to the well-house, attracted by the fragrance of the honeysuckle with which it was covered.

g. I stood still, my whole attention fixed upon the motions of her fingers.

h. As the cool stream gushed over one hand she spelled into the other the word *water*, first slowly, then rapidly.

2.

a. The community needed (and, of course, still needs) men who could read and write, conduct complicated business, sing elaborate music, build cathedrals, lead armies, frame and administer laws.

b. – to provide for the children of the poor something of what the benefactor acknowledged to be his duty to supply for his own children.

c. The visitor to an old parish church will often see on the walls a list of parish charities and among them, often enough, gifts for the education of the poor

d. To meet this need there were founded schools so that 'there may never be wanting a succession of persons duly qualified to serve God in church and state'.

e. Entangled here, as always, are the twin conceptions of education.

f. – his gift was a form of capital investment.

g. And so, today, as the methods by which wealth is produced become ever more complicated, new colleges are founded that the supply of men trained in their operation and development may not fail.

h. Look at it one way and the gifts are designed as a form of social service

i. But from another point of view, he was indirectly providing for a supply of craftsmen to maintain the wealth of the community

j. or for enabling orphans or poor boys to be apprenticed to a good trade.

3.

a. No young novelist should ever dare to imitate the style of Dickens.

b. Of Dickens's style it is impossible to speak in praise.

c. But the critic is driven to feel the weakness of his criticism, when he acknowledges to himself – as he is compelled in all honesty to do – that with the language, such as it is, the writer has satisfied the great mass of readers of his country.

d. If such a one wants a model for his language, let him take Thackeray.

e. Both these great writers have satisfied the readers of their own pages; but both have done infinite harm by creating a school of imitators.

f. To readers who have taught themselves to regard language, it must therefore be unpleasant.

g. It is jerky, ungrammatical, and created by himself in defiance of rules – almost as completely as that created by Carlyle.

Exercise G

Prepare an outline plan on the work of (*a*) the BBC or (*b*) the Post Office or (*c*) your local technical college.

Chapter 3

Clear Wording 1
(Problems of Semantics)

I. THE VERBAL COMMUNICATION PROCESS

A perfect act of communication takes place when the idea in the mind of the Tx is transferred, unchanged, into the mind of the Rx. *Idea* is here used very broadly, to include a piece of information, a question, an appeal, an order etc. as well as the more usual meaning of 'a notion or concept'.

To communicate by means of words the Tx codes his idea into words (or, frequently, recodes it, as it is in words of some kind already) and transmits these words by speech or writing. The act of communication has not taken place, however, until the Rx has received and decoded these words to establish the 'idea' in his own mind.

As the message passes from Tx to Rx it is subject to distracting and distorting factors which (borrowing again from the vocabulary of the electronic engineer) may be called '*noise*'. 'Noise' is, in fact, frequently ordinary physical noise which, in a factory for example, substantially reduces the efficiency of spoken communication, or it may be electronic noise which interferes with communication by telephone or loudspeaker system. But it is used here to refer also to such things as illegible handwriting, smudged copies of duplicated typescript, poor telephone connections, and all distractions (whether toothache or a pretty girl passing your desk) which reduce the concentration of either Rx or Tx.

Fig. 5

For perfect communication A and D must be identical. This is something extremely difficult to achieve because of the combined effect of noise, and distortion at B and C.

We have all had experience of the strain of communicating when attention at either end is distracted or when the medium itself is in some way defective, and we must in fact recognise that conditions will sometimes exist where noise causes complete communication breakdown. Such conditions are unusual, however, and the effect of noise can generally be overcome by will-power, by increasing the effort put into concentration. Noise too is most often encountered in spoken communication, where there is usually the possibility of asking immediately for a repetition of that part of the message that was interfered with.

The distortions at B and C are less simply overcome – at those points we confront the fundamental difficulty of communication by means of words. The key questions are:

1. How accurately do the words used at B express the idea A?

2. How can we be sure that the Rx will at stage C assign the same value to those words as the Tx did at B?

This chapter considers some of the problems inherent in our use of words to convey meaning (*semantics*) and attempts to show how the Tx should choose his words so that his meaning is conveyed to the Rx with minimum distortion, maximum clarity.

II. WORDS AS SYMBOLS

When we use words, we are using symbols. As the Union Jack can be said to stand for our country, so a certain sound made by our breath passing over our vocal chords while tongue and lips move into various positions stands for the male parent. When we write the word down, *father*, we employ a double symbolism, since the letters that represent this sound are themselves symbols.

We are free to assign whatever value we choose to our symbols; but we shall not get very far in communicating with others unless our symbols are recognised by them. Thus if I choose to symbolise Great Britain by means of a yellow flag with purple stripes and the male parent by the word *ogboo*, I shall meet continual incomprehension when I attempt to use my symbols.

When we are speaking to fellow Englishmen we do not have to worry when we use the word *father* that the Frenchman uses *père* and the German *Vater* as their symbols for the male parent. We know that our particular audience will understand. Similarly it is not necessary for the whole community to recognise our symbols. An economist writing for fellow economists uses a vocabulary of symbols, many of which (such as *value, wealth, margin*) have a rather different meaning for the majority of the community from that which they have for his readers. There is no confusion, because the economist knows his readers will be familiar with his use of these symbols before they start to read. If he does not know this, he must make his special use clear immediately. A prime cause of communication breakdown is the unsound assumption by the Tx that the Rx knows already the special interpretation to be given to his symbols (the economist lecturing to a general audience who forgets that they will interpret *value, wealth, margin* in their way, not his).

The Tx should endeavour, as far as possible, to confine himself to symbols which he believes to be familiar to the Rx in the interpretation that he (the Tx) is putting upon them. It is, however, sometimes necessary to introduce unfamiliar symbols (which may be new words or old words with a slightly changed meaning). A number of symbols probably unfamiliar to the reader are employed in this book. In this chapter, so far, *semantics* is an example of an unfamiliar word and *idea* and *noise* are used in unfamiliar interpretations. The interpretation of these special symbols was made clear as soon as they were used – essential if misunderstanding is not to result.

All this may be formulated as rules:

1. Prefer words that are familiar to the Rx in the interpretation you wish him to give to them.

2. If you want the Rx to give an unfamiliar meaning to a familiar word within the context of your communication, make this clear the first time you use this word.

3. If you use a word likely to be unfamiliar to the Rx, make its meaning clear the first time you use it.

You will realise that for you to be able to apply these rules efficiently you will need to have:

1. a fairly accurate impression of the vocabulary of the Rx.

2. an extremely accurate knowledge of the accepted meanings of words (with particular realisation of which words your own trade or profession uses with meanings differing from the generally accepted ones).

When we are communicating with men and women of more limited vocabulary than our own, breakdown may occur when we use what seem to us familiar words in their most everyday senses – simply because these words are not known by, or are only distortedly known by, the Rx. Judging what will, or will not, be familiar vocabulary for the Rx demands imagination, continual alertness to the other man's point of view, and a good knowledge of the Rx.

When you yourself are the Rx you too may make errors of interpretation because the words you hear or read are unfamiliar. You can reduce the number of occasions on which you make such errors by improving your vocabulary. The more words you are familiar with, and the more accurate your interpretation of those words, the better you are as an Rx. You improve your vocabulary by reading and listening, with reference to a dictionary when you come across a word you are not certain about. The more demanding the material you read and listen to, the faster your vocabulary will develop; do not be satisfied with material already well within your range. Continued subjection to communication material intended for a Tx of smaller vocabulary than your own (and this will include much popular newspaper, magazine, and television material) cripples development.

III. AREAS OF MEANING

You will already be realising that it is a fallacy to believe that there is one 'correct' meaning for every word. The decoding process at C is never as simple as $15x + 27y$ where $x = 8$ and $y = 6$, because the symbols of language can stand for more than one idea each.

Radium is a metal of great value. What does this mean? That radium costs a great deal of money or that it does a great deal of good? Or both? Consider these sentences:

What is the value of this ring?
What is the value of learning about communication?
I value my good name.
I got good value for my money.
There is something wrong with the tone values in all his paintings.
A crotchet has twice the value of a quaver.

What is the meaning of *value*? Even without bringing in the economist, *value* is seen to have a series of meanings or, more accurately, a series of *areas of meaning* (since each sentence illustrates a group of meanings). Notice too that it is only when we meet *value* in context that we know how to interpret it. We can often form only an approximate idea of the meaning of a word out of context, since we cannot tell which area of meaning to assign to it.

IV. THE USE OF DICTIONARIES

The feeling that somewhere there must be a final court of appeal where 'correct' meanings are laid down dies hard. 'Look it up in a dictionary', people say. But the dictionary, if it is a good one, will not attempt an $x = 8$ type of answer but will show as many areas of meaning as there is space for within the limits of the cost of the dictionary.

Furthermore the dictionary is not a legislator telling you what you are to do; it tells you only what other people are already doing. A dictionary is compiled by a large number of scholars each of whom is assigned a small part of the dictionary alphabetically (say FEA to FEV). Each notes examples of written uses of the words in his section, especially unusual uses, as he reads an immense number of previously selected books. From the large number of contexts for each word supplied him by his assistants the editor subsequently deduces the areas of meanings which are (1) current (2) have been accepted in the past but are no longer live. Thus a dictionary provides a systematic record of usage, not a series of rules for linguistic behaviour. But this is exactly what we want. If you as a Tx are in any doubt about a word you propose to use, you can – and should – check it in a dictionary – not to find out its 'correct' meaning but to find out, approximately, what meaning or meanings the Rx is likely to assign to it. The authority of the dictionary arises partly from this, but also from the fact that the Rx in turn, if he is uncertain of this word, will check it in a dictionary. Thus the dictionary acts as code-book to both Tx and Rx and in the end does influence their view of what the word means. Certain dictionaries (notably the Oxford series in England and Webster's in America) have greater authority than others, partly because they are those that have been compiled on sound research lines and are not simply taken from other dictionaries, but partly because they are known to be those most frequently consulted. If you use a cheap dictionary there will not be space in it for sufficient areas of meaning to be shown, and if you use a little-known one you may find yourself with a different code-book from the one your opposite number is using.

Buy therefore the largest dictionary you can afford and let it be one of wide repute; it will be the most useful aid to communication you will ever find.

A good dictionary supplies not only definitions of each word's areas of meaning but also illustrative contexts, its grammatical function(s), an indication of its origin (derivation), and a guide to its pronunciation. For some words it will supply still more information – if you look up *penny*, for example, in even the pocket version of the Oxford dictionary you will be amazed at the amount of information crammed into so small a space. It is certainly a pity to use a dictionary just to check spelling, or to buy the kind that has entries so brief that they lead you in a circle (e.g. you look up *value* and find 'worth' – you look up *worth* and find 'value').

An inevitable limitation to the usefulness of a dictionary is that it is always out of date. While the compilers have been busy, the language has changed; by the time the dictionary is printed the language will have changed again. Dictionaries are very expensive to compile so one compilation will have to stand for many years; though from time to time additions to, and revisions of, the original edition will be made by a conscientious publisher, these will never keep us with the continual vocabulary changes of a living language – new words entering the language, old words shifting their meaning. This is not quite such a serious limitation as it would at first seem, as changes in the use of existing words establish themselves fairly slowly and new words are often generally familiar words that do not need to be checked in a dictionary. However, it is something that should be borne in mind by those who tend to look to the dictionary as the final authority on meaning.

V. MAKING MEANING CLEAR

We saw in Section II that we are often in the position of having to make clear the interpretation we expect the Rx to give to a word we are going to use. Three devices are particularly useful in making meaning clear – *illustrative contexts*, *glossing*, and *definition*.

A. Illustrative contexts

We have learned the meanings of nearly all the words we know from the contexts in which we have heard or seen them; from childhood on, we all carry out a similar process to that which is the task of the dictionary editor. As an Rx reads what we have written he will start to assign a meaning to a new word from the contexts in which it appears. This is the natural way for him to learn our meaning.

This process can sometimes be speeded up and made more accurate by supplying illustrative contexts as soon as the word is first used – this method is used at the beginning of Chapter I of this book in an attempt to establish the critical word *communication* quickly for the reader.

As we need one context for each area of meaning it can, however, be a cumbersome device and is in fact little used outside dictionaries and examination answers.

'Write sentences to bring out clearly the meaning of . . .' or 'Illustrate the use of the following by means of sentences . . .' are common questions in English papers. Two points should be noted about answering such questions:

   1. only one area of meaning is required.

   2. the sentence used must, as far as possible, 'fix' the meaning of the word – a good test of this is to see if you can substitute a word of opposite meaning. Thus to illustrate *courageous* the sentence *The soldier was very*

courageous is valueless as we could in fact substitute *cowardly*. We need something like *The soldier was courageous for he stood his ground although attacked by three of the enemy*.

It is not easy to fix the meaning of a word by means of a single sentence. The fixes we obtain in the normal communication situation are the result of comparing a number of contexts each one of which helps to limit the field of meaning of the word and sharpen our interpretation of it.

It should be noted, by the way, that an attempt has been made to indicate the author's use of *fix* in this section by illustrative context only.

B. Glossing

A *gloss* was originally a note inserted in the margin to explain a word in the text. Today we use footnotes or put the gloss in parenthesis. Sometimes the word glossed comes after the gloss itself, as in example 4. below.

1. *In general they are extremely ductile – that is they pull out very easily.*

2. *The outer parts of the atom are occupied by electrons – that is by particles of pure negative electricity.*

3. *Work hardening (toughening under strain) is a common behaviour of metals.*

4. *If any polished metal is lightly attacked with acid – 'etched' as it is called . . .*

The essence of the method is that a simple equivalent of the word glossed is put beside it: it is a form of paraphrase. It is a very useful device as it gives the Rx a rapid indication of how he is to interpret a word, without holding up the communication for a full explanation. It is particularly suitable where the Tx is not sure whether the Rx will know the word or not, or where he thinks the Rx will need only a reminder. Because it uses few words it is frequently employed in business communication, especially firm-to-customer communication where technical language appropriate to the firm must be briefly explained for the non-technical Rx.

C. Definition

When we define a thing we separate it from every other thing in the universe. We do this by first classifying the thing and then subclassifying for as long as possible. Finally the smallest amount of additional information is added that will separate the thing defined from all other things in the last subdivided class. Things outside that subdivided class are ignored. Thus a violin falls into the general class 'musical instruments' and can be subdivided first as 'stringed' and subsequently as 'four-stringed' and 'played with a bow'. *A violin is a four-stringed musical instrument played with a bow* puts the violin into the correct subdivided class but is not a definition as it permits the violin to be confused with the viola, the cello, and the double-bass. *A violin is the smallest of the four-stringed musical instruments played with a bow* is a sound definition of a violin although it would give no idea of what violin was like to a man ignorant of musical instruments and leaves for a second definition the question of what constitutes a bow.

Your Rx would get a very much better idea of a violin if you could take him to a concert and point one out. The fact that you can point out makes a difference between words like *violin, potato, volcano* on the one hand and words like *value, idea, definition* on the other. When we define *violin* we do not readily think about whether we are defining the word or the object that the word stands for; but this does concern us when we have to define *value*. It is perhaps safest when attempting to define words that refer to ideas in our heads rather than to objects in the world appreciated by our senses to use a form of words such as '*value* refers to' rather than '*value* is'.

This difficulty becomes more pronounced when we turn to the definition of other parts of speech than nouns. Some modification of the system of definition applicable to things becomes clearly necessary when we start to define *to radiate* or *small*. Since definition is so much associated with nouns it is usual to convert verbs to nouns (i.e. to define *radiation*) and to associate adjectives with the noun they are to be used with (e.g. *For the purpose of this paper, the term 'small boiler' is taken to mean a boiler with a heating surface not greater than 3 sq m and an output not in excess of 30 kW*).

VI. DISCRIMINATION BETWEEN SYNONYMS ON A BASIS OF MEANING

The English language is unusually rich in synonyms (words of similar meaning) chiefly because so many languages have contributed to ours. Thus we have *regal* (directly from Latin *regalis*) alongside *royal* (from Old French *roial*). Synonyms, although closely connected in meaning, are rarely fully interchangeable; we cannot talk about 'the Regal Family', and 'he surrounds himself with furnishings of royal magnificence' sounds a little strange. Even where meaning is identical, as in the pair *violin* (from Italian *violino*) and *fiddle* (from Middle English *fithele*) there is usually a difference of tone (e.g. *fiddle* is used contemptuously or in rather undignified contexts). We shall have to consider the effect on our communication of these differences of tone in Chapter 5; at this stage it is the small differences of *meaning* that exist between so many synonyms that concern us. If we are aware of these differences we can improve our communication by selecting the word which most exactly conveys our meaning. On the other hand, uncertainty as to the precise degree to which two synonyms are interchangeable can lead to blurred transmission of our ideas.

Many words are treated as synonymous, by those unskilled in language, that are so different in meaning that it is questionable whether they can be called synonyms at all (e.g. *illicit* and *illegal*). It is convenient however to consider such words at the same time as true synonyms and in this book the word *synonym* is therefore used subsequently to include such near-synonyms.

Often the key factor in discriminating between words closely connected in meaning is their *relative narrowness of application*. *Illicit* is more limited in use than *illegal* since it refers only to those actions which offend against the law because they are performed without a licence or permit. *Illegal* refers to the general range of actions contrary to the law. Generally there is a gain in precision of meaning by choosing words of narrow application, but sometimes circumstances require us to prefer the broader word. If in a report we mention the necessity either to *oil* or *grease* a certain appliance when in fact both processes are necessary, either word is too narrow and we should have preferred *lubricate*, broad enough to include both processes. *Maintenance* of an appliance is broader still as it includes lubrication along with, for example, cleaning and checking.

Another type of difference between synonyms is that of *intensity*. *Tired*, *weary*, *exhausted* represent increasingly intense forms of the same state of being. We should choose the one that has just the right degree of intensity for our subject matter and – especially in factual communication of the sort that is the subject of this book – avoid trying to add drama by choosing words that exaggerate the situation.

Some words carry an overtone or suggestion of emotion along with their more factual meaning; this *emotional connotation* is another way by which synonyms can sometimes be differentiated. Thus *lonely* has an emotional connotation absent from *solitary* or *unaccompanied*. (These in turn, by the way, can be distinguished by the fact that *unaccompanied* is limited to those animate objects which can be accompanied; *solitary* is the broader word.) Often the emotional connotation of a word is disapproval. Such words are often said to have a *derogatory* or *pejorative* connotation. Thus *notorious* is distinguished from *famous*; *cunning* from *astute*; *obstinate* from *unwavering*. There are many such pairs and sometimes the one of the pair which is not derogatory carries a connotation of approval. Frequently we have a group of synonyms which represent the range; disapproval, neutrality, approval – as *gross, fat, plump.*

All these factors should be borne in mind when choosing between synonyms, but they will not always be applicable and many synonyms have slight but important differences in their areas of meaning that cannot be fitted into these categories. It is a matter of familiarising yourself with the contexts in which these words appear and deciding for yourself what governs which word goes into which context.

Synonyms should not be looked upon as merely a device for avoiding the same word used several times. Too much attention to this (a practice known as 'elegant variation') is a waste of the Tx's time and a source of confusion to the Rx who has to keep on readjusting to new symbols. They should be looked upon primarily as a way of improving the accuracy of our coding. It is not the similarities between synonyms that matter – it is the differences.

VII. CAUSES OF CONFUSION

A. Homophones

Friend, Charles Lamb is reputed to have called to a poacher he passed in the fields, *is that thine own hare or a wig?*

Opinions may differ as to whether puns are all that amusing, but there is no doubt that unconscious puns that arise through confusion between homophones (words spelled differently but sounding alike) harm communication. It cannot be often that genuine misunderstanding arises (*There is a boy adrift in the harbour mouth*) but the attention of the Rx is distracted while he laughs at the mistake, and the Tx loses authority.

We need to be particularly careful in checking dictated material for misspelling of homophones, and it is as well to spell out the word when dictating if the context is likely to cause any doubt in a sectretary's mind.

B. Malapropisms

Malapropisms are words which are used in error for other words somewhat like them in sound or appearance. They are named after Mrs Malaprop, a character in Sheridan's *The Rivals* who describes another character as *the very pineapple of politeness* and hopes that her daughter who has just been told to *illiterate* a young man from her memory will never become a *progeny of learning.*

They are more common in speech than in writing and are very damaging to the Tx. Since the confusions often occur between words which are long and unfamiliar the Tx lays himself open to the accusation of conceit-edly attempting a vocabulary beyond what he can master.

A similar error occurs when the Rx misinterprets a somewhat unfamiliar word because he confuses it with one rather like it in appearance or sound.

C. Colloquial meanings

Some words with well established areas of meaning in writing develop an additional area of meaning (or more than one) in speech. *Catch on*, *drag*, *square*, *fabulous* are examples – many thousands could be listed. Quite apart from the effect on the tone of what we write (separately referred to on page 61) confusion over meaning may result if we employ such words in writing intending them to carry a meaning they have only in speech.

Such colloquial extensions of meaning do gradually become absorbed into the written language, first in such informal contexts as newspaper articles but eventually in even the most formal writing. The complete process takes many years and it is often difficult to decide just how far a colloquial extension of meaning has become acceptable in writing (i.e. with what sort of Rx and in what sort of writing it can be used without misunderstanding). Some of the words in Exercises H and J at the end of this chapter illustrate this. Certainly, local and central government and the world of business will be among the last sectors to recognise such colloquial extensions of meaning, and this is therefore a point of some importance for the readers of this book.

Occasionally the colloquial meaning of a word is so well known (while still considered suitable only for speech) that we are unable to use it in its original sense except with a very conservative Rx and are virtually deprived of the use of the word altogether. An outstanding example of this is the word *nice*. This has acceptable written contexts which include:

This is a matter for nice judgment.
A nice balance is maintained throughout the report.
The factory works to nice tolerances.
Very nice stitching will be necessary.

The area of meaning of all these is 'precise and delicate'.

In colloquial use *nice* is a handy blunderbuss of a word to be aimed vaguely at everything one approves of – *nice weather*, *nice girl*, *nice food*, *nice work*, *a nice fit*, *nice stitching*. These familiar speech uses blur the response of the Rx to the written contexts so that he is, for example, quite at a loss to know what the Tx means by *nice stitching* in the last sentence above.

In commerce and local or central government the safest advice for the Tx is:

1. Avoid using words in their colloquial sense in writing.
2. Avoid using in writing, in any sense at all, a word which has a very well established colloquial sense.

VIII. EXERCISES

NOTE: The intention of these exercises is not so much to expand your vocabulary as to make you more aware of the kinds of problem involved in selecting words to convey your meaning. Reading, and listening to, material expressed by those whose vocabulary is wider than your own is the natural way to expand your vocabulary. The majority of these exercises will prove most useful if attempted orally in a class so that group discussion can follow; if you are working on your own the best substitute for this is to write down your answers and check them in a good dictionary.

Exercise A

Write sentences (similar to those on page 28 for *value*) to provide contexts for as many separate areas of meaning as you can distinguish, for the following words:

leaf   try   plant   point   heart

Exercise B

Write sentences to bring our clearly the meaning of:

1. alien impenetrable individual deteriorate emigrant interim irrelevant pacify analysis inconclusive
2. determination alternate sinecure menace eradicate contemporary predicament reconnaissance exonerate
3. temporal crustacean phenomenon machiavellian polytheism jejune intrinsic obviate allegation eclectic

Exercise C

With the aid of a dictionary compose a logical paragraph to include all the following words, in any order:

responsibility stultify induction assiduous conducive environment innate initiative crucial procrastinating

Exercise D

1. Make one-sentence definitions of the following:
   a trombone   a pencil   a table   a canal   an axe
2. Attempt definitions of the following:
   democracy   efficiency   justice   beauty   love

If you try the second part of this exercise in a group, you will almost certainly find important differences between your definitions because your ideas of what you are defining differ. See how many different kinds of definition you can think of (for example how *love* will vary according to the definer's age, sex, nature). You will realise that the man who, in a discussion, says, 'It all depends what you mean by . . .' is not splitting hairs; he is trying to make sure you are both talking about the same thing.

Exercise E

In the following groups of sentences the words in italics are synonyms, yet the sentences will not make good sense until these words are re-distributed amongst the sentences. Carry out this redistribution and try to decide what has made the change necessary.

    A

1. The judge sentenced the prisoner to six months' hard *work*.
2. No sooner had I finished one *toil* than he set me to another.
3. When do you start *labour* again?
4. There is too much *task* in farming for it to be a suitable occupation for one who likes an easy life.

    B

1. The speaker had an attentive *crowd*.
2. The *audience* swept the speaker off the platform and trampled him underfoot.
3. A *mob* had by now collected round the speaker and many were listening seriously to his words.

    C

1. The solicitor spent an hour advising his *patient*.
2. The butcher was always polite to a new *client*.
3. The doctor's *customer* complained that the waiting-room was uncomfortable.

    D

1. She is *liable* to give me a present at Christmas.
2. It is *apt to* sink at any moment now.
3. In all the years I have known him I have found only one fault in him – he is *likely* to tell lies.

E

1. The *antique* lady could walk only with great difficulty.
2. Many people consider an *obsolete* warming-pan a suitable decoration for the wall of a timbered room.
3. The wardrobe mistress had spent weeks making the *old* dresses for the company.
4. As a weapon of war, molten lead is now *old-fashioned*.

F

1. The new secretary appeared to be quite *effective*.
2. His stern reply seemed to be *efficient* for the man immediately returned to his bench.
3. The lighting in the last scene of the play was particularly *effectual*.

Exercise F

Arrange the words in the following groups in ascending order of intensity:

tepid   hot   warm
frighten   alarm   terrify   scare
momentous   significant   weighty   important
reprehensible   wicked   iniquitous   improper
idiotic   stupid   injudicious   foolish
ugly   ill-favoured   plain   homely   hideous
quickly   hurriedly   rapidly   swiftly   precipitately   briskly

Exercise G

Distinguish the following on the basis of emotional connotation:

home   residence
childish   childlike
politician   statesman
helpful   officious
pious   sanctimonious

Exercise H

Distinguish between the colloquial and the accepted written meanings of the following words:

decent   hectic   literally   putrid   lovely

Exercise I

1. Distinguish between the following synonyms or near-synonyms.
2. Are there any words that you consider identical in meaning and fully interchangeable?

3. If any are identical in meaning but not fully interchangeable why is this
so?
synthetic   artificial   imitation   manmade
expensive   dear   costly
illegible   unreadable   indecipherable
lady   woman
man   gentleman
reticent   secretive   taciturn
short   brief   concise
tall   high   lofty
personnel   staff   employees   workers
presumption   assumption   hypothesis   postulate
massive   huge   vast   colossal   gigantic
merry   gay   happy   jovial   jolly
confirm   verify   endorse   corroborate
constantly   continually   continuously   perpetually   incessantly
make   construct   form   create   build   shape   manufacture
    fabricate   erect   produce   contrive   generate   run up
payment   wage   salary   fee   remuneration   emolument   stipend
    gratuity   honorarium

Exercise J

For each of the following words indicate which of the 'meanings' given is
closest to the accepted written meaning:

1. *unique:* unexpected   the only one   very rare
2. *aggravate:* irritate   make worse   become bigger
3. *livid:* lead-coloured   brilliant   red-faced
4. *chronic:* long-lasting   incurable   very bad
5. *anticipate:* do something in advance   wait for something to be done
    expect something to be done
6. *transpire:* become known   happen   change into another language
7. *hypercritical:* over-sensitive   over-critical   pretending to be virtuous
8. *rostrum:* list of duties   a platform for public speaking   a patent
    medicine
9. *disinterested:* bored   not interested   without self-interest
10. *unexceptionable:* ordinary   out of the ordinary   above reproach

Exercise K

Distinguish between the words in the following pairs or groups, which
are sometimes confused because of similarity of sound and/or appearance.

If any of these words are unfamiliar to you, use a dictionary to discover their areas of meaning but do not attempt the exercise with the groups in which they appeared.

persecute prosecute
imminent eminent
draft draught
observance observation
ingenious ingenuous
expedient expeditious
affect effect
defective deficient
flaunt flout
deprecate depreciate
credulous creditable credible
consul counsel council
luxurious luxuriant
perspicacity perspicuity
statue statute stature status
resort resource recourse
exotic erotic esoteric
illusion allusion elusion delusion

Exercise L

1. Write the following words and phrases in a column and, at the side of each, give a word or phrase which expresses the same idea disappiovingly:

   astute generous famous esprit de corps collaborator new idea
   ingenious plan delicate hint wide discretion shrewd thrust

2. Write *brief* explanatory notes on the *difference in meaning and use* between the words or phrases in each of the following pairs:

   impassable dependant judicious compare with truism
   impassible dependent judicial compare to axiom
   [*Royal Society of Arts, English Language Stage III*]

Exercise M

1. Make a numbered list of ten words which could be used to fill the ten numbered spaces in the passage given below. You may use *six only* of the following nine words and must therefore repeat one or more of them.

*principles   methods   standards   philosophical   philosophy   science
results   scientific   principal*

There are two different ways in which a philosophy may seek to base itself upon ... 1 ... It may emphasise the most general ... 2 ... of science, and seek to give even greater generality and unity to these results. Or it may study the ... 3 ... of science, and seek to apply these ... 4 ..., with the necessary adaptations, to its own peculiar province. Much ... 5 ... inspired by science has gone astray through preoccupation with the ... 6 ... momentarily supposed to have been achieved. It is not results, but ... 7 ..., that can be transferred with profit from the sphere of the special sciences to the sphere of ... 8 .... What I wish to bring to your notice is the possibility and importance of applying to .. 9 ... problems certain broad ... 10 ... of method which have been found successful in the study of scientific questions.

2. State the central idea of the passage in one sentence and in your own words.

3. Give other words or phrases, one for each, which could be used to replace the following in the passage without either altering the meaning or disturbing the flow of words:

seek to base itself   emphasise   generality   adaptations   peculiar
inspired   preoccupation   transferred   sphere   possibility

[*Royal Society of Arts, English Language Stage III*]

Chapter 4

Clear Wording 2
(Problems of Handling)

I. WORDS IN SENTENCES

The responsibility of the Tx to ensure that his wording does not obscure or distort his meaning does not end with his choice of words. When he begins to build his sentences new problems arise from interaction between words. Words (especially those next to each other in the sentence) influence each other in a way perhaps not expected, producing a surprising second meaning (ambiguity); the order in which the words are set down has more effect on the total meaning than he realised; the construction of the sentences becomes muddled, causing a blur in transmission – these are the kinds of problem of syntax which confront the Tx every time he speaks or writes.

Besides determining the best order for his words – and this has a direct effect on the quality of the transmission of his meaning – the Tx will also have to decide a number of more purely grammatical points (do the subject and verb agree in number? Is that the right case for the relative pronoun? can I use that word as a preposition?). These matters are of subordinate importance, but they are not without effect on the clarity of his wording; and he will certainly want (especially when writing or talking in a business context) to appear 'correct', as he will feel that if he does not conform to educated usage he will be putting himself in a position of inferiority to his Rx.

Faults of handling may produce four types of unsatisfactory sentence: (1) the unintelligible sentence (2) the sentence which conveys two or more meanings at once (3) the sentence which by faulty syntax or failure to conform to accepted usage makes the task of the Rx harder than it need be (4) the sentence which conveys its meaning, but ineptly or in a manner which reveals its author's unfamiliarity with educated usage.

II. AMBIGUITY

A. *Types of ambiguity*

To produce a sentence capable of one meaning only every time you write (or speak) a sentence must be your aim as a communicator. Second meanings have a way of appearing in what we write without our being aware of them. We know what we want to say and we are amazed when the Rx sees something quite different in our words. You will have to be alert to the possibility of ambiguity all the time, but especially when you are reading through, and revising, what you have written.

Some sentences are completely ambiguous – that is to say with the best will in the world the Rx cannot detect which meaning the Tx had in mind. *John told Tom that he had passed the examination* is an example of such a sentence. More often the second meaning is a ridiculous one, obviously not intended by the author, as in the well-known *If the baby does not thrive on fresh milk, boil it*. Although the first type of ambiguity is certainly the more important, it is no defence to say, 'Anybody can see what I meant.' If the Rx is laughing at you he is not concentrating on what you are telling him. Even the most ridiculous second meanings are therefore harmful to communication; and in business nobody wants to be laughed at.

B. Causes of ambiguity

1. VAGUE REFERENCE OF PRONOUNS. The trouble with both the ambiguous sentences above is that we are not sure of the reference of the pronoun – does *he* mean John or Tom, does *it* refer to the milk or the baby? Notice that it cannot be assumed that the Rx will always associate a pronoun with the last noun mentioned – in the second sentence *milk* is the last noun but almost everybody who hears that sentence thinks of the baby as the antecedent of *it*.

In the following sentence from a national newspaper, context revealed that the first *he* referred to the unit sergeant-major but it remained a mystery whose men were being persuaded by whom to transfer to another TA unit.

When he returned to the drill ground a week later he was 'ordered off' by Major Starling, who told him he had been trying to persuade his men to transfer to another TA unit.

Although, for convenience, ambiguity is discussed here in terms of single sentences it may, of course, manifest itself in more than one sentence. A *this* or *these* at the beginning of the sentence leaving the reader uncertain which of two things mentioned in the previous sentence is referred to is a common form of this sort of ambiguity.

2. THE RULE OF PROXIMITY IGNORED. Words to be associated together by the Rx should be physically together in the sentence; otherwise

the Rx, assuming you are observing the rule of proximity, associates the wrong things together.

Writing desk for sale by lady with Queen Anne legs. (A common type – some improvement can be made by commas round *by lady* but fundamentally unsound.)

The meeting will be held in the old Men's Staff Room. (Devastating when spoken, not ambiguous at all when written, because of the use of capitals.)

The man on the horse with the wide-brimmed hat was the one who told me. (Commas after *horse* and *hat* produce very little improvement.)

Less obviously, it was difficulty with the rule of proximity that betrayed the film critic of a great newspaper into writing of *a beautifully observed study of a man who commits suicide in the last day of his life.*

3. INDECISIVE PLACING OF ADVERBS. There is an important difference between *He did not win luckily* and *He did not win, luckily.* Doubt is avoided by rearranging the order of the second sentence as *Luckily, he did not win.*

All adverbs need to be placed where there can be no doubt what word they are modifying, but some adverbs (*hardly, scarcely, almost, even,* and, above all, *only*) need special care.

Her mother only guessed the cause of her tears. (Does this mean only her mother guessed, or the mother guessed only, i.e. she was not certain?) Note the differences between:

That student passed only in Economics (he had only one success).

Only that student passed in Economics (only one candidate was successful).

That student only passed in Economics (he did not get a very high mark).

4. FAULTY PUNCTUATION (see also Appendix I). Although punctuation is a poor aid for a sentence ambiguous through neglect of the rule of proximity, some sentences are ambiguous purely because a comma has been omitted or, sometimes, wrongly introduced.

She likes coffee and rolls in bed has quite a different sense with a comma after *coffee.*

5. AMBIGUOUS WORDS. Words which have two or more areas of meaning can cause ambiguity if care is not taken to ensure that context makes it clear which area is required, e.g.

If you wish to retain the book after fourteen days you must ask for a renewal or telephone or the unfortunate pharmaceutical chemist who took as his slogan:

> *We dispense with accuracy.*

Occasionally two areas of meanings of the one word are used in close proximity, with baffling effect:

> *The two little girls took nearly twenty minutes to reach the pillar-box only to find they could not reach it.*

In reviewing a film about archery, a magazine devoted to that sport referred to *the unselfconscious shooting of children* leaving the reader in doubt whether the children were shooting arrows, being shot by cameras, or being shot by archers. A correspondent to a local paper combined this type of ambiguity with the falsely related participle (see page 48) to produce *Being on a bend one has to drive through 'blind' hoping no one is coming from the other direction* – thus apparently publicly confessing to drunken driving.

Probably the most serious ambiguities are of this kind, when the Rx is uncertain which of several possible meanings to assign to a word used by the Tx or the Tx uses the one word in more than one sense. Often such ambiguities are not just the results of carelessness in choice of word but reveal a basic uncertainty in the Tx's original ideas. Persistent ambiguity is a sign of woolly thinking and cannot be put right by mechanical means or the application of rules.

III. COMMON FAULTS OF SYNTAX AND USAGE

A. Faulty agreement

1. The verb agrees in number with its subject – this is familiar enough but there are many points of difficulty.

> *A man is walking down the street*
> *A man and his wife are walking down the street*

BUT

> *A man with his wife is walking down the street.*

The multiple subject is here joined together by a form of words that makes one part of the subject so much subordinate to the other, that we have to treat the subject as singular. *With, together with, as well as* are the principal links that produce this effect:

> *Mr Tomkin, as well as his secretary, is to be present at this meeting.*

Sometimes even multiple subjects joined by *and* are treated as singular if they are felt to combine together to form a unity:

> *Fish and chips is a nourishing food.*

On the other hand, items consisting of two parts invariably used together (e.g. *pyjamas, scissors, pliers*) are always treated as plurals and can cause awkward sounding constructions:

Pliers are a useful tool.

The neatest solution here is to add *a pair of* and treat as a singular:

A pair of pliers is a useful tool.

There are a few words which are plural in form but singular in agreement (e.g. *news, measles, mathematics, economics*). *Means* can be either singular or plural.

2. Collective nouns can also be troublesome.

The congregation is bigger this week, we say, but not *The male congregation on entering the church takes off its hats*. The second context forces us to think of the individual heads belonging to the individual members of the group and as soon as we do that we find the singular unsatisfactory.

Alternatively, if we were to say *The congregation are bigger this week* it would suggest that the individual members had become larger since the previous week (as they well may have done). We prefer the collective, then, as a singular – unless something in the context forces us into thinking of the individual units of the whole, when we treat it as a plural:

The fleet is in port again

BUT

The crew of one ship are quarrelling amongst themselves.

The same noun can hardly be treated as both plural and singular in the same sentence, however:

NOT *As the jury have disagreed it will be dismissed.*

A collective followed by *of* plus a plural noun (*a case of instruments, a team of athletes, a flock of sheep*) is often wrongly treated as a plural subject.

NOT *A collection of valuable paintings are on display*
BUT *A collection of valuable paintings is on display.*

3. *Each, every, everyone, everybody, anyone, anybody* are all singulars.

THUS *All of the workmen are to get a rise*
BUT *Each of the workmen is to get a rise.*

None is now treated as a plural, in defiance of all logic (it is hard to see how what is less than one can be more plural than one) and constructions such as *None of our soldiers is missing* have now a very old-fashioned look to them.

Kind, sort, type are all singular nouns.

NOT *I do not care for those kind of people*
BUT *I do not care for that kind of people*

OR (better, because it avoids the clash of singular and plural that worries some readers)

> *I do not care for that kind of person.*

Either, neither are also singular:

> *Neither of the gardeners knows much about gardening.*

For *either ... or, neither ... nor* constructions, the grammatical rule is that the verb agrees with the nearer of the subjects.

THUS *Neither my brother nor I am very interested in gardening* is sound grammar but reads a little strangely and would seem distinctly affected if spoken. In writing, the solution is not to substitute unsound grammar (*are*) but to rephrase the whole sentence to avoid the construction:

> *My brother and I take no interest in gardening.*

In speech the informal *are* is usual.

NOTE: This is one of many cases where the dictum of the grammarian clashes with what the ear is used to. The grammarian's role should really be, like the dictionary compiler's, that of recording usage, not laying down rules, but over the years he has become an accepted legislator in matters of doubt. In the business world where so much stress is laid on 'correctness' you will be ill-advised to stray far from orthodox grammar in your formal writing. Speech is much freer, and it is in fact our greater familiarity with colloquial forms that makes us sometimes unprepared for the grammatically 'correct' forms.

B. Faults connected with verbs

1. The tenses of a passage should not be changed unnecessarily between past and present. If the main verb is in the past, all subordinate verbs must usually be in the past too:

NOT *He told me he will carry out the work immediately*
BUT *He told me he would carry out the work immediately.*

2. The perfect infinitive (*to have spoken*) is often used unnecessarily:

NOT *I should have liked to have spoken to him*
BUT *I should have liked to speak to him.*

There is no difference in meaning between these sentences and the clumsy perfect infinitive has been used in the first only as a result of a quite unnecessary attempt to treat the infinitive as a subordinate verb and turn it into the past tense after a past tense main verb.

> *He was believed to have visited their office in Milan*

does not mean the same as

> *He was believed to visit their office in Milan*

and the perfect infinitive serves a purpose in the first of these two sentences.

3. Verbal nouns (gerunds) and present participles are often confused.

The mother was watching the child dancing
The mother was watching the child's dancing.

A valuable distinction is made here. In the first sentence *dancing* is a present participle having an adjectival function with *child*. The mother is interested in her child who is clearly the direct object of *was watching*.

In the second sentence it is the dancing which is the direct object of *was watching*; it is what the child dances that interests the mother. *Child* is reduced in strength to its adjectival equivalent *child's* so that the noun function of *dancing* comes to the fore (i.e. *dancing* is a verbal noun in the second sentence). Similarly,

NOT *Do you mind Brenda coming with me*
BUT *Do you mind Brenda's coming with me.*

Nobody is minding Brenda. The object of *Do you mind* is *coming*, the verbal noun.

4. Participles, both present and past, are often used without the noun, or pronoun, they are intended to serve as adjectives to. These 'unrelated participles' frequently then appear to the Rx to attach themselves to other nouns with which they either make sense not intended, or no sense at all:

NOT *Standing on the bridge the river flows away to the south* (the river is not standing on the bridge)

BUT *Standing on the bridge you can see the river flowing away to the south*

NOT *Being summer I spent most of my time at the seaside*

BUT *As it was summer, I spent most of my time at the seaside*

NOT *When detonated at the ground, the surrounding air is heated to a very high temperature*

BUT *When the bomb is detonated at the ground . . .*

The noun or pronoun that the participle is to be associated with by the reader must be expressed, not understood. Even if there is no noun for the participle to relate itself to falsely, a participle left hanging gives an impression of slack slovenly writing.

Where *regarding, considering, concerning*, and *failing* are used IN THEIR PREPOSITIONAL FUNCTIONS the question of false relation does not arise.

Thus *Considering the improvement in output, the capital expenditure involved does not appear excessive* is a sound sentence, while *Considering the improvement in output justified the expenditure, his vote was in favour* is unsound, *considering* being unrelated.

5. Perhaps the best known fault of syntax amongst those ignorant of English grammar, the 'split infinitive', is often not a fault at all. It consists

in placing a word or words between the *to* and the word that with *to* forms the infinitive (e.g. *to finally correct*). The objection to doing this seems no more than a meaningless taboo having no connection with clear writing. In fact the determination to avoid splitting the infinitive sometimes leads to ambiguity, as in *He failed completely to understand what I was telling him*. If the writer meant that the failure to understand was only partial he might have done better to put *He failed to completely understand what I was telling him*.

However, since the taboo against the split infinitive is strong amongst business men (and examiners in English) it is probably best to avoid it.

C. *Difficulties with relative pronouns*

1. Relative pronouns have a dual function. They stand for a noun already used (the *antecedent*). They also serve as a linking device. Consider the sentence:

He completed the report that had been asked for by the manager.

This can be looked upon as a linked version of:

He completed the report. This report had been asked for by the manager.

The relative pronoun *that* (1) stands for the noun *report* (2) links the two sentences into one by making the second into a clause.

The principal relative pronouns are: *who, whom, whose* (for persons); *which* (for things); *that* (for either). *That* is in fact not very often used as a substitute for *who*. As a substitute for *which* it should be used only when the clause it introduces is 'defining'. (Defining clauses identify the antecedent for the Rx by answering such questions as *Which one?*)

THUS *The river that flows through London is the Thames* (defining)

BUT *The River Thames, which is usually mud-coloured, flows through London* (non-defining).

We can use *which* instead of *that* in the first of these sentences – although *that* is preferable – but not *that* instead of *which* in the second.

For the effect of commas in distinguishing non-defining from defining clauses see page 256.

2. Separation of the pronoun from its antecedent sometimes causes it to appear to refer to the wrong noun:

He left the message on the table that he intended for the manager.

Still worse, the antecedent sometimes does not appear in the sentence at all:

He decided to ignore the advice of his committee which was extremely foolish.

What is foolish? The committee? The advice? Most probably his decision – but a pronoun can hardly refer to a noun which is not there.

3. The relative pronoun takes its case from its own clause but its number from its antecedent:

> *There is the man who is going to win the race*
> *There is the man whom I saw yesterday.*

When words in parenthesis such as *I think, We believe* are introduced, confusion sometimes occurs between these two basic sentences:

NOT *There is the man whom I think is going to win the race*
BUT *There is the man who, I think, is going to win the race.*

Where the antecedent is expressed, little difficulty is experienced in making the relative pronoun agree in number with it (this agreement being revealed only by the subsequent verb, as relative pronouns are alike in form for plural and singular):

> *These are a few of the films that are to be shown next year.*

But where the antecedent is 'understood' there is sometimes confusion:

NOT *This film is one of the best that has been shown this year*
BUT *This film is one of the best that have been shown this year.*

4. A relative pronoun preceded by *and* or *but* should be used only with a clause which both (1) follows an earlier clause introduced by the same relative pronoun and (2) refers to the same antecedent as the earlier clause does. Furthermore, both clauses should be defining, or both non-defining. Thus:

> *He completed his report, which occupied fifteen sheets of typescript and which, incidentally, was most unlikely ever to be read*

NOT *He completed a report occupying fifteen sheets of typescript and which, incidentally, was most unlikely ever to be read*
> (no earlier clause introduced by same relative pronoun)

NOT *The river which flows through London is the Thames and which is usually mud-coloured* (first clause defining, second non-defining).

D. *False ellipsis*

Ellipsis is a process, of leaving some words to be 'understood' in a sentence, whereby we avoid using the same word twice in a sentence to do the one job.

Thus

> *He had worked for and he had waited for this post many years*

by ellipsis becomes:

> *He had worked and waited for this post many years.*

False ellipsis occurs when we attempt to make a word do the work of a completely different word as well as its own:

NOT *I should be grateful if you would send me further details and application form for this post*

BUT *I should be grateful if you would send me further details of, and application form for, this post*

NOT *Goldcrest cigarettes are as good, if not better than, full-priced cigarettes*

BUT *Goldcrest cigarettes are as good as, if not better than, full-priced cigarettes*

NOT *At Southampton one can see liners coming and going from many different parts of the world*

BUT *At Southampton one can see liners coming from and going to many different parts of the world.*

E. Confused construction

Sometimes two legitimate constructions are in the mind of the writer at once and he produces an inadmissible mixture of the two:

NOT *No sooner had she reached the church door when the organ began to play*

BUT *No sooner had she reached the church door than the organ began to play*

OR *Scarcely had she reached the church door when the organ began to play.*

The man who wrote *On some of these islands the population has more than halved in the last thirty years* was trying to apply the *has more than doubled* construction to *has fallen to less than half*.

F. Faulty constructions with correlative conjunctions

The correlative conjunctions are:

not only   but (also)
neither   nor
either   or
both   and
rather   than

The construction following the second half of the correlative should balance that following the first. The easiest way to ensure this is to check that the same part of speech follows both halves:

NOT *We were not only interested in his achievements but by his potential*

BUT *We were interested not only in his achievements but by his potential* (both followed by preposition)

OR *We were not only interested in his achievement but impressed by his potential* (both followed by finite verb).

G. Difficulties with negative sentences

1. In English two negatives equal a positive as they do in mathematics. This is not true of all languages – in Italian for example a sentence which literally translates as '*I did not never send you a letter*' is just a more emphatic negative. Theoretically this means that if you want a positive in an English sentence you can put in two negatives and if you put in three negatives you are back to a negative again; but multiple negatives are best avoided. At best they give the Rx unnecessary trouble in sorting them out, and at worst an extra negative creeps in, as in

> *It must not be assumed that there are no circumstances in which a profit might not be made.*

In speech, double negatives are surprisingly common as

> *I shouldn't wonder if he didn't do it*

where the speaker means

> *I think he did it.*

2. *Nor* and *or* following a negative can be confused easily. After *neither* it must be *nor* and after *either* it must be *or*. If the negative is merely a *not* or *no* it is not quite so easy to decide. If the effect of the negative in the first part of the sentence continues into the second part *or* is used, but if the negative is confined to its own part *nor* is used.

NOT *The blame for this rests not with the pupils or with the teachers but with the parents*

BUT *The blame for this rests not with the pupils nor with the teachers but with the parents*

OR *The blame for this does not rest with the pupils or the teachers but with the parents.*

H. Words of limited function

A small number of words are at the stage of having their grammatical functions extended in colloquial usage (i.e. they are being used as parts of speech that they were not used as previously). Those that follow – although appearing in written contexts in these extended functions more and more frequently – cannot yet be said to be sufficiently established to justify their employment in formal business writing.

1. Grammatically, 'due' is an adjective. It is becoming quite common to see 'due to' used as a prepositional phrase:

> *We were unable to keep to schedule due to fog.*

It is better to substitute one of the accepted prepositional phrases *owing to, because of* or *as a result of*:

We were unable to keep to schedule owing to fog.

Due to is best confined to constructions such as noun +*due to* or noun +verb *to be +due to,* where it has its true adjectival function:

Fog due to industrial smoke is widespread
Fog is due to industrial smoke.

Notice that *Fog, owing to industrial smoke, is widespread* has quite a different meaning from the first of these two sentences.

2. *Quite* is best confined to an adverbial function in writing. As used colloquially (*quite a crowd, quite an ovation*), it is an adjective. Constructions employing *quite* as an adjective are becoming widely accepted but still have a makeshift look to them that precludes them from use in the most formal contexts. They have the further disadvantage of vagueness of meaning – what is *quite a crowd?* a considerable number? more people than expected? very many people? In practice it often means 'a small crowd' i.e. not a crowd at all.

3. *Like* is not acceptable as a conjunction in formal English (though it is in American English), and its colloquial use in this function should be replaced by *as*:

NOT *I prune my roses in February like the gardening expert on Television does*
BUT *I prune my roses in February as the gardening expert on Television does*
OR *I prune my roses in February like the gardening expert on Television*
    (where *like* is employed legitimately as a preposition).

4. *Than* is not accepted by conventional grammarians as a preposition. This colloquial use (as in *I think I know better than him what to say*) is, however, well established and the 'correct' form (*I think I know better than he what to say*) is beginning to seem a little pedantic to many people. Perhaps the way to satisfy everybody is to add the verb (*I think I know better than he does what to say*).

IV. EXERCISES

Exercise A

How many separate meanings can be given to the words *In Palladonia the burganders bud only on the chalk hills* by changing the position of the *only?*

Exercise B

A town council put up the notice ONLY DOGS ON LEADS ALLOWED IN THIS PARK but the objection was raised that there was little point in having a dog on a lead unless someone was holding it and in any case it was unreasonable to reserve the park for dogs. It is clear enough what the council intended to say – rephrase the notice so that it is completely free of ambiguity.

Exercise C

Correct the ambiguities of the following letter by a golfer:

I must write to tell you how sorry I am my golf ball narrowly missed you yesterday. I certainly thought for a moment I had hit you behind the bunker. When I got there you had already passed on so I decided to waste no time in writing.

What happened was that as I was about to stroke the ball my eye was caught by a passing squirrel which deflected the ball to the right where you were standing. I have said for years that somebody would get hit there and something needed doing badly about it, so I am particularly distressed at coming so near to offending myself.

Exercise D

Point out and correct the ambiguities in the following:

1. After Jackson was out, Tomkins appeared to play probably the best innings of the season.
2. When did you arrange to meet him?
3. I am not going out because it is cold.
4. During the winter the 15.20 train (which during the summer runs on weekdays but not on Sundays) will not run on Saturdays.
5. I regret to inform you that nobody has been in this office for three weeks.
6. I shall hope to see you some time next week.
7. You will not catch many germs walking in the open air.
8. Despite the traffic noise that kept her awake for hours she slept some time during the night.
9. Jack and Brenda met Tom and Sheila at their usual restaurant by chance. This was fortunate as they had been wanting to meet her, but Brenda had felt sure she would not come if invited as they had never got on well together. In the event she asked them both to come round to their place for a second meeting, so she felt the whole thing had gone off very well.
10. All men are animals and you're a man; so you must be an animal. I don't care to go out with an animal.

Exercise E

Each of the following sentences contains one fault of the type discussed in this chapter. For each sentence, point out the fault and rewrite the sentence with the minimum rewording.

1. Due to the trading losses we have suffered we are unable to maintain our annual profit-sharing bonus.
2. George Thompson even knows the combination of the office safe.
3. This is a reform overdue for years and which will immediately improve the position of clerical officers.
4. At the end of the year we found that our trading in this country had not only increased beyond expectations but also our overseas sales.
5. The herbaceous border has been replanted and most of the shrubs died since you were last here.
6. I am unable to find proof that either of the accounts have been paid.
7. There is no reason to doubt that what he said in his second statement is not true.
8. It is my considered opinion that he never has, and never will, behave in such a manner.
9. Equipped with several years' legal training, the demands made on him in his new post proved well within his powers.
10. Candidates are recommended to divide their time equally between each question.

Exercise F

Criticise the following sentences carefully and correct them:

A

1. The solution to the problem, and which should have been obvious from the first, was to alter the filing system, so the new manager ordered this to be effected forthwith.
2. When it was announced that the biggest majority of the electors vote for the Progressive Party, the listeners were so disinterested that they turned off their wireless sets.
3. We intended to have gone to the festival, but Arthur and I was prevented due to a very foggy morning.

B

1. It seems as if you and me are likely to be unlucky in getting a raise in salary from what the secretary let fall about the company's position yesterday.

2. Not having heard from you to date you will not be surprised at me supposing the answer is in the negative to my request to you to kindly support my application for the post in London.
3. Who do you propose as the new Manager? Above all tact and evenness of temper is what is needed and I would not hesitate to say Smith was the man if you ask me.

[*Corporation of Secretaries, Intermediate*]

Exercise G

Criticise the following sentences from students' work and rewrite them making no unnecessary changes.

1. Youth today is fashion-conscious and nearly all young people follow fashion trends, especially girls.
2. In that year membership was 547 000 with the total retail sales being £15 million.
3. Many of these sort of teenagers result from homes where parents either are unable to control them properly or the mother is at work and has no time for her children.
4. The amount of people devoting their lives to youth work and the work and skill that is put in is amazing.
5. The most effective of the main effects is the concluding rocket display.
6. It is impossible to predict the path of clouds of radioactive dust due to variation of local wind direction.
7. These kind of developments were not encouraged in the nineteenth century.
8. Because sea voyages were so long and dangerous there was very little sea travel where unnecessary.
9. Most decisions are only taken by the Council of Ministers as a last resort.
10. The Transport Commission aim to produce a railway system of which the nation will be proud to use.
11. Although traffic is dense in these regions it occurs only at peak periods.
12. British Rail derive the greater part of their revenue from freight than from passenger traffic.
13. Charles Howarth together with William Cooper were constitution makers which still is used today.
14. In the early days of the cooperative movement buying a share not only entitled the customer to dividend on purchases but also to a vote in management.
15. On returning the drawer to its position the next article drops into place.

16. All conditions can be created in the tanks under which the ship models can be tested.
17. At an early stage each cell looks alike.
18. Having ascertained the minimum resistance hull shape, the shipbuilders are given the relevant information and build accordingly.
19. Relatively few families in the whole world have record players and cannot therefore buy and appreciate records.
20. After feeding the plant with liquor containing very slight traces of ammonia it is concentrated into pure ammonia.
21. There was a period of expansion in new areas and then more slowly until it reached a peak in 1903.
22. Very little or even no changes occurred in the next few years.
23. Trade fairs are a commercial feature today many being in new exporting markets.
24. When removing the carburetter the float chamber unfortunately broke in two.
25. It is designed so that the cement being mixed can be emptied into a wheelbarrow which can be placed under the drum when it is upside down.

Exercise H

Comment on the wording of the following sentences from students' work:

1. The court of justice has several judges appointed mutually amongst the Six.
2. Many ministers were completely disinterested in the maritime aspects of their country's affairs.
3. We have, during the last few weeks, been inundated with forms that have not been returned to us.
4. The surplus between cost and selling price steadily arose.
5. The trading methods of the different cooperative societies are not necessarily the same.
6. The import of foodstuffs into this country is particularly important.
7. The idea of this machine is to test materials before they are used in the factory.
8. This is a small but sturdily built grinder and has a wide range of uses, the maximum height of the wheel being 300 mm.
9. Such a man is still sometimes seen cycling down a country lane, with a large suitcase strapped to the carrier, peddling his goods.
10. Older children take up smoking because they think it makes them look older.

Chapter 5

Appropriate Wording

I. TONE

We are all familiar with the way the tone of voice in which somebody speaks to us affects us, quite apart from what he has to tell us. We may feel the speaker dislikes us; or is friendly towards us; is bullying us or seeking our help; despises us or respects us – just because of the way he speaks. When we are ourselves the Tx it pays us to remember how we felt about certain tones of voice when we were the Rx.

Similarly in writing, an attitude towards the Rx, or the subject matter, can be conveyed by the wording and the sentence structure. It is useful to employ the word 'tone' for this also. Many advertisers, for instance, adopt a bullying tone – *Try some today. Act now; don't delay. Buy it now.* With so many people shouting imperatives at him the consumer begins to develop a self-protective deafness. The older tone for this sort of thing was ingratiating, even obsequious: *May we venture to intrude upon your valuable time in order to bring to your attention the advantages to be obtained from the use of our duplicating machines.*

Impersonal constructions and a stilted vocabulary produce a cold tone: *Your request has been received and the matter is under consideration. As soon as a decision has been reached notification of this will be sent.*

Emphasis on 'I' and 'you' and a less formal vocabulary produce a warm friendly tone much more conducive to good communication: *I have received your request and am looking into the matter now. As soon as I have made up my mind I shall let you know.*

But this degree of informality may not always be felt to be justified in business, although it is certainly on the increase in letters and internal memos. Deciding just how formal the tone should be and keeping the tone consistent are the two aspects of tone most likely to present difficulty in written communication.

Most people find the way a policeman gives evidence faintly comic (unless he is giving evidence against them). This is because the tone of his vocabulary often seems a little too dignified for what he has to say, especially considering he is speaking, not writing: *Acting on information received I was proceeding in the direction of Ayrton Park when I observed the accused behaving in a suspicious manner.*

It does sound a little unnatural; but the policeman is in the same difficulty that a manager is in when dictating letters – he is speaking, but what he speaks is going to be read. Policemen are trained to speak like that so that what they say will be uniform in style and dignified, and will not offend against accepted written English when it appears in a transcript of evidence. We would all recognise that the tone was completely wrong if instead he said something like: *We'd had a tip off so I was legging it for Ayrton Park when who should I see but Jimmy the Creep here up to something fishy by the look of him.* This, however, might be something like the appropriate tone for telling his mates about it – if he used his court-of-law tone in the canteen somebody would soon point out his mistake.

Words, then, are chosen not only for their meaning but also for their tone; and their tone must be appropriate not only to the subject matter but also to the circumstances and the Rx. To a friend we may write: *Let me know what I owe you*; but to a firm: *Kindly render your account*; and these are not interchangeable. A firm will write to a customer not: *If you can't get our make in the shops round your way drop us a line* but: *If you are unable to obtain our product locally write to us direct.* The post office may properly make the proviso: *Payment will be made subject to the possession by the Postmaster of sufficient funds*; but you could hardly write to a friend who had lent you a pound: *Repayment will be subject to my possession of sufficient funds next month.*

If, as in this last example, we use in speech or writing extremely formal language in an informal situation or seek to gain effect by using long or unfamiliar words where simpler words would do equally well, we are being pretentious. The opposite fault is, in writing, to lower the tone by writing too much like we speak; in speech, to make excessive use of informal and slang expressions.

The worst fault of all is to swing from one extreme of tone to the other when we talk or write. We must aim at a consistent tone and one that is appropriate to the circumstances.

In written business communication we frequently require rather a dignified and formal tone. When all the other factors in choosing our words have been given consideration, we must also give some weight therefore to the aspect of tone, eradicating those words and expressions that seem beneath the dignity of what we are writing but at the same time avoiding the pretentious and trying to write as simply as possible.

II. TONE LOWERERS

A. Dialect

A dialect is the minority language of a region or class. It may vary from the form most widely accepted amongst educated English people (what is rather oddly called 'Received English') not only in pronunciation but also in syntax and vocabulary. The old Devon woman calling down from her window *Oi be up 'ere eatin' winkles* is employing a different conjugation of the verb 'to be' that runs *I be, thou beest, he be*. North of Trent the local ruling for the distinction between *shall* and *will* is opposite from that of Received English. Most areas have their special words (e.g. *griskins* in Wiltshire, *pyklets* in the North Midlands) not widely understood outside, or special uses of words (in the area north of Trent *to mash the tea* is not the same sort of process as *to mash the potatoes* and *mending the fire* has nothing to do with repairing it). A University of Leeds survey team visited eight Wiltshire villages and found six words for 'left-handed' – *wotty-'anded* (Ashton Keynes), *kek-'anded* (Burbage), *gammy-'anded* (Steeple Ashton and Whiteparish), *skwippy* (Sutton Veny), *skwiffy* (Fovant), and *Marlborough-'anded* (Avebury and Netheravon – which are near Marlborough, of course.)

Class dialects are mostly a matter of pronunciation. In London (as in most great cities) 'low' areas and areas considered of good class frequently abut upon each other. There is an old anecdote of the two churches, one each side of a road which was the boundary between two such contrasting districts. On the one side of the road the congregation is singing *Prize 'im fer iz grice and fiver* and on the other side, *Preeze Him for His grease and fever*. The point of the anecdote is that both versions are variants from Received English, both are class dialect forms; from this point of view one is not 'better' than the other.

A business man who has dialect elements in his speech is at an advantage when dealing with people of his own region or class; the familiar dialect inclines them to be friendly towards him, prepared to trust him. It is a very different story once he moves outside his own region or class. Regional elements will make him at best the odd man out, something of a figure of fun – at worst, incomprehensible. Class difference shown in his voice will antagonise his Rx; whether the latter feels that the Tx is revealed as either superior or inferior to him in social class he will tend to be suspicious of him just for being different.

It would seem then, perhaps regrettably, that the young manager needs to cultivate a rather colourless neutral voice devoid of all but the merest trace of dialect background. Many, to retain the advantages which the dialect offers on home territory, become virtually bilingual.

Since dialect is a minority language it is automatically ruled out from formal written communication, the aim of which is to be as widely understood as possible. If therefore you come from an area where dialect is strong it is important to be quite sure that you know which words and constructions are for local use only, so that these do not become unconsciously absorbed into your formal writing.

B. Colloquialisms

Colloquialisms are expressions properly employed only in speech or which can have a certain meaning only in speech (see page 35). Such expressions are perfectly suitable to all spoken communication and add flavour to private correspondence (after all in a private letter we do want to sound as if we are talking to the person we are writing to) and other kinds of informal written communication. Their use in formal written communication results in an immediate loss of the dignified tone required, though there may be occasions in business correspondence where this is worthwhile for the sake of the improved friendliness of tone.

C. Slang

Slang consists of the intentional substitution of an undignified equivalent for the Received English expression. Its origin would seem to lie in a combination of dissatisfaction with, or embarrassment over, the standard expression when speaking and a need for novelty. The genius who invents the slang expression is seldom recorded in history. Nobody knows who first substituted *browned-off* for *melancholy* or *disillusioned* in such a sentence as *I'm feeling properly browned-off today* but it was certainly a *squaddy* (soldier). Nor who later decided that *browned-off* was losing its novelty and substituted *cheesed-off*.

In moderation, such expressions are a valuable addition to our spoken communication but we have to be careful to use them with the right Rx. It must be remembered too that the conscientious use of up-to-date slang by the kind of Tx who would not normally use such expressions is a kind of inverted pretentiousness and is frequently (and rightly) seen by the Rx as condescension. The use of out-of-date slang has nothing to be said in its favour.

Since slang is, by definition, undignified it is ill suited to formal writing. It becomes no more acceptable by enclosure between inverted commas. *All students are requested to refrain from 'kicking up a row' while in the library* is no improvement on the same words without the inverted commas.

III. PRETENTIOUS LANGUAGE

Pretentious language arises when too much attention is paid to dignity of tone. If an over-colloquial style can be described as writing in your shirt sleeves, a pretentious style is writing in medieval armour, so weighed down with words that you can hardly communicate at all. It is the fault of inability to call a spade a spade, so that it becomes *a horticultural implement for the excavation of terrestrial matter*. An obsession with long and unfamiliar words at best is time and space wasting and irritates the Rx with its conceit, at worst substantially reduces the number of people who can understand what is meant.

The practice of substituting the unfamiliar (but more dignified) for the familiar is on the increase. Barbers long ago became hairdressers (and some hairdressers, friseurs) but undertakers are scarce too today and funeral directors and morticians are to the fore; rat-catchers are more socially acceptable as rodent operators and the London County Council found some years ago that it could improve recruitment of road-sweepers by advertising for street orderlies.

One can hardly object to these little concessions to human vanity; but what is one to make of the doctor, quoted in *The Lancet*, who converted what in colloquial language would be *feeling full* into *sensations interpreted as a satiety associated with ingestion of food*, or the report on the suspected use of poison gas bombs in the Yemen in 1963 which referred to these as *munitions used to disseminate chemical warfare agents?* What of the teacher who in an article on team teaching (in *Education* 15 May 1969) produced this impressive-sounding piece of non-communication: *The large group element provides good communication across all small group and individual activities but it also provides a gravitational counter to the centrifugal effect of so much satellite activity?*

Some years ago the government of the time interested itself in what was to prove a costly failure, a scheme to import on a large scale from West Africa what were then commonly called 'monkey-nuts'. It was understandable that when referring to these the more dignified term *ground-nuts* was preferred, somewhat surprising that when they were shelled to take up less space on a ship they became *decorticated ground-nuts*, but downright amazing that once this term was established the nuts with the shells still on became *undecorticated ground-nuts*.

Politicians seem to excel at this sort of thing. A recent Commonwealth Relations Secretary made this pronouncement to the House: *We have proposed to the Six that while maintaining the objective of comparative outlet, the arrangements for the initial period should be reviewed from time to time and, where necessary, amended to take account of changes in the situation or of world-wide commodity agreements which might have been concluded in the meantime.* But business men do not lag far behind. An impresario seeking to interest an actor in an open-air theatre project wrote: *The ultimate success of our venture will be completely dependent on the climatic conditions.* The actor is reported as replying: *I suppose you mean, you hope it won't rain.*

There is nothing wrong with using a long or unfamiliar word if it does a job no other word will do (and provided the Tx satisfies himself the Rx will know how to decode it). There is certainly something wrong with the deliberate use of unfamiliar vocabulary in an attempt to impress the Rx ('blinding with science', as the Services call it).

Even where the word preferred is not long enough or unfamiliar enough to cause any decoding problem for the Rx it is a little odd that so many business men seem automatically to select the longer of a pair of synonyms: *inform, tell; commence, begin* or *start; assist, help; purchase, buy; locate, find; proceed, go.* In certain contexts the longer and very slightly more formal word probably has its justification. *A course of lectures on Cybernetics will commence on January 16th* – it could be argued that here *commence* has a little more authority than *begin* and that the context supports this. But *The new clerk will commence work on January 16th* borders on the pretentious.

It is possible that English teaching at 'O' level sometimes inculcates attitudes towards language that are not helpful in business communication. In essay writing at school the pupil is frequently exhorted to display his width of vocabulary; and an ostentatious display of vocabulary is exactly what pretentious writing is.

IV. JARGON

The word *jargon* is most useful if reserved for derogatory reference to the special language of a trade, profession, or field of study. We may apply it when we consider a Tx is using a specialised vocabulary, or complicated constructions, to impress, or in such a way as to isolate himself from his Rx. Jargon is thus in some ways analogous to both dialect and pretentious writing.

The architect talks of *fenestration* when he means the number of windows in a building; the hospital almoner uses *domiciliary patients* to refer to patients in their own homes and *ambulants* to refer to those that can walk. This is the jargon of vocabulary. Sir Ernest Gower quotes in *The Complete Plain Words* this piece of legal jargon, the jargon of construction: *Separate departments in the same premises are treated as separate premises for this purpose when separate branches of work which are commonly carried on as separate businesses in separate premises are carried on in separate departments in the same premises.*

Two forms of jargon are specially noticeable in business and local or central government communication:

1. use of the specialised vocabulary of a trade, industry, government department etc. without explanation even though the Rx is from outside that trade, industry, or department.
2. commercial jargon – fragments of that curious style of writing once called 'business English' that was at its heyday before the 1914–18 war.

If you are forced to use a word from the jargon of your job (because no other word exists) you should enclose it between inverted commas and – if the Rx is unlikely to have met this use of the word before – supply a gloss. Such inverted commas mean 'as we call it' and are not to be confused with those that some people put round slang or colloquial expressions, which seem to mean, 'I cannot be bothered to think of the formal equivalent for this'.

  Commercial jargon makes a letter or report seem stilted and old-fashioned. Here are a few examples of the kind of commercial jargon still encountered, with their modern equivalents:

under separate cover	*separately*
we are able to quote you ...	*our quotation is* ...
on Friday next	*next Friday* (but date better)
your valued/esteemed order	*your order*
we shall have pleasure in arranging for ...	*we shall arrange for* ...
inst., ult. and *prox.*	give the date
we beg to	meaningless – omit
and oblige	omit
re (or, worse, *in re*)	*with reference to, about*
per (*per goods train*)	*by*
as per (*as per my*)	*as* (stated) *in*
advise	*inform, tell*
same (*return same immediately*)	*this, it*
enclosed please find	*I enclose*
We acknowledge receipt of ... *I have to acknowledge receipt of* ...	} *Thank you for* ...

V. OBJECTIVE AND SUBJECTIVE LANGUAGE

An objective statement tells us about the object that the statement is about. A subjective statement tells us about the reaction of the Tx to the object; i.e. it really tells us about the Tx. Thus if John says: *Mary is pretty* he only appears to be telling us something about Mary. What he is really telling us is something about what he considers prettiness. Harry may say: *Mary is not very pretty*, and George: *Mary is plain*. Mary remains the same – what is emphasised is the differences in the three men's ideas of prettiness. Thus *Mary is pretty* is a subjective statement, and *pretty* in this context a subjective word. *Mary's height is 167 cm* on the other hand is an objective statement; it is not dependent on who says it and is capable of external checking (Mary can be measured). If we substitute for this: *Mary is tall*, we have a statement still objective but considerably less objective than the previous one. Interpretation of this statement depends partly on the Tx's opinion of what constitutes 'tallness' for a girl. A Swede and a Japanese would probably have differing views on this. We may feel therefore that it is the impression of tallness made upon the speaker that is being referred to and that the statement is to this extent subjective. Nevertheless we know that there is substantial agreement about what is meant by 'tall' for a girl, especially within members of the same racial group, and we are prepared to accept 'tall' as a predominantly objective word in this context. For the statement to be completely objective we would have to associate it with a definition of 'tall' girls in terms of measurement (cf. the definition of 'small' boilers on page 32).

It is important then to be aware, both as an Rx and as a Tx, whether the words we are using are subjective, objective, or predominantly objective. There is a place for subjective wording in business, when we are seeking persuasion and to communicate attitudes (in advertising, for example), but the bulk of business communication is factual and demands objective or predominantly objective writing. This is not to say that even in reports (one of the most objective forms of business communication) the occasional subjective word which serves a special purpose may not be employed. For example, in a report, *During this stage of the operation the mixture reaches a temperature of 180°C* is completely objective; but *During this stage of the operation the mixture reaches the dangerously high temperature of 180°C* may be much more helpful to the Rx. The great weakness of subjective wording in business communication is that it intrudes the Tx's opinions and viewpoints into what should be factual matters and the Rx may be betrayed into accepting as a fact what is only an opinion. When you are the Rx you should check carefully to make sure you are not making this mistake yourself.

VI. CLICHÉS AND VOGUE WORDS

Vigorous lively language leaps from Tx to Rx demanding his attention. Tired over-worked expressions (and that is what clichés are) have little impact on the Rx – he has met them so often before. It is part of the craft of communication to avoid slipping into the use of clichés.

Today imitation of the inventiveness of others is so rapid and so widespread that within a few months what was a new and perhaps effective use of language becomes a cliché, obsessionally used by everybody. Here are a few examples of fairly recent clichés of this kind (some people call contemporary clichés 'vogue words'):

instant
(major) breakthrough
factor (as *consideration of the price factor*)
massive (build-up)
escalate
psychedelic
target, ceiling (as *production target*)
image (as *the image projected by our advertising*)
affluent/permissive (society)

The student will probably be able to add his own up-to-date examples without great difficulty.

It must be admitted that *communication* itself is well on the way towards becoming a vogue word, expecially in such loose contexts as *It's all a matter of communication* which seems sometimes to have little more meaning than the old cliché *It's all done by mirrors*.

Older clichés are still popular with senior staff and it is necessary for new entrants to the business and government worlds to familiarise themselves with expressions such as *Hobson's choice* or *He'll not set the Thames on fire*, not so that they can use them themselves but so that they will understand their meaning when employed by others.

VII. SUMMARY OF RECOMMENDATIONS

It will be seen that in choosing his words the conscientious communicator has to give consideration to a large number of criteria, some of them possibly contradictory. His first consideration must always be to ensure that meaning is conveyed as exactly as possible by the words selected; the points raised in this chapter are therefore of secondary importance. These points may be summarised as the attempt to choose words appropriate to (a) the type of subject matter (b) the circumstances under which communication is taking place, and (c) the Rx – his educational standing, width of vocabulary, specialised knowledge of the subject etc. The communicator must (1) decide the degree of formality or informality required (2) choose words which give a tone appropriate to this decision but (3) choose the simplest words that will fulfil his purpose. He will (4) decide whether objective or subjective writing is called for and (5) choose words appropriate to this decision. He will (6) endeavour to write freshly and vigorously, avoiding clichés. Finally he must (7) at every stage keep his Rx in mind and seek the words that will best suit that particular Rx.

VIII. EXERCISES

Exercise A

The following is adapted from a letter in a Malayan newspaper. Rephrase the young man's letter for him so that it is consistently dignified, but not pretentious, in tone.

I am handsome Sikh teenager whose betrothed is beseeching him to purchase motor vehicle. At last at great expense I am proud possessor of 100 per cent car but my driving lacks proficiency. Sometimes I am exchanging brake for exhilerator and other times I am passing wrong side oncoming traffic at great rapidity.

My beloved covers eyes with hands and moans softly and now declares she will be accompanying me only by public transport or Shanker's pony. Shall I bow to feminine whim or seek Another to occupy hot seat?

Exercise B

Rewrite the following in a more consistent tone.

Whatever may have been true of the early prospectors who began to poke about in the earth for oil in a slap-happy fashion nearly a century ago, nowadays we try to hunt it out scientifically. Often the oil is hidden quite a way down and before drilling is done we have to make scientific observations and measurements on the earth's surface to try to spot where the oil is. First the geologist gets going and tries to put his finger on those regions where he reckons oil is likely to have piled up in underground beds of rock or sand. But often the geologist cannot get enough 'gen' to go on because the rock formations are completely covered up. Then the geophysicist comes in on it. His first ploy is to measure the force of gravity as accurately as possible over the whole area where the presence of oil

seems 'on'. This is because oil-bearing rock is usually denser and therefore has a bit more gravitational pull than the rocks lying above it. He
cannot as yet pin-point the oil itself but he can get a hazy idea of which
rocks might contain oil.

Oil fields have an awkward habit of turning up in tricky places, render-
ing field operations frequently hazardous. Much prospecting is done in
the 'back of beyond' where jungle and swamp make the going pretty slow.
It says a lot for the gravity meters employed that they stand up to the
belting they get on the job and yet are capable of such delicate measurement.

Exercise C

Consider the following pairs of words. Indicate for each a context in
which you would prefer the first to the second, and one in which you
would prefer the second to the first. Are there any pairs where you would
prefer one word to the other in all contexts? Justify your answers.

think	give	show	start	make
consider	donate	evince	initiate	render
end	try	watch	necessary	get
terminate	attempt	observe	requisite	obtain

Exercise D

1. Which words in the following passage do you consider subjective?
2. List the *facts* you know about the COPY-BOX 5 after reading the
   passage.

The widely-acclaimed COPY-BOX 5 produces perfect copies in up
to five colours, more cheaply than any other duplicator. Operation is
extremely simple and wonderfully clear copies result. Paper pressure can
be manually adjusted and it copies on all thickness of paper in sizes up
to 20 × 30 cm. The duplicator is supplied with foolproof automatic paper
feed and an easily removable damping pad. The large-capacity fluid
tank is pump-fed, exactly the right degree of damping being achieved by
regulation of the accurate control disc.

The COPY-BOX 5 is clean, fast, and remarkably versatile. Elegantly
styled and finished in corrosion-resistant enamel (black or cream) this
precision-built appliance will form a handsome and valuable addition to
your office equipment.

Exercise E

Write an *objective* description of one of the following in about 150 words:

1. a relative or friend
2. your home town or village
3. your vehicle
4. your usual classroom.

Exercise F

Write a short speech (about 200 words) for one of the following occasions, *to include the maximum number of clichés*:

1. A distinguished Old Boy presenting the prizes at his old school
2. A senior executive urging harder work and higher production from his factory
3. A shop steward on 'Management and the Workers'
4. A politician on 'The Future of England'.

Exercise G

What is the meaning of the following figurative expressions, now clichés? Do you know the origin of any of them?

A Parthian shot
To cross the Rubicon
A nest-egg
On the knees of the gods
A flash in the pan
A bone of contention
The fourth estate
The thin end of the wedge
Caviare to the general
Pearls before swine
An Achilles' heel
A square peg in a round hole
An olive branch
The devil's advocate
To view the world through rose-tinted spectacles
A red herring
To take the bull by the horns
To change horses in mid-stream
Between Scylla and Charybdis
To go cap in hand
Making bricks without straw
Under the aegis of
To have too many irons in the fire
To rob Peter to pay Paul
A sop to Cerberus

Exercise H

Comment on the following with special reference to the use of inverted commas.

1. This is a useful 'gadget' that will probably prove to have a considerable sales potential in the home market.
2. The highly polished surface is first lightly 'etched' with acid.
3. I am not entirely satisfied that the method by which we obtained this information was completely 'above-board'; there does seem an element of the 'wangle' in what was done.
4. We send out 'crews', groups of operators specially trained to make geophysical survey in the field, at regular intervals.
5. We should be very grateful if you would give the 'tip-off' when the process is ready for development.
6. A group of parasites of particular interest to this department is that causing 'scours' in sheep. Losses from this disease can be reduced by phenothiazene applied by drenching or, in pellet form, by means of a 'balling gun'.
7. On the fifty-third flight, four more approaches to the stall were made with the aircraft 'clean'.
8. This time the stall, or 'G break', was large and abrupt, causing the aircraft to drop but with its nose still up in the flying position.
9. The word 'stock' is derived from Old English *stocc*. His word stock is less than 3,000 words.
10. We signed for the goods 'unexamined'. We signed for the goods unexamined.

Exercise I

Improve the expression of the following sentences giving special attention to (*a*) suitability and consistency of tone (*b*) avoidance of pretentious language, jargon, and clichés.

1. Anthony in the funeral oration tends to down Caesar for his vaulting ambition.
2. In this modern world too many people devote their leisure to things like television, the cinema, and football, where they have everything laid on for them.
3. Re your order *Sexual Customs in Togoland* of 15th ult. we beg to advise this volume out of print.
4. Customers are requested to obtain a check from the waitress and to present same at cash-desk prior to departure.
5. Maximum expedition in plant installation is envisaged subject to early site availability and adequate recruitment of personnel.

6. We thank you for your esteemed order for quality rose trees which will enjoy our most careful attention. Notification will be forwarded a few days prior to dispatch.

7. *Extension to Boxhead Golf Club*
   We would be pleased to receive tender from you in respect of the above. Enclosed please find specification, tender form, tender envelope, and Drawing No. S26/1/2 in connection therewith.

8. This agreement is likely to be instrumental in effecting no inconsiderable amelioration of present conditions of employment of company executives not least with reference to the remuneration factor.

9. Although we have left no stone unturned in our investigation into the causes of the delay in forwarding this consignment success has been conspicuous by its absence. We deeply regret the inconvenience inevitably occasioned you by our procrastination.

10. Mr Tompkins has been employed in this department in a subordinate capacity for six months and has done his job pretty well; it would be a good idea to provide him with an opportunity to demonstrate his potential for initiative.

Exercise J

The words *lady dog, edifice, inquire* may be described as 'genteelisms' for *bitch, building, ask*. Give genteelisms, one for each, for the following 'normal' words:

read   sofa   toothpaste   servant   before   underclothing   boarder jam   go   stop

[*Royal Society of Arts, English Language, Stage III*]

Chapter 6

Concise Wording

I. THE IMPORTANCE OF CONCISE WRITING IN BUSINESS COMMUNICATIONS

When a young man working in an office is first entrusted with dictating letters on his firm's behalf or is called upon for his first written report, it is natural enough that he tends to spread himself – short letters seem inadequate letters, a short report seems an insignificant report. Nevertheless, this tendency should be resisted from the start; the habit of verbosity, once entered upon, is difficult to shake off, and in fact grows more pronounced as the years go by. Verbosity in written business communication has nothing to be said in its favour. Conciseness, on the other hand, offers the following advantages:

1. reduction in typist time
2. saving in paper, and wear and tear of typewriters and ribbons
3. saving in storage space when material has to be filed
4. reduction in printing costs when material has to be printed
5. saving in reading time for the Rx (the most important consideration).

Conciseness must come last of the points to be considered when choosing our words – accuracy, clarity, and appropriateness of language must never be sacrificed to brevity. In practice, however, observation of sound principles in selecting words – particularly discrimination between synonyms and avoidance of pretentious language and jargon – usually in itself takes the writer well on the way to maximum conciseness. After that, it is mostly a matter of substituting for the initial tendency to pad out what one has to say an awareness that words are precious and easily wasted, and the determination not to use any word that is not doing a necessary job.

II. THE TRUE MEASURE OF CONCISENESS

We usually judge the length of what we write by the number of words used. This can be deceptive. *The lateral fenestration of domestic accommodation units* is only seven words long while *the number of windows in the sides of houses* is nine words long. These figures are irrelevant when conciseness is thought of in terms of the advantages listed above. The relevant count is that there are fifty-five letters and spaces in the first sentence and forty-four in the second. The pretentious sentence is not shorter than the simple one – it is 25 per cent longer. Except where we are preparing copy for a certain limited space (in an advertising block for example) we shall probably never count letters and spaces; but we should always remember that the more convenient word-count is not a reliable measure of conciseness if we are addicted to long words.

III. REDUNDANCY

Grammarians distinguish various types of redundancy and give these special names. For communication in business it is sufficient to recognise the types that exist and to avoid them.

1. The simplest form is where a second (and therefore redundant) word is used to give meaning already conveyed by a first word. *He arrived tired and weary. He has returned back to the office. The reason why … is because …*

2. A second type occurs when words are used to specify something which can already be understood from the rest of the sentence. *As they strolled back the sun was setting in the west.*

3. A third type consists in the addition of adjectives to nouns that need no adjective – *actual facts; definite decisions; serious dangers* – and intensifiers added to words that should not be intensified – *very perfect; very perceptible: extremely dead.*

4. A fourth category is brought about by the meaningless introduction of adverbs or adverbial phrases. *Definitely* and *of course* are widely used in this way.

In the days before the death penalty was discontinued in 1965, Sir Alan Herbert dealt with *definitely* in inimitable fashion: 'I offer a prize to the first foreman of a jury to announce a verdict of *definitely guilty* and another to the judge who informs the prisoner that he will be *definitely hanged by the neck until he is very definitely dead.*'

Of course is often tucked into a sentence with no motive at all except to pad it out, but sometimes produces the irritating effect of making the Rx appear an ignorant fool: *This matter should, of course, have been dealt with at branch office level* (and nobody but you would have thought otherwise).

Relatively, comparatively, unduly, although capable of precise meaning, are frequently used in contexts where they can have no meaning. *The new process is comparatively inexpensive* means nothing unless the cost of the old process has been mentioned. *Delivery of this order has been unduly delayed* is meaningless unless we expected delivery to be delayed but not for so long as it was.

In sentences of the type, popular in business and government circles, *Our research department is actively engaged in investigation of the cause of this phenomenon*, *actively* is redundant as it is not possible to be inactively engaged in an activity.

In the sentence *Man's direct influence on geography is really quite negligible*, *quite* is ambiguous. If it is intended to mean 'completely, entirely' it is redundant because *negligible* includes this idea; if it is intended to mean 'tending towards, somewhat' it is redundant because such a qualification of *negligible* is meaningless. Removal of *quite* necessitates removal of *really* (independently redundant, anyhow, because there is no distinction to be made between *quite* and *really quite*). Two words are saved, and the sentence gains in vigour and impact.

5. Finally, there is legal redundancy. Lawyers must be particularly careful to avoid ambiguity; redundancy is a clumsy but automatic check on ambiguity; legal documents are therefore deliberately repetitive, avoiding generalisations and naming each specific instance.

Thus in typical bye-laws controlling behaviour in a public park we are told that we must not (*a*) *remove, cut, or displace any soil, turf, or plant*, (*b*) *pluck any bud, blossom, flower, or leaf or any tree, shrub, or plant*.

This cumbersome kind of writing arises from the attempt by the man drafting the regulations to envisage every possible infringement and to deal with it specifically so that no loop-hole of escape exists for the offender. It is a style – whatever its merits or demerits for the legal profession – not to be imitated by business men. Local and central government officers have frequently to write to members of the public about matters that are the subject of such regulations. There is no need to copy the redundancies of the original, except where interpretation of the legal point involved depends upon the exact wording.

IV. CIRCUMLOCUTION

Redundancies are easily enough detected in revision and, even if overlooked, will cause only minor inflation of your wording. Circumlocation is altogether more serious. Its essence is an unconscious preference for the long-winded and roundabout over the short and direct. It arises deliberately rather than accidentally and runs right through a man's writing (and often his speech as well). It is closely allied to pretentiousness; the man who employs a pretentious vocabulary will almost always be addicted also to circumlocution. It is important to detect the symptoms early; circumlocution quickly becomes a lifetime habit.

Here are some tendencies which should be looked upon as warnings that you are moving that way.

1. Preference for

in this connection	*with regard to*
in connection with	*as regards*
in regard to	*with reference to*
in respect of	*as to*

instead of their simple prepositional equivalents:

I am writing to you in connection with your application ... for
I am writing to you about your application ...
Your estimate as to the number to be ordered ... for
Your estimate of the number to be ordered ...

Use of these expressions, especially as a lead into material, often results in gross inflation of the wording:

With reference to your Order 591/A, these goods were despatched on the 15th ult. for
We sent your Order 519/A on May 15th.

(80 letters and spaces against 37.)

2. Compulsive use of *case* and *instance*:

A large number of students have left the College this year, in many cases before taking their examinations – for
A large number of students have left the College this year, many before taking their examinations.

The substitution of *instance* for *case* does not improve such sentences.

Particularly absurd are unnecessary uses of *case* where its meaning as 'a container' is brought to mind by the context:

These were very large ships for the period carrying twenty or more rowers and cargoes of cattle in many cases.

3. Preference for

as/so far as ... *is concerned*
from ... *viewpoint/angle/standpoint/point of view*
in view of/owing to/in spite of/the fact that ...

Thus *This post is not so well paid* can become

This post is not so attractive so far as salary is concerned or
This post is not so attractive from the remuneration viewpoint.

As your application was not received before the closing date … becomes
*In view of the fact that your application was not receieved before the
closing date* …

Although becomes *in spite of the fact that*; *because* is replaced by *owing to
the fact that* or – often and ungrammatically – *due to the fact that.*

4. Love of abstract nouns. It is difficult enough to be sure that the Rx
decodes as the Tx wants him to even when they are dealing in concrete
nouns. When the Tx writes *table* he has a certain picture of a table in his
mind unlikely to be identical with the table that comes into the Rx's
mind when he reads the word, since no two tables are absolutely alike.
The semantic problem becomes much greater as soon as the communicators start using abstract words. It is curious, then, that a certain type of
Tx will deliberately force abstract nouns into what he writes, even if it
means a longer sentence, e.g.

This material is of a resilient character for
This material is resilient or, better,
This resilient material …
Owing to the expensive nature of this operation … for
As this operation is expensive …
*Completion of this contract should be delayed until the position in regard
to availability of raw materials has been clarified* (Note: *completion,
position, availability, in regard to*) for
*This contract should not be completed until we are sure that the raw
materials will be available*
*Admission must be made of a certain lack of due carefulness on the part
of our staff in this connection* (Note: *admission, lack, part, in this connection*) for
We must admit our staff were rather careless about this.

5. Excessive use of the passive voice. The verb is the mainspring of
the sentence. As its name implies (from Latin *verbum*, a word) it is *the*
word. As we have just seen, emphasis on nouns, especially abstract
nouns, at the expense of verbs weakens our sentences. Adjectives in turn
weaken nouns (they have been called 'the enemy of the noun'). The verb
itself is weakened if it is put into the passive voice. The passive is favoured
for reports because it is impersonal. Just because it is impersonal it is
unsuitable for much business communication. It puts a distance between
Tx and Rx. The passive is usually at least one word longer than the active
equivalent, and can, especially when associated with abstract nouns, produce considerable circumlocution.

ACTIVE *Mr Jones will pay this account next month.* (8 words)

PASSIVE *This account will be paid next month by Mr Jones.* (10 words)
PASSIVE WITH CIRCUMLOCUTION *Payment of this account will be made by Mr Jones next month.* (12 words)
ACTIVE *In cricket, the batsman sometimes hits a six.* (8 words)
PASSIVE *In cricket, a six is sometimes hit by the batsman.* (10 words)
PASSIVE WITH CIRCUMLOCUTION *The hitting of sixes is an activity occasionally engaged in by cricketers when acting in the capacity of batsman.* (19 words)

V. VERBIAGE

Verbiage is a convenient term for reference to a particularly cumbersome accumulation of words in an attempt to communicate. Verbiage will include redundancies and circumlocution but its characteristic is a sustained disproportion between the number of words used and the amount of information conveyed. It most commonly results from a combination of the desire to pad out material to make it seem more important, or to impress the Rx with a grand manner, and sheer linguistic ineptitude (see Example 1 below). Occasionally however, as in Example 2, it appears to be employed consciously, with the aim of disguising from the Rx how little is really being said.

Whatever its source, verbiage is a use of words that is diametrically opposed to communication principles.

EXAMPLE 1 – an extract from a schools circular issued by a local education authority:

GAMES. *In view of present pitch conditions attributable to the long spell of dry weather, staff responsible for games (particularly competitive matches) may find it advisable to pay particular attention to this aspect with a view to deciding in connection with any particular activity whether it can be proceeded with with safety to the pupils or should be changed to a practice or should be postponed.*

Rephrasing to remove the verbiage reduces this to less than half the length (30 words against 66) and greatly increases the readability:

During the present dry spell, staff responsible for games should assure themselves before starting any game that the pitch can be used with safety. This applies particularly to competitive matches.

EXAMPLE 2 – an announcement by an estate agent:

The property is joined on to one other similar character property on one side, but otherwise is equivalent to being detached.

In other words, the property is semi-detached.

VI. CONDENSATION

So far we have considered conciseness only as a matter of not putting in unnecessary words. For most communication purposes this is all we have to worry about. When we are making a précis, or reducing advertising material to fit into a limited space, we may have to adopt more positive measures to condense our wording. Condensation consists in a combination of three principle devices:

1. substitution of single words for phrases
2. substitution of phrases for clauses
3. elimination of adjectives and adverbs (and adjectival and adverbial phrases and clauses) not essential to meaning.

1. WORDS FOR PHRASES. Substitution of single words for phrases is usually only possible if the initial selection of words has been a little clumsy. As we saw in Chapter 3 one of the principal advantages of choosing just the right word for the job is that it saves using a phrase. Thus *The alterations were carried out with the least possible degree of interruption of normal business* can be more concisely expressed as *The alterations were carried out with minimum interruption of normal business*. This in turn can be expressed still more concisely as *The alterations were effected with minimum interruption of normal business* provided it is felt that *effected* is an appropriate word for the subject matter and type of Rx.

2. PHRASES FOR CLAUSES. *This employee, who has now passed his qualifying examinations, should be considered for a Grade III appointment* can be slightly shortened by substituting a participial phrase for the adjectival clause – *This employee, having passed his qualifying examinations, should be considered for a Grade III appointment* – and considerably shortened, at the expense of an insignificant loss of detail, as *This employee, now qualified, should be considered for a Grade III appointment*.

3. ELIMINATION OF NON-ESSENTIAL ADJECTIVES AND ADVERBS. We have seen (pages 73–74) that adjectives, adverbs, and adverbial phrases are frequently redundant as used in business communication. Where they (and adjectival phrases and clauses and adverbial clauses) although not redundant do no more than add descriptive detail, they may be omitted to condense a piece of writing. Thus in the first example above, *normal* can be omitted; and in the second example, *now qualified*.

Somerset Maugham is reported as having advised a young writer to go through what he had written striking out every adjective. Reduction in the number of adjectives, and adverbs, probably improves any piece of writing; all that can be left out, therefore, without loss of essential meaning should be left out. Factual communication particularly gains by this treatment as the objectivity of a passage rises with the elimination of qualifying words, which are those where subjective elements are most to the fore.

VII. EXERCISES

Exercise A

Comment on the following expressions:

foot-pedal   assembled together   renovated as new   sole monopoly
time-clock   facilitates easier assembly   leading protagonist
the larger majority   as from   as and from.

Exercise B

Today is 1 March. Approximately when will it be:

1. soon
2. in the future
3. in the near future
4. in the very near future
5. in the foreseeable future?

If you find difficulty answering this question, what have you learned?

Exercise C

Shorten the following passages by removal of redundancies. The first is another extract from park bye-laws; the second is from a committee report on a proposed NATO nuclear fleet.

1. A person shall not affix any bill, placard, or notice to or upon any wall or fence in or enclosing the park, or to or upon any tree, or plant, or to or upon any part of any building, barrier, or railing, or any seat, or of any other erection or ornament in the park.
2. The size of the nuclear resources at the disposal of the NATO Allies is so considerable in quantity that any increase in it is superfluous. This would only increase the existing 'overkill' for which from a military point of view there is no need whatsoever.

Exercise D

Shorten, and increase the vigour of, the following sentences.

1. A relatively sharp increase in prices has been apparent during the week.
2. A marked improvement in quality has been effected since the introduction of quality control was brought about.

3. Destruction of the entire central section of the building took place as a result of the conflagration.
4. Refusal by management to consider an outlined scheme for staggered working-hours which had been put forward by the works committee was a cause of grave dissatisfaction on the part of the latter.
5. The application of time and motion study to this section will, of course, result in appreciable improvement from the production standpoint.

Exercise E

Rephrase the following sentences to remove redundancies and circumlocutions.

1. Diesel and electric traction engines have been substituted in place of steam power on the railways.
2. Malnutrition is widespread in China and many thousands of children die at a young age.
3. The need for consumer protection organisations has become very necessary over the last few years.
4. The other methods of financing available are too innumerable to mention.
5. In some societies a share must be first obtained by accumulating dividends before the customer can become a voting member.
6. It is fact that at this time of year there are more deaths on the road caused by drunken driving than at any other time of the year.
7. Finally, to conclude my remarks, I want to pay tribute to all those who, unnoticed and unrewarded, have unobtrusively helped throughout the year with nobody until this moment to draw attention to the support and assistance they have rendered the organisation at all times.
8. The subject of our lecture tonight will be about Cybernetics.
9. We must apologise for the delay in delivering your order the cause of which was due to staff absences in the packing department as a result of the present epidemic of influenza, which is as you know extremely widespread, and has forced several of our men to take time off from work.
10. The situation of these exporting countries is in a most advantageous position in so far as foreign trade is concerned as they are so placed as to have easy access to other countries.

Exercise F

Reduce the following passage of 290 words by at least 100 words by removal of redundancies, circumlocutions, and other unnecessary wording only.

Many stories and tales of a most exciting kind are told of how in the old days of the past men used to adopt all sorts of various disguises in order to penetrate, without being recognised, into the factories of their competitors to try to steal their competitors' secrets that were jealously guarded. Even in the nineteenth century this was not by any manner of means entirely unknown as a method of procedure, and it is said that not more than five people only were ever allowed into one of Bessemer's early factories. Nowadays, information about new processes and products is usually widely published to all concerned or interested and we do not have to adopt measures of such a desperate nature to be in a position to obtain it.

On the other hand, there is a great deal more of it to be had. Thousands of widely scattered firms and institutes all over the world are carrying out research into finding out about the applications of science in industry and it is vitally essential that results are made known to the right people relatively quickly. More and more scientists with their long tradition, stretching back for so many years, of prompt and speedy publication are coming increasingly into industry. Industrial processes are developing all the time a more and more complex character as the years go by. In fact we have actually reached a stage when a great deal of knowledge is required to be in the possession of the makers of our present-day high quality products. It is a sobering thought, one which is bound to make us seriously consider the present situation, that any electrician of today now knows more about electricity than Faraday did in his time.

Exercise G

This passage of 130 words can be halved by condensation, and removal of redundancies. How near can you get to 65 words?

Prices which can be maintained at a constant and unchanging level are the essential prerequisite to peace in the industrial world. Increases in the workers' pay-packets which coincide with upward trends in prices provide no solution at all. The question we have to ask ourselves is, 'Can we have, at one and the same time, simultaneously full employment, prices held at a steady level, and negotiations freely entered upon for increases in the workers' wages?' In my opinion, I think that the aim of seeing that each and every member of the community has employment should be removed from the sphere of party politics. If we are unable to achieve all three of these very desirable goals that we are all aiming at, let us at least achieve that one.

Part II

Chapter 7

Summaries

I. PRACTICAL APPLICATIONS

The most obvious occasion when concise writing is necessary is the preparation of a summary.

The student tends to think of summarising exclusively in terms of the form he knows best – précis for examinations; but he will probably later on meet many practical applications in his work. It is true that précis for examinations is governed by certain conventions – notably that it is written in continuous prose, not note form, and that it avoids the words of the original – which are not obligatory when preparing summaries in the course of business, but all types of summary are likely to be better executed as a result of training in précis.

Précis for examinations is almost invariably set in the form of the reduction of a short continuous passage to a third or a quarter of its length (occasionally, a fifth). Précis in business is more likely to be of correspondence, of a report, of evidence – material not already in continuous prose form. Illustration of the kinds of minor differences of technique necessary for handling this sort of material is provided in Chapter 8 under the heading: 'Précis of correspondence' (pp. 117–121). Where material already in continuous prose has to be changed to a more concentrated form to save reading time for a senior executive, this is likely to be lengthy material (e.g. papers read before learned societies, articles in magazines, or even whole books, or sections of them, relevant to a firm's products), and the reduction required much greater than for précis, perhaps to one-tenth or even less. Reductions of this order are usually referred to as *abstracts*. Where material is concentrated still further (as would normally be necessary with a book) the term *digest* is often used. The particular type of highly concentrated summary which is prepared by a solicitor to put the facts of a case before a barrister is called a *brief*. This word is also used with extended meaning; for example, the notes prepared by a secretary for the chairman of a committee so that the latter will have an adequate grasp of the main facts about an item for discussion may also be referred to, at least colloquially, as a 'brief'.

As the kind of summary required in business is usually much more concentrated than the examination précis it is useful to practice reducing some passages to a ninth or a tenth of the original. A strongly recommended exercise is to reduce a passage first to a third, then to a third again – thus producing a reduction to a ninth in two stages. The passage can then be further reduced to a single sentence of, say, twenty-five words (see Example, page 89, and Exercises).

The situation also often arises where material has to be reworded so that it takes up slightly less room with no loss of content (to fit space left for copy in an advertising block, or to avoid extending a pamphlet by another four pages for the sake of an extra couple of hundred words, for example). Such tasks are very like the final stages of précis-writing and are the easier for previous précis practice.

Thus it can be seen that the examination type précis is not just an end in itself, but provides valuable training for various types of practical summary. It also encourages the utmost economy in the use of words, and that is a valuable attitude to acquire for anybody who expects to make much use of words in his business career.

II. PRÉCIS IN EXAMINATIONS

The essence of précis in examinations is the scizing of the original author's principal facts and arguments and their reproduction in the student's own words (except where use of the original wording is specifically permitted, as in Institute of Bankers) as sound continuous prose of a length prescribed by the examiner. To achieve this successfully the student must be competent in three aspects of communication.

1. He must be able to understand the original passage in detail and also to form an overall view of its principal purpose. His ability as an Rx is under review.

2. He must be able to divide the author's points into the relevant (which must be included) and the irrelevant (which must be excluded). The relevant he must further divide into the essential and those which are relevant but not essential; and balance the proportions of his version according to the priorities he allocates to these points. His powers of logic and organisation are under review.

3. He must reduce the material to the requisite word limit. His facility with words and especially his capacity to write concisely are under review.

When we remember that the resultant summary must also satisfy the examiner as a piece of well-written prose of a high standard of 'correctness', we can see that précis in examinations represents a very demanding test of a student's linguistic ability.

III. PRÉCIS METHOD

1. Check the instructions given. Is reported speech compulsory? Is a title asked for? *In not more than* 150 *words* means just what it says. *In approximately* 150 *words* may be taken as meaning in 140–160 words. If no word limit is mentioned it is usual to assume that reduction to one-third of the original length is required.

2. Read the passage through quickly to grasp the general sense. Reread if necessary.

3. Read through slowly, noting the divisions of subject matter in the passage and trying to give meaning to every word. Some students prefer to write down headings for the principal divisions; others can get the outline clear in their heads without writing anything down (see Example p. 89). Whichever method is used, this stage must not be shirked.

4. Give a title to the passage. This should be specific, not vague, and should cover all the subject matter. It is not likely to be a one-word title, but rather a phrase that expresses the whole passage in miniature. Even if a title is not asked for, you should still try to form one, if only for your own benefit to ensure that you understand what is the essence of the passage.

5. Some examining bodies expect the source of the original to be incorporated in the précis. (It may be assumed that this is required if the examiner himself shows the source of the passage he sets.)

There are two ways of doing this:

a. by starting with a form of words such as: *James Dogsbody in an article in 'The Times' of 4th May* 19.. *writes that* ...

b. by a title such as: *Précis of an extract from an article by James Dogsbody in 'The Times' of 4th May* 19...

With the second method, if a title has been asked for by the examiner a descriptive title will have to be linked on as well by a connective such as 'concerning' or 'referring to'. Thus the final title may become (cumbersome but impeccable):

Précis of an extract from an article by James Dogsbody in 'The Times' of 4th May 19.. *concerning the high incidence of shoplifting in self-service grocery stores.*

The second method (*b*) has the advantage of not consuming any of the permitted words (titles are not included in the total of words); the first (*a*) has the special disadvantage that unless a present tense verb is used, as in the example, the writer is committed to past tense reported speech.

6. It is usual to summarise spoken material (e.g. an extract from a speech) in past tense reported speech, i.e. as if introduced by a clause such

as *The speaker said that*, though these words need not be actually included unless to show source by method (*a*) above. A few examining bodies expect this for written material too. (It may be assumed that this is what is required when 'reported speech' is specified in the instructions.)

Otherwise, for written material there is no reason why present tense reported speech should not be used, i.e. as if introduced by a clause such as *The writer says that*.

For further distinction between past tense and present tense reported speech see Appendix II.

7. Write out a rough draft. Except for the few examinations where use of the original wording is permitted, this should be in your own words, substituting simpler words for unusual ones in the original. Material should be selected on the basis of the categories: essential; relevant but not essential; irrelevant. Endeavour to make some reference to all material that is not irrelevant to the main theme. A good rough draft is always rather longer than is required.

8. Avoid questions, and convert rhetorical questions into statements.

9. Change the order of the material if it is to your advantage to do so.

10. Briefly, everything to do with expression is your responsibility; everything to do with subject matter, the original author's. Thus you must not change his 'facts' even if you know them to be wrong, or indicate your disagreement with his viewpoint or arguments.

11. Illustrations, examples, analogies, must be omitted except where they take up a very large part of the original or are essential to the argument. Particularised statements should be replaced by generalisations, specific examples by a statement of the tendency that the example illustrates.

12. Omit all figurative language.

13. It is useful to write the rough draft on alternate lines to leave room for revisions.

14. Check the number of words in the rough draft and reduce to the required limit. Every effort should be made to achieve this by rewording, not by removal of material. The ways of achieving conciseness discussed in Chapter 6 will be useful at this stage. Rewriting of complete sentences is usually more effective than the removal of a word here and a word there. A running score of words saved should be kept in the margin and the process continued until this equals the number of words your draft was above the limit.

15. Reread your revised draft. Check that it still makes sense, is grammatically sound, in full sentence form, properly punctuated, and is not too jerky. With a considerable reduction there is bound to be some

loss of smoothness, as the passage is now over-packed with facts. This effect can be minimised by the use of connectives, avoiding very short sentences, and keeping the paragraphs of normal length. Avoid the common mistake of converting each paragraph of the original into a separate little paragraph in your shortened version. Short passages can be summarised as one paragraph and no examination is likely to produce a passage long enough to require more than three paragraphs for its summary.

16. Write out a fair version of your précis, making further improvements in the expression if this can be achieved without adding words.

17. Check the number of words in the final version and write this in at the end of the précis.

18. In examinations, the timing of the précis is important; if more time is spent on it than was allowed for by the examiner, insufficient time will be left for completing the rest of the paper. A useful formula to give an approximate idea of the time that should be spent is 15 minutes for each 50 words of completed précis. Thus a reduction to approximately 150 words should be completed in 45 minutes.

IV. EXAMPLE

NOTE: The student working on his own is strongly recommended to attempt the following exercise for himself before reading the notes and model answers that follow. The complete exercise should take not more than 1¼ hours.

A. The Exercise

Make a précis of the following passage
    a. in not more than 150 words
    b. in not more than 60 words
    c. in one sentence not exceeding 25 words:

Whatever may be its wider implications, the explosion of a hydrogen bomb is, for the meteorologist, simply another atmospheric disturbance and therefore to be classed with certain rare natural occurrences, such as a volcanic eruption. But there are certain features of a manmade disturbance that require special examination.

As with all events on this scale, it is impossible to describe what happens in detail, but we can be reasonably sure of the main effects, and the most impressive of these arise from pressure waves.

The immediate result of the detonation is that the air surrounding the bomb is raised very rapidly to an enormously high temperature. The hot gases expand violently as a great fireball, compressing the air around them into what is called a shock wave, or 'blast wave', that is responsible for much of the terrible destructive power of the weapon.

Another kind of wave arises because of the weight of the air. The force of the explosion lifts the atmosphere around the bomb and causes what are known as 'gravity waves', resembling ordinary ocean waves. Waves of this type are not normally felt by human beings, and they have no effect on weather.

The most significant feature of a nuclear weapon is the production of radioactivity. When the weapon is detonated near the ground a vast mass of highly radioactive matter, solid and gaseous, is thrown upwards. Because of the high temperature, the gigantic 'bubble' ascends to very great heights, possibly 35 000 metres or more.

The heavy debris soon falls to earth again, but the fine dust settles very slowly and drifts for many miles with the wind. The result is that a large oval area, equal in size to the whole of Wales, is contaminated by radioactive debris. The gases and the smallest particles remain high in the atmosphere.

Changes of speed and direction of wind mean that clouds of radioactive dust and gases are broken up and drift in different directions at different heights. If the main mass continued to move, say, westwards in a wind of 80 km/h it would, in theory, travel round the world in about three weeks, but in reality it is far more likely that it would be caught up in local wind systems, and it is almost impossible to predict its path.

Some of the radioactivity decays rapidly, but much is long-lived and remains potentially dangerous for considerable periods.

The Daily Telegraph

B. Notes on passage

1. This passage falls into three principal divisions – a short introduction establishing the topic (i.e. the atmospheric effects of a hydrogen bomb explosion); the pressure waves; the production of radioactivity. The second division is subdivided into 'blast' waves and 'gravity' waves, and the third has three subsections – heavy debris; fine dust; gases and smallest particles. About this last subsection further information is supplied, concerning its unpredictability of movement, which is important since we are also told that some of the radioactivity remains active for a long time. This is the kind of grasp of the subject matter and its divisions that should be achieved in the first reading.

The structure and content of the passage could be represented by the following outline:

i. *Introduction*

Meteorologist, to introduce topic of special atmospheric effects of a hydrogen bomb explosion.

ii. *Pressure Waves*

    a. Blast waves – how caused – principal destructive force

    b. Gravity waves – how caused – harmless.

iii. *Radioactivity*

    a. Heavy debris – soon falls (i.e. vertically)

    b. Fine dust – contaminates large oval area

    c. Gases and smallest particles – drift unpredictably with wind – radioactivity remains dangerous.

2. It is now easy to formulate a title for the passage – 'The Atmospheric Effects of a Hydrogen Bomb Explosion'. A typically unsatisfactory title (because not sufficiently specific) would be 'The Hydrogen Bomb'.

C. *Model answers*

The Atmospheric Effects of a Hydrogen Bomb Explosion

1. To the meteorologist a hydrogen bomb explosion is just another atmospheric disturbance, comparable with a volcano erupting, though it does produce certain special effects.

Two types of pressure wave result, a 'blast' wave occasioned by the rapid expansion of hot gases round the bomb, and a 'gravity' wave caused by the raising of the atmosphere over the bomb. The second is harmless but the first is the chief destructive force of the explosion.

The most important effect is the throwing up – often to great heights – of radioactive matter. Although heavy particles settle again quickly, smaller ones spread over a large oval area, while the finest remains in the atmosphere indefinitely together with radioactive gases. It is not practical to estimate the direction such radioactive clouds will move in, as they shift with the wind. Some of the radioactivity remains dangerous for a long time. (144 words)

2. The atmospheric disturbances caused by a hydrogen bomb explosion included harmless 'gravity' waves and highly destructive blast waves. Most important was the production of radioactivity. Although the fall-out of larger particles could be predicted, gases and the smallest particles formed radioactive clouds that would shift with the wind and could remain dangerous for a long time. (56 words)

3. Hydrogen bomb explosions produce destructive pressure waves and also radioactive debris some of which remains dangerous a long time and may fall anywhere. (23 words)

D. Notes on model answers

1. Answers 1. and 3. are in the original tense, but 2. is in past tense reported speech to demonstrate the difference.

2. Note the attempt to avoid the language of the original (*important effect* for *significant feature* for example – *significant feature* is exactly the kind of phrase that students tend to 'lift' unconsciously). *Meteorologist* is retained as a technical word difficult to replace and one which you may be assumed to know the meaning of by the post 'O' level stage.

3. In answer 2. a simpler subdivision of the third section of the passage is used – predictable and nonpredictable fall-out. The causes of the types of pressure wave are judged the least important material and are excluded, as in the introduction.

4. In answer 3. destructive pressure waves are mentioned but harmless ones ignored. Similarly, predictable fall-out is ignored.

5. To show the source, the title could be amended to something of this kind: *Précis of an extract from a 'Daily Telegraph' article referring to the atmospheric effects of a hydrogen bomb explosion.*

V. EXERCISES

NOTES: *Exercises A* and *B* are fairly easy passages to provide a bridge between 'O' level précis and the kind set in ONC (OND) in Business Studies or Public Administration and intermediate professional examinations. The other passages are all of the length and difficulty to be expected in such examinations and the word limits are those most commonly prescribed, a third or a quarter. You are strongly recommended to attempt to reduce at least some of these further, to 60 words and to 25 word sentences, as in the example above.

Concerning supplying a title, use of reported speech, and showing the source, no special instructions are given; you should conform to the requirements of the examining body for whose examinations you are preparing.

More varied précis practice with longer passages is provided by 'Passages for comprehension and summary' (pages 227–253).

Exercise A

Reduce the following passage to not more than 130 words (one-third):

Britain's industrial and commercial management is a key factor in the solution of our foremost economic problem – how to restore national solvency and earn the standard of living which science and technology

have made possible to first-class industrial nations. True, there are other
important influences, such as the political and economic actions of governments, some of which are beyond our control; but the one big factor which
is thoroughly within our control and which would really boost our
country's fortunes is a massive increase in our overall industrial and commercial efficiency.

Better product design, better cost-competitiveness, better marketing
and after-sales services, can win new export customers and retrieve sections of the home market which have been captured by other countries.
Yet our overall productivity still lags sadly behind that of the United
States; alarming advances are being made in Japan, and other countries
are rising fast in the international league table. Much of the blame for the
plight of the British economy has been placed on the attitude and performance of British managements. Is it, in fact, all their fault? Probably not;
but a good deal of it must be – and what is more important, managements
are the only people who are likely to be able to put it right.

Many years ago, my first 'chief' in the consulting business taught me a
golden rule: 'Get managements to manage, and you won't have too much
difficulty getting the workers to work.' There are few things, if any, which
British managements could not do just as well as American, German, or
Japanese if they would only equip themselves with the necessary knowledge and then make up their minds to manage! The difference between
the 'thrusters' and the 'sleepers' of the world's industries is not in the
workers, the salesmen, the clerks, the typists; it is in the ability, education,
and above all the 'will to manage' of the managers.

The ultimate responsibility of management is, of course, to the shareholders who own the business, to secure the best return it can – in the long
term rather than the purely short term – on the assets or resources which
it employs and which are entrusted to its care. But this is too narrow a
view; in an enlightened society most people believe that managements also
have responsibilities to the community which embraces suppliers, customers, and employees, and obligations to recognise national policies.

Donald J. Lockyer in Journal of the Institute
of the Motor Industry, January 1969

Exercise B

Reduce the following passage to not more than 140 words (one-quarter):

Free holidays, especially holidays in the sun, encourage workers to
reach their productivity targets. This seems to be a recent realisation by
British employers. Some of the biggest names in British industry now use

this form of employee incentive. The reasons are clear. First, the holiday incentive has been shown conclusively to produce results in terms of increased output or sales; secondly, there are bonus returns on the employer's investment in the form of increases in employees' loyalty and productivity.

For some time Americans have been induced to put in 'that little extra effort' by the offer of the big prize – in cash, merchandise or travel – for those who exceed the basic norm. And it seems to work. Big incentives and high performance are part of the American industrial tradition. Very often the incentives take the form of free holiday travel, and it is not unusual for an entire boatload of sales staff or dealers to set forth on a major holiday jamboree earned by achieving set targets.

In providing holiday travel awards – as in many other business practices – the Japanese have followed the Americans, and with remarkable success. When Honda moved into Europe one of their first operations was to set up a holiday award scheme for UK motor cycle dealers. The fifty dealers who achieved top sales performance were flown for a two-week holiday in Japan. Honda quickly achieved dealer – and thereby market – domination, and the holiday award scheme has operated nearly every year since.

The Russians, too, seem to acknowledge the value of holidays as incentives, and there are many 'workers' holiday camps' on the balmy Black Sea coast for workers who reach and exceed their targets.

Thirdly, the holiday award is sometimes tax-free, an element of special attraction to boss and worker alike.

The provision of holiday award schemes will not bring automatic increases in output and sales. The holiday incentive, like other kinds of sales promotion, is a highly specialised business, and is becoming increasingly sophisticated. What is extremely important is to set targets which are not only attainable but which, when reached, give the company an adequate return on the investment. Moreover, the type of holiday provided must act as a real incentive. Recent market research shows a strong preference for incentives in the form of holidays, particularly in higher socioeconomic groupings, where presumably taxation bites deepest. But in the lower groupings there is some preference for cash. The holiday award must be an 'additional' holiday. Otherwise employees feel cheated, thinking that they are receiving no more than their rightful dues.

The features constituting the main attractions of an incentive holiday are sun, comfort and water. Therefore the best places are undoubtedly the Mediterranean and the tropical and subtropical islands, the Canaries and Bahamas rating highly in the eyes of would-be award-winners. But the United States and cruises are also clearly popular. The facility must definitely include wives, and indeed they often have a considerable part to play in motivation and the drive to increased achievement.

Travel is now increasingly recognised as an effective work-incentive; and it can undoubtedly boost sales. But the travel award must be used as a weapon, not a bouquet. The subject of the incentive – whether production worker, salesman or dealer – should be closely inspected; great care should be taken with the choice of holiday and careful consideration given to the setting of targets. In this way the employer is sure of receiving a fair return on his enlightened investment.

Patrick Davies in *The Daily Telegraph*,
26 February 1969 (*adapted*)

Exercise C

Reduce the following passage to approximately 150 words (one-third):

Language is a tool for the expression and communication of thought. Failure to communicate may be caused either through inadequate knowledge of, or through deficiencies in, the language, such as misleading grammar or the possibility of ambiguity of words. No single language exists, however, which is sufficient both for expressing all thoughts and feelings and for precluding nonsense. Some languages in fact seem to encourage the consideration of meaningless questions and the expressing of nonsense.

However, as language is the use of certain symbols according to certain conventions, it should be possible, by the choice of a suitable symbolism and a suitable set of conventions, to minimise the number of meaningless questions which can be asked and to preclude to a large extent the uttering of nonsense.

An ideal language would obviate both of these difficulties. It would be so clear and precise that it would preclude all nonsense and so rich that it would be sufficient for expressing all possible thoughts and feelings.

The construction of such an ideal language is, of course, an impossibility. But in certain restricted fields, such as mathematics and physics, we are able to construct more exact languages which serve as more efficient tools of expression and communication than the language of everyday speech.

Such specialised languages have certain definite advantages.

For example: they are extremely precise, and therefore economic in use; they are known to people throughout the world, and therefore to a certain extent transcend natural language barriers. (It is possible to translate a Russian scientific text into reasonable scientific English by means of an electronic computer.)

Finally they serve as an aid to thought and therefore help progress. But on the other hand they have their disadvantages: they are harder to learn than the natural language which we learn at our mother's knee; they are known only to specialists in the various fields and, therefore, tend to be 'parochial' preventing the specialist from communicating with other people, and indeed with other specialists; and they tend to degenerate into 'jargon'.

Such languages, which of course are not restricted to the scientific field, tend to be more artificial than our normal speech. Think of some of the examples of legal or religious phraseology that you have met. Even so they spring from the same type of cultural background as does our everyday speech and so they are not so artificial as the experimental 'International Languages'. Thus the specialised languages have survived and grown whereas all such experiments as Esperanto and Interlingua, to name but two, are, I feel, doomed to failure because they ignore the cardinal point that a language arises by necessity out of, and along with, a culture.

> Eric Nixon in notes on the Granada
> TV programmes *Man to Man*, 1964

Exercise D

Reduce the following passage to approximately 150 words (one-quarter):

It is said of the Emperor Caligula that he used to write his laws in very small characters and post them on the top of the highest pillar in Rome, 'the more effectively to ensnare the people'. In a different way, it seems that we are heading for a somewhat similar state of affairs.

It is not just the sheer volume and complexity of new laws passed by Parliament, or the subtle nuances of judicial decisions, which add to our daily burdens – though admittedly these do not exactly help. Nor does the incomprehensible jargon of legal terminology make life any easier.

Basically, the problem is largely one of communication. The non-specialist non-lawyer is left in a state of utter ignorance about the mass of legal rules and, without knowledge, there can be no understanding.

The maxim that 'ignorance of the law is no excuse' is one of the silliest utterances ever made. Its validity presupposes the existence of several important conditions, among which are:

That there is a limit to the sheer quantity of legal rules which are capable of being known;

That ordinary people can readily understand those laws which do exist;

That there is no room for variation of legal rules by the techniques of judicial interpretation;

That everybody has his own tame lawyer who can advise him of the legal consequences of his actions.

In our present society, none of these factors exist. The result is that the overwhelming majority of the population are totally uninformed about provisions of English law which affect their vital interests. It is true that there are various organisations which assist in preventing this ignorance. Newspapers and journals provide articles and features, specialist organisations and societies give advice and help to their members, and so forth. But such a service is not comprehensive and, however valuable it may be, it only skims the surface of the problem.

The remedy seems to be either fewer legal provisions, or great publicity and education. The former situation is unlikely to come about. Each year, the annual output from Parliament increases; each year, more and more judges give an increasing number of judicial decisions, which have to be analysed, digested, compared with and distinguished from previous decisions. Law is becoming so complex that even lawyers are having difficulty in coping with problems which arise. Not many lawyers could explain with complete confidence some of the more abstruse provisions of the Land Commission Act or the Leasehold Reform Act, to name but two recent pieces of legislation.

Clearly, greater publicity and education is the only effective way of drawing the attention of the general public to legislative provisions and judicial decisions. The Ministry of Transport seems to be the only government department which really understands this, for it alone carries on effective campaigns (other ministries have a habit of publishing 'explanatory leaflets', which are more complex than the Acts they are intended to explain!). But something more than this is required. We could expand existing services, like the Citizens Advice Bureaus, or the Legal Advice scheme, but this too is not likely to be very effective.

A more radical solution was put forward recently by the legal correspondent of *New Society*, who suggested that local Legal Centres should be established throughout the country. Staffed by full-time salaried lawyers, they would be able to deal with queries and legal problems, as well as help to publicise legal rules generally. One can visualise the local Legal Centres operating on lines similar to local Health Clinics, and performing a function no less valuable.

Norman Selwyn in *The Daily Telegraph*, 25 October 1968 (*abbreviated*)

Exercise E

Reduce the following passage to not more than 150 words (one-quarter):

The most extraordinary feature of life in the next 40 years is likely to be the pace of technological change. This, of itself, is something the country has been through before. The original Industrial Revolution brought profound changes in Britain. The population increased rapidly and a vast amount of building development took place.

Millions of people were born into miserable conditions – with bad housing, bad factories, bad or non-existent schools, and sweated labour. But out of their endeavours Britain became a great industrial nation, with a dominant position in the world.

At the root of the Industrial Revolution was steam power based on coal and, although steam was later coupled with electricity and supplemented by petroleum, it can be argued that the curve of technological progress flattened out after the first great surge forward in the application of steam. The two wars, separated by 25 years, were not greatly different in their sources of energy.

But right at the end of the Second World War nuclear energy made its first shattering appearance. This, and the more subtle development of radar, with all its electronic implications, now seem likely to usher in a second Industrial Revolution as profound in its effects as was the first.

This time, however, as far as Britain is concerned, there will be two striking differences. Instead of being the sparsely populated country it was when the first Industrial Revolution started, Britain now has a population of 54 million. Many people say the country is full. And instead of having the markets of the world open and waiting, Britain is now fighting for its life against the competition of many other industrial nations.

This is the main prospect – that this milling population of 54 million, which according to official forecasts is expected to increase to 74 million soon after the end of the century, confined within its island home, will be subjected to strains and stresses as violent as any that have occurred during the last two centuries.

Old standards and long-cherished values will tend to be thrown into the melting pot. Society will be turned upside down and inside out as new ideas surge in, as new prospects open out and great wealth – assuming we maintain our position – accrues. It is in this condition of flux and confusion, when old ideals are threatened before new ones have been hammered out, that the danger to the physical environment will be at its greatest.

It can be assumed that in this process of rapid change there will be many individual developments for the better. Slums will be replaced by new dwellings. The factories of the nineteenth century will give way to light, airy and spacious buildings. The old office blocks will be rebuilt. Schools and hospitals are likely to be incomparably better. Open spaces may be provided where none existed previously.

But the acute risk is that the synthesis will be wholly unsatisfactory, that the new development will be thrown together in a series of hotch-potches, spread and sprawled, wrongly located, inconvenient in use, ugly in appearance, at fault socially, and that in the process of change much that was previously cherished will disappear.

This process, with its paradoxical contrast between the improvement of the environment in microcosm and the utter failure to create the macrocosm, can be seen happening all over the country even now, in spite of the controls exercised under the Planning Acts. There are some things we can be proud to take a foreigner to see; but much of it – starting perhaps with the journey in from London Airport – must make us want to hang our heads in shame.

Professor Colin Buchanan in The
Observer, 19 January 1964

Exercise F

Reduce the following passage to approximately 150 words (one-quarter):

Nothing works without order, be it a watch, a train, or the globe in orbit round the sun. The degree of efficiency with which they work is determined by the degree of order maintained in them. The same principle applies to the home, the farm, the business, the community, and the state. But here other elements enter in: human relations and the need constantly to adapt to changing circumstances. It might be said that the business man is only truly efficient when he is operating both on his own behalf and for the good of the community. By and large, governments evolve controls – taxation, for example – which are designed to ensure this cooperation. Laws reinforce the controls; penalties can be imposed for non-compliance. These are the instruments of order.

If, therefore, we search for world order, we are looking for the means whereby the world, with all its peoples, can function in something of the same orderly manner. We hope for cooperation, but we recognise that there must be controls that would, if necessary, enforce it. What I suspect we are less willing to consider is what order on this scale would demand of us.

What we must think of is not order between individuals but order between organised states. The trouble here is that – as the German philosopher Schopenhauer put it – states coexist like hedgehogs in a bag, in close and prickly contact. Thirty years ago, when the champions of the League of Nations talked of world order, it was security in Europe they mainly had in mind. If they had achieved it, the task we face today might have been infinitely less complicated. In the intervening years, states have grown in power to hurt one another; so has the jealousy and fear between them. One reason for this is that it is now technically possible to govern the world from one centre. So that behind the rivalry of the Great Powers is the fearful sense that the side which wins the struggle may provide the eventual world government.

That would be domination by one power, not world government and world order in which *all* nations might cooperate; and it must be admitted that nothing in the foreseeable future seems likely to lead in this direction. Even in western Europe, countries which have every reason for submerging their independence under one government – and have talked of doing so for many years – still hesitate on the brink. Why do they do so? In part it is because federation is no longer merely a matter of creating a common authority to take care of external affairs and defence. (It was when the United States came into being in 1789.) Nowadays, the internal and external affairs of nations are so closely interwoven that government shapes almost all the circumstances of life. The important point is that the more all-embracing state control becomes, the more the order which it imposes is related to a particular scheme of values – to its chosen ideology. This is easy enough to see in an authoritarian regime, less easy to see in a democracy. In eastern Europe, order equals the enforcement of communism, in South Africa of *apartheid*; in Britain it might be called the safeguarding of the freedom of the individual by law.

Each state, then, has its own set of values. So before people demand world government they must know what kind of values they want government to protect. Until they are clear about that, world government – even if it could be established – would soon break down.

F. S. Northedge in The Listener,
7 December 1961

Exercise G

Reduce the following passage to not more than 160 words (one-quarter):

There have been fundamental changes in the pattern of holiday-taking since Victorian times, when many of our large resorts first came into existence. The approach of the Victorians to travel was essentially a passive one – they preferred 'seeing' to 'doing'. They would generally arrive at a resort by train and stay in the one place throughout their holiday. The hotels of the day were designed to provide comfort, while reflecting in the lavish decoration and expansive rooms, the extravagance of the times. Holidays followed much the same pattern for all, and therefore a resort was able without much difficulty to cater for all tastes by providing a promenade, a bandstand, a pavilion, and entertainment in the centre of the town.

Today's holidaymaker asks for much more than this. The emphasis has shifted towards more active forms of enjoyment and there is a tremendous variety of pursuits to choose from, ranging from sailing and ski-ing to golf and pony-trekking. So great is the demand for participation that we are witnessing the commercialisation of hobbies.

Holiday traffic is no longer homogeneous. There are now many different types of holidaymaker each with an entirely different set of requirements. Some look for solitude while others like plenty of company. Touring has become an important feature of the new pattern of holiday-taking but there are still those who like to stay in one resort throughout their holiday, particularly if they have children.

The 'do it yourself' approach has become increasingly popular and has been marked by a sharp growth in demand for caravans and holiday flatlets in recent years. On the other hand this has been accompanied by an equally rapid rise in the popularity of the holiday camp, which works on the reverse principle providing everything the visitor could need within the confines of the camp, and a high degree of service.

It is clear that the requirements of the different types of holidaymakers are not always compatible and resorts today cannot attempt to cater for all tastes as they did in the past. The answer to this problem of diversification within the industry almost certainly lies in specialisation on a regional scale.

Today reference is made as frequently to a holiday region, e.g. the Lake District, the Costa Brava or the Cornish Riviera, as it is to an individual resort. The growth in the popularity of touring as opposed to static holidays has been largely responsible for this. In Britain certain regions are undoubtedly better equipped in terms of amenities to deal with a particular type of holiday traffic than others, and within the region certain resorts and towns stand out as ideal centres for certain types of activity.

It appears likely that in the next decade the trend towards area specialisation will grow. Already some regional organisations have been set up to study present trends in visitor traffic and from there decide which types of traffic the region is best suited to attract and serve. The planned development of tourist facilities within the region can then follow taking into account the requirements of the particular category of visitor the area will cater for. It will be more important than ever for a holiday area to create a clear cut image in the minds of prospective holiday-makers.

All branches of the holiday industry face a challenging period of opportunity in the years ahead. Competition from foreign resorts, already considerable, will certainly grow as the level of prosperity increases. The inclusive tour has already brought the cost of a holiday in some continental resorts to a level very little above that of a holiday at home.

> L. J. Lickorish, General Manager of
> the British Travel and Holidays
> Association, in the *SIA Journal*,
> January 1964

Chapter 8

Business Letters

I. BUSINESS LETTERS AND COMMUNICATION PRINCIPLES

It is in the letters he writes (or dictates) that the junior manager has most opportunity to apply communication principles, and the greatest need to do so.

It has been said – more than once – that a firm's letters are its ambassadors. Customers (and other firms and organisations too) base their impression of a firm on its letters as much as anything. To many it seems that correspondence reveals what a firm is really like, as distinct from the picture of it projected by its publicity and advertising. Every letter sent out, therefore, to some extent changes the standing and prestige of the firm. This is even more true of public administration. The principal contact that the man in the street has with government departments is through correspondence; at a local level the public impression of 'the Council' is largely created by the letters sent out by its officers.

The standard of business letters generally in this country is not high. Far from achieving such aims as establishing an atmosphere favourable to business and increasing goodwill for the firm, correspondents frequently fail even to make it clear what they are trying to say. While the firm is seeking – by its publicity material and such details as its office furnishing and the quality of its stationery – to give an impression of efficiency, modernity, and style, its letters are often ungrammatical, old-fashioned, and clumsy. Here is an example from a firm of national repute – the only alteration the name of the product:

> *We are pleased to note your interest in our Tiles and accordingly have pleasure in enclosing herewith literature giving details of these materials. Prices depend to some extent upon the type and conditions of sub-floor, area required to be laid, and in connection with Nutred Decorative Tiles, the colour or colours selected for use.*
>
> *We should be pleased to provide you with an estimate for any work you may have under consideration if you would kindly let us have the aforementioned details, together if possible with a small drawing or dimensioned sketch of the spaces concerned.*

> *We trust this is in accordance with your requirements and in the mean-time await to hear from you further.*

It is difficult to imagine many customers receiving this letter as a reply to a first enquiry feeling encouraged to proceed further. Here is another, again exactly as received, except for the omission of the stockist's name:

> *We thank you for your enquiry and are pleased to note your interest in our fireplace designs. We have much pleasure in enclosing our brochure incorporating only a small selection from our varied range of fireplaces, however, a comprehensive catalogue also prices are available at our stockists showroom.*
>
> *We are requesting our nearest stockist, namely, Messrs … to contact you and doubtless they will be very pleased to render any assistance possible.*
>
> *If we can be of any further assistance to you in making your selection we hope you will advise us. It would be very much appreciated if, in due course you would let us know if one of our designs has met with your requirements.*

What is wrong here goes much deeper than the punctuation errors (which could be blamed on the typist).

A minimum communication standard for the business letter should be that it is expressed in clear and exact English and contains no errors of syntax, spelling, or punctuation. For all but completely routine letters, however, more should be aimed at than the minimum. The following are typical points that require attention:

1. suitability of tone to subject matter
2. friendliness and warmth of tone
3. selection of material and choice of wording to suit the Rx (his probable vocabulary level, knowledge of the subject and its technical jargon, the type of person he seems to be etc.)
4. psychological factors (tact, courtesy, special care when conveying unwelcome information -- which is liable to be misunderstood simply because the Rx *wants* to read it in a sense different from that which you intend)
5. freshness of language (freedom from clichés and commercial jargon).

The letter should contain no padding or wasted words, and be as concise as is possible without sacrifice of any of the aims enumerated.

II. CONVENTIONS AND LAYOUT

The business letter has developed over the years certain conventions which – however odd or illogical – must be subscribed to or your letter will not be accepted by the Rx as a 'proper' business letter. Layout too is decided rather by what is traditional and accepted than by what will be most effective. Most business men, and local and central government officers, rely on secretaries in these matters; the examining bodies in typing and secretarial duties thus indirectly exert a very powerful influence. If a private person is sending a handwritten letter to a firm he is well advised to follow much the same rules that typists obey or his letter may seem amateur, or even bizarre, to the man who receives it. These matters are to some extent subject to fashion and the model layouts and notes that follow represent the conventions accepted at the time of writing.

Business letters may be classified as:

1. private person to firm (or organisation)
2. firm (or organisation) to private person
3. firm (or organisation) to firm (or organisation).

If the conventions and layout for the first two are known, the third, which is a combination of these, can be easily deduced.

A. Private person to firm (or organisation)

> *10 Hilltop Road,*
> *Hightown, Wiltshire.*
> *SN26 6KA*
> *20th November, 19..*

The Colton Engineering Co.,
Tottenham Street, London.
SE12 4QD

Dear Sirs,

....
....
....
....
....
....

> *Yours faithfully,*
> *James Thompson*

NOTES

1. It is assumed that this letter is handwritten. In this book italic type is used in all examples of letters to represent handwriting (including signatures).

2. Both addresses are shown with progressive indentation, the more usual form with handwritten letters. The punctuation shown for the addresses is still the most widely accepted, although 'open style', omitting the commas at the ends of lines and the full stop after the county, has increasing support. A comma after the house number is not recommended.

3. The placing of postcodes is illustrated. Further details are given in Appendix III on page 265.

4. The date is in the most widely accepted form. Permissible variants are dropping the comma and substituting 20 for 20th. Abbreviated forms are out of fashion.

5. The inside address is a particular characteristic of the business letter, and is employed even when no carbon copy is being kept and therefore no practical advantage is being gained.

If the appropriate departmental head is known, the letter is better addressed to him, but by his official title not his name. Thus a letter concerning purchasing should be addressed to:

The Sales Manager,
   The Colton Engineering Co.,
      Tottenham Street, London.
        SE12 4QD

Dear Sir,

The device of addressing as 'Messrs' companies whose trading name incorporates the names of members of the firm is out of fashion. It is correct to write:

Jackson, Broadbridge & Co. Ltd,
Address

Dear Sirs,

6. The subscription *Yours faithfully* is always correct in formal business letters although other subscriptions may be right in certain circumstances. *Yours sincerely* is correct when the addressee is known socially by the writer, and the situation is no longer completely formal (see also NOTE 5 on page 108).

B. Firm (or organisation) to private person

THE COLTON ENGINEERING COMPANY
Tottenham Street, London.
SE12 4QD

OUR REF: AJH/PFL   22 November, 19..

J. Thompson Esq.,
10 Hilltop Road,
Hightown, Wilts.
SN26 6KA

Dear Sir,
                        ...
                Yours faithfully,
            for Colton Engineering Co.
                A. J. Harland

NOTES

1. Firms use stationery with a printed head to ensure that – at the minimum – all letters from the firm show its correct trading name and address. Much more information (i.e. telephone numbers, telegraphic address, names of directors, even an advertising slogan or picture of the works) may be included. The address is frequently centred under the firm's name. There are many variants and you should collect a number of examples of firms' stationery to compare.

2. A firm will always assign a reference to correspondence, and this is intended for quotation in the reply. This ensures that the reply goes to the right man, or in a large organisation may be the key to a complicated filing system. The simplest reference consists (as here) of the initials of the man sending the letter combined with those of the girl typing it. When firm writes to firm each will give a reference to the correspondence and to avoid confusion these are marked OUR REF and YOUR REF. References should always be quoted in replying to a firm (the top left-hand of the first sheet opposite the date is the place for this). It may be impossible to put your second letter on a certain matter alongside your first letter unless you do so.

3. The inside address is shown in 'block' form, most usual for type-written letters. Each paragraph of a typewritten letter starts an arbitrary distance from the left-hand margin, usually five spaces.

4. The firm is almost certain to address Mr Thompson as 'Esq.'. This complimentary mode has been applied so freely that there is little compliment left in its use and it is now a mere convention. It cannot be used except with the initials of the addressee – if these are unknown 'Mr' must

be employed. There is no equivalent for women, who must be addressed as *Miss* — or *Mrs* —, *Dear Madam,*.

5. The form as shown with *Dear Sir* and *Yours faithfully* is for very formal or routine correspondence. If Mr Thompson is known to the firm at all he would probably be addressed as:

> *J. Thompson Esq.,*
> Address
>
> *Dear Mr Thompson,*

with the subscription:

> *Yours sincerely,*

Many firms now employ this form even if the correspondent is not known to them, with the commendable motive of establishing a warmer and more personal note in the letter. Eventually this too will become a convention and thus lose its present advantage.

6. The firm's letter may be signed in a number of ways, according to the degree of importance given to the correspondence. In ascending order these might be:

> *a.* name of firm only
> *b.* name of firm plus initials of Tx
> *c.* name of firm plus signature (as example on page 107)
> *d.* signature with office held (e.g. *A. J. Harland, Sales Manager*).

Styles *a* and *b* should not be used for any but the most routine letters. Persons having delegated authority to sign on behalf of their firms sometimes sign 'p.p.' or 'per pro' (*per procurationem*), e.g.

> *p.p. Colton Engineering Co.*
> *A. J. Harland*

but this custom is steadily being replaced by *d* above, where the exact degree of authority is indicated by the name of the office held.

III. SOME POINTS OF STYLE

Many firms have an accepted 'house style' which makes at least their run-of-the-mill letters all look and read as part of one family. Where such local rules prevail they must be obeyed, regardless of any clash with the suggestions that follow.

Some firms seek to impose consistency and minimum standards on their letter writers by the use of 'form letters' – stereotypes to suit all routine occasions, which can be copied by the inexperienced. These 'form letters' may be necessary where many routine letters and postcards have to be sent out by very junior members of staff but they are a prime cause of conservatism in a firm's correspondence, perpetuating outmoded expressions as well as producing a lifeless and unnatural letter that often does not quite fit the circumstances for which it is being forced into service. The best letters are produced, fresh, for the particular occasion and the particular Rx.

Starting the letter off is a matter that should be given some thought. Many correspondents favour a 'subject head' (centred and underlined, immediately below the *Dear Sir*,) instead of a topic sentence. Thus:

```
Dear Sirs,
            Television Repair Job No. 553
```

may conveniently replace

```
Dear Sirs,
     I am writing to you about my television set
which you have now had for repair for over six
weeks.
```

The subject head has the advantage of appearing brisk and to the point. Sometimes it seems a little too much so, and the more leisurely topic sentence gains in friendliness and courtesy. Where there are bound to be a number of letters on the same matter it is certainly worth while inventing a subject head for the correspondence that will probably be repeated by the Rx with a subsequent gain in speed of reference.

Replying to a letter, the correspondent must first acknowledge this letter and refer to its date. Old-fashioned expressions such as *I have to acknowledge your letter of 15 ult. in which you refer to* ... are better replaced by simple direct expressions such as *Thank you for your letter of 15th October, 19.*. If the date of the letter and its reference number or subject head (or both) are quoted there is no need to give a précis of the other man's letter in the opening sentence. Such constructions as *referring to, and with reference to* are, as we saw in Chapter 6, better avoided. Thus *With reference to your order of 15th October, 19.., we are pleased to advise you that the Zapp pre-coated panels now await your collection* becomes (modernising the language throughout) *We are glad to tell you that the Zapp pre-coated panels ordered by you on 15th October, 19.., are now ready for you to collect.*

Letters may be written in:

1. the first person singular: *I have received your application and shall be bringing it before the Board for consideration next week*

2. the first person plural: *We have received your application and shall be considering it at a board meeting next week*

3. the impersonal passive: *Your letter has been received and will be considered by the Board next week.*

The first person singular can be used only by somebody of weight and authority in a firm, as he is reporting his personal actions or expressing his personal opinion yet they also represent those of the firm. A junior member of a firm is advised to associate himself with the whole firm by using the plural. The personal element in these two styles is usually their principal advantage but this can be a disadvantage if the letter· writer is very junior or if the matter is exceedingly formal, when the impersonal style is to be preferred.

There is, of course, no reason why the styles should not be combined – for example, using the first person singular so long as the writer's personal actions or views are mentioned but shifting to one of the other two styles where a matter concerning the entire firm is involved.

Letters predominantly in the first person singular are signed by the writer; letters in the first person plural or impersonal passive are usually signed with the name of the firm, the writer's name, if shown at all, appearing beneath. Some correspondents insert the line *I am* or *We are* (according to whether the letter is singular or plural in style) before *Yours faithfully*. There is no point in this unless the letter ends with a participial construction, when this addition is needed to complete the sentence:

> *Trusting this action meets with your approval,*
> *We are,*
> *Yours faithfully,*

However, these participial constructions (*Awaiting your further instructions*, *Anticipating an early reply*, *Assuring you of our best attention* etc.) are for the most part clichés from Edwardian commercial jargon and best avoided.

I am, We are (and their absurd variants *I remain, We remain*) have therefore little justification in modern correspondence.

IV. EXAMPLES

A. Enquiry and reply

> *46 Rawdon Road,*
> *Bamber, Kent.*
> *BR31 7NP*
> *5th April, 19 . .*

The Solid Fuel Centre,
> *Gloucester Close, London.*
> *W1 9XL*

Dear Sirs,

> *I should be very obliged if you would send me a copy of the booklet* '*Warmer Homes with Solid Fuel*', *currently advertised in the press.*

I should like also to raise a point that is of some concern to me as I am considering buying a new boiler. Considerable publicity has recently been given to the Condor Thermostatic Boiler No. 3 but I notice it is not included in your list of recommended appliances. Is this an oversight or is there in fact some defect in this boiler that has prevented it from passing the Centre's tests?

Yours faithfully,
John Cole

NOTES

1. Two points for action are raised in one letter. The writer prepares the second point carefully and will probably get both his booklet and a reply to his query. With more complex material it would be better to write two letters even if both are enclosed in one envelope. Raising several points, involving more than one department, in one letter is not the best way of making sure that all points are dealt with.

2. Having reached the end of his query at paragraph two, the writer does not waste time on a vague closing paragraph – he has been polite enough all through to have established goodwill without this.

THE SOLID FUEL CENTRE

Gloucester Close
London   W1 9XL

WP/VGF   7th April, 19..

J. Cole Esq.,
46 Rawdon Road,
Bamber, Kent.
BR31 7NP

Dear Sir,

Thank you for your letter of 5th April, 19.. As requested, I am sending a copy of 'Warmer Homes with Solid Fuel', which I hope you will find of interest and use.

The Condor Thermostatic Boiler No. 3 is not yet included in the recommended list, but I have no doubt that it is only a question of time before it is added. With all new appliances a certain amount of time has to elapse before the necessary tests can be carried out, and as this

model has been available for only a few weeks it
may be several months before information is
received that it has become an approved
appliance.

Yours faithfully,

W. Perching

Technical Information Officer

NOTES

1. First sentence acknowledges letter received and quotes its date.

2. At paragraph two NOT *With regard to the Condor Thermostatic Boiler No. 3 this boiler is not yet* ...

3. Tone throughout friendly and helpful. Writer is not afraid to use a few extra words to obtain this effect, yet the letter is concise.

B. Complaint and letter of adjustment

Grey Walls,

Tenderham, Kent.

BR33 2JM

9th December, 19 . .

The Krispikorn Co. Ltd,

    Shawford, Birmingham.

        B81 5KJ

Dear Sirs,

    My little boy has been very disappointed on no less than three occasions by finding no British Battleship cards in packets of Krispikorn. All three packets had wording on them which implied that these cards were in the packets.

    I feel that as this has happened more than once it is reasonable to bring the matter to your attention.

Yours faithfully,

(Mrs) Muriel Wyman

NOTES

1. The most important point about a letter of complaint is to avoid rudeness or sarcasm. A good firm will put the matter right if the facts are laid before it fairly. Rudeness only makes the recipient defensive and uncooperative. This is a calm and sensible letter and deserves favourable treatment.

2. Mrs Wyman does not put *Mrs* in front of her name simply because she is proud of her married status. She is, very properly, making it easy for the firm to address her correctly in their reply.

KRISPIKORN CO. LTD
Shawford   Birmingham   B81 5KJ

SJH/MLG   11th December, 19..

Mrs M. Wyman,
Grey Walls,
Tenderham, Kent.
BR33 2JM

Dear Madam,

We were sorry to learn from your letter of
9th December, 19.., that your little boy had
been disappointed in not finding his British
Battleship cards in three packets of Krispikorn.

We must apologise for these deficiencies.
It seems that there was a fault on one of the
packaging machines at the time these packets
were being processed. We are grateful to you for
taking the time and trouble to bring this matter
to our notice.

We enclose with this letter six replacement
British Battleship cards and hope that your son
will be just as pleased with them now as he
would have been when he opened the packets to
look for them.

We are also sending you separately two
packets of Krispikorn which we trust you will
accept with our compliments.

Yours faithfully,
for Krispikorn Co. Ltd.

S. J. Heward
Consumer Relations Officer.

NOTES

The letter of adjustment presents considerable difficulty. First it has
to be decided whether the complaint is justified. The customer always
has to have the benefit of the doubt but if the customer is clearly in the
wrong a tactful letter must be sent pointing this out (not easy). If the
complaint is justified, the adjustments department (or equivalent section)
must: (1) find out what went wrong so that an explanation can be sent to
the customer (2) decide what action is best to put the matter right and

restore the customer's good opinion of the firm (3) write a letter admitting the fault, apologising (but not crawling), and endeavouring to prevent the loss of the customer's future trade (without letting the customer see too obviously that this is the aim).

C. First collection letter

H. AND C. CORNCROFT & CO. LTD

Rose Growers

Wallington   Essex   CO51 7AB

```
J. Morris Esq.,                      30 January, 19..
The Grange,
Hillford, Somerset.
BA42 6DE

Dear Sir,
                    Account 58236
     According to our records, you have not yet
settled your account with us for rose trees
supplied to you on the 10th October of last
year. We enclose our detailed statement. You
will note that the amount outstanding is
£21.68.

     We trust the quality of tree supplied was
to your satisfaction and would appreciate your
early settlement of this account.
                    Yours faithfully,
                    H. and C. Corncroft & Co. Ltd.
Enc.
```

NOTES

1. Letters seeking payment of money owed (collection letters) must be very carefully written, as it is easy to give offence. Firms will often submit statements several times with perhaps the addition of a phrase such as 'Account overdue; please remit' before writing the first collection letter. In a first letter of this kind a very cautious approach should be adopted; the wording should be of a kind (as here) that allows for the possibility that the firm is itself in error. Just as well that this letter was so carefully worded in view of the reply (below).

2. The *Enc.* at the bottom left of the letter serves as a reminder both to the person who puts the letter in its envelope and to the person who opens the envelope that there is an enclosure (here the detailed statement).

                                    The Grange,
                                    Hillford, Somerset.
                                    BA42 6DE
                                    3rd February, 19..

H. and C. Corncroft & Co. Ltd,
Wallington, Essex.
CO51 7AB

Dear Sirs,

                        Order 58236

        I have received from you a letter dated
30 January 19.., which asserts that I have not
settled the above account. In fact this account
was paid at the time of ordering by my cheque
Barclays SC 305388. As you have apparently
mislaid this cheque, which I note has not been
cashed, I have instructed my bank to withhold
payment on it, and enclose a second cheque for
the amount due.

                        Yours faithfully,

                            J. Morris

NOTES

    A dignified letter in the circumstances. He makes his points firmly, but
refrains from pointing out the inconvenience he has been put to by the
firm's inefficiency.

    Although in this example the customer turns out to be in the right, there
will be many occasions when no satisfactory reply is received and the firm
will have to send a series of letters, gradually hardening in tone, in its
attempt to obtain payment without losing a customer. Threat of legal
action is reserved to the third or fourth letter in the series.

D. Second and third collection letters

    (SECOND)

Dear Sir,

                        Order 58257

    On 30th January 19.., we wrote to you
drawing your attention to what appeared to be an
unpaid account amounting to £42.85 for rose

trees supplied to you on the 15th October last
year.

    We are surprised to have had no reply from
you on this matter and would be grateful to
receive your cheque at your earliest
convenience.

                Yours faithfully,

  (THIRD)

Dear Sir,

Order 58257

    We have now submitted our statement in
connection with the above order three times, and
wrote on 30th January and 14th February
reminding you that the account was still
unsettled.

    We have received no reply to our letters
and have therefore no alternative but to put the
matter in the hands of our solicitors if your
cheque for £42.85 is not received by 1st
March.

                Yours faithfully,

E. Third person invitation and reply

The Chairman and Directors of James Hargreaves
and Sons Ltd request the pleasure of the
company of James Thompson Esq. on the occasion
of the Open Day and Presentation of Apprentice
Awards at 15.15 on Tuesday 7th January 19..

RSVP to Education Officer,
James Hargreaves & Sons Ltd,
Hillborough, Kent BR49 6DM
before Friday, 13th December, 19..

Mr James Thompson thanks the Chairman and
Directors of James Hargreaves & Sons Ltd for

```
their invitation to attend the Open Day and
Presentation of Apprentice Awards on 7th
January 19.. (1) at which he will be very happy
to be present or (2) but regrets that owing to a
prior commitment he will not be able to be
present.
```

NOTES

Form and wording are highly conventional. The invitation will often be a printed card with only the name of the Rx added by hand. A third person invitation is usually taken as committing the Rx to a third person reply. This should be unsigned and have no inside address. It has been customary for the address of the person replying to appear at the end, bottom left, followed by the date, but if the reply is sent on headed paper this is not possible.

Except for invitations, third person correspondence is becoming very rare. Its formality is out of keeping with modern ideas of directness and simplicity in correspondence.

V. PRECIS OF CORRESPONDENCE

Circumstances sometimes arise – for example, when making a report, or when seeking legal advice – when it is desirable to reduce a lengthy correspondence to an easily assimilated piece of continuous prose. The final version can easily be made very much shorter than the original as there is inevitably much repetition in a sequence of letters. It is not always necessary to précis every letter of the series, but the dates at which the various stages of the correspondence are reached are sometimes critical and must always be made clear. Some ingenuity is required to avoid a monotonous sequence of sentences starting *On the 15th May the company wrote, saying* . . .

A business-like title making clear the exact names and addresses of the correspondents and giving a very brief indication of the subject is useful for reference purposes, and is also advantageous because it permits the correspondents to be referred to in a more cursory manner in the body of the précis.

In the example that follows a correspondence consisting of six letters is reduced to 130 words, excluding the title. These letters may also be read as a more extended example of business correspondence than has been provided in the preceding section.

PIDDERMINSTER TECHNICAL COLLEGE

Pidderminster   Somerset   BA25 2PJ

Department of Business Studies

14th May, 19..

The Library Supply Co.,
Paddington Street, London.
W2 9XZ

Dear Sirs,

<u>Our order 5931</u>

I have received the above order from you
consisting of two dozen copies of Fraser:
Cybernetics in the Office (Holton & Co).
Unfortunately three copies were wrongly bound,
pages 31-46 being omitted and pages 47-62
inserted twice in each. I am returning these
three books, separately packaged, for your
replacement.

Yours faithfully,
T. F. Smythe
Head of Department

THE LIBRARY SUPPLY CO.

Paddington Street   London   W2 9XZ

JHL/JFT   17th May, 19..

The Head of Department of Business Studies,
Pidderminster Technical College,
Pidderminster, Somerset.
BA25 2PJ

Dear Sir,

<u>Your order No. 5931</u>

We have received your letter of 14th May,
19.. and the three defective books to which you
refer. We shall be taking this matter up with
the publishers and shall send you the
replacement volumes as soon as we receive them.
We must apologise for the inconvenience this has
caused you but you will understand that we sent
the books to you in good faith, not realising

that Holton & Co. had supplied us with defective
volumes.

Yours faithfully,
for The Library Supply Co.,
J. H. Langton

PIDDERMINSTER TECHNICAL COLLEGE
Pidderminster   Somerset   BA25 2PJ

Department of Business Studies

Your ref: JHL/JFT   18th June, 19..

The Library Supply Co.,
Paddington Street, London.
W2 9XZ

Dear Sirs,

Our order 5931

It is now more than a month since I wrote
requesting replacement of three defective books
supplied on the above order. I hope this matter
has not been overlooked and that I can expect
the books very soon.

Yours faithfully,
T. F. Smythe
Head of Department

THE LIBRARY SUPPLY CO.
Paddington Street   London   W2 9XZ

JHL/JFT   21st June, 19..

The Head of Department of Business Studies,
Pidderminster Technical College,
Pidderminster, Somerset.
BA25 2PJ

Dear Sir,

Your order No. 5931

Thank you for your letter of 18th June,
19.. We are very sorry that there is this delay
in replacing the defective copies of Fraser:
Cybernetics in the Office. As you will perhaps
know, Holton & Co. have recently transferred
their business from London to Brighton; since
then it has been very difficult to obtain books

from them. We are, however, sending them a
reminder, and hope that we shall soon have the
replacement volumes ready for despatch to you.

Yours faithfully,
for The Library Supply Co.

J. H. Langton

PIDDERMINSTER TECHNICAL COLLEGE
Pidderminster   Somerset   BA25 2PJ
Department of Business Studies

Your ref: JHL/JFT   26th June, 19..

The Library Supply Co.,
Paddington Street, London.
W2 9XZ

Dear Sirs,

Our order 5931

We have just received a second statement
from you for the above order, which has been the
subject of some correspondence. I must make it
clear that I do not propose to pass this account
for payment until we have received the three
replacement volumes referred to in my previous
letters. It is now six weeks since I first wrote
to you about this matter on 14th May, 19..

Yours faithfully,
T. F. Smythe
Head of Department

THE LIBRARY SUPPLY CO.
Paddington Street   London   W2 9XZ

JHL/JFT   29th June, 19..

The Head of Department of Business Studies,
Pidderminster Technical College,
Pidderminster, Somerset.
BA25 2PJ

Dear Sir,

Your order No. 5931

Thank you for your letter of 26th June.
We have still not received the replacement
copies of Fraser: Cybernetics in the Office from

Holton & Co. However, we have managed to obtain
three copies from another bookseller and are
sending these to you by today's post, in order
that this matter can be settled without further
delay and inconvenience to you.

                    Yours faithfully,
                 for The Library Supply Co.

                        J. H. Langton

In the précis that follows it is assumed (as is usual in exercises) that an
outsider is making the précis. In practice this is not usually so and the task
is that much easier as, for example, The Library Supply Co. could refer
to itself throughout as 'we' and 'us', if it was itself making the précis.

Précis of a correspondence between T. F. Smythe
Esq., Head of Department of Business Studies,
Pidderminster Technical College, Pidderminster,
Somerset, and The Library Supply Co. of
Paddington Street, London. Subject: the
college's order No. 5931.
On 14th May, 19.. Smythe acknowledged receipt
of two dozen copies of Fraser: Cybernetics in
the Office (Holton) but drew attention to three
defective copies returned, separately packaged,
for replacement. The Library Supply Co.
acknowledged receipt of these on 17th May and
undertook to obtain replacements from the
publishers. On 18th June a reminder was sent by
Smythe which was replied to by the company on
21st June blaming the delay on the publishers.
On 26th June Smythe wrote again referring to a
second statement sent for this order and
stressing that he would not pass the account for
payment until the replacement volumes were
forthcoming. On 29th June the company wrote that
these volumes had been obtained from another
bookseller and were being despatched.

VI. EXERCISES

In attempting the following exercises you should invent additional details
where necessary to give verisimilitude to your letters, which should be

properly laid out and complete in all relevant details such as dates, addresses, references.

Exercise A

Write an application for a post of the kind that you would like to hold. This should consist of a brief letter of application together with a schematically presented data sheet indicating under headings your personal details, education, qualifications, and experience, and providing the names and addresses of referees.

Exercise B

1. Imagine you have moved to another area. Write to the local technical college enquiring about courses similar to the one you are now following.
2. Write to a distinguished sportsman, writer, or television personality, inviting him to address a students' society of which you are secretary.
3. Write to a local coach-hire firm seeking a quotation for an outing which you are organising on behalf of a group of students.

Exercise C

Write a typical letter of enquiry of the sort received frequently by your firm and a reply to it, or (if not employed) a letter of complaint about a purchase you have made and the firm's reply.

Exercise D

Jackson, Hobart & Co. Ltd, who have been good customers of your firm for several years, owe £320·65. Write letters for use when payment is (a) six weeks overdue (b) ten weeks overdue (c) three months overdue. You may assume two statements have been sent before your first letter.

Exercise E

Write letters to suit the following situations:

1. Your firm has received an order for goods to the value of £4 200 from a new customer, James Blishford & Co., who do not quote credit references.
2. Your firm has received an order from John Jimpson of 19 Holly Park, London SE11 9KB, for a 'Windstop De-Luxe' folding beach shelter and a cheque for £10·55. This is the price quoted in your advertising for the 'Windstop' standard quality folding beach shelter. The 'De-Luxe' is advertised at £13·75.
3. A Mrs J. Hanbury of Orchard Cottage, Temple Ruiston, Gloucestershire GL48 3ML, has asked you to supply and fit a 'Valiant' No. 3

boiler. Your firm will sell only through the trade and does not do any
fitting of appliances itself.

Exercise F

Write one of the following pairs of letters:
1. To the Town Clerk of your nearest town protesting at a scheme to
   cut down trees as part of a road-widening scheme and drawing attention to the ugly lopping of trees throughout the town; and the Town
   Clerk's reply.
2. To the Parks Superintendent suggesting the provision of greater
   facilities for games and an increased number of flower beds, in the
   principal park; and the Parks Superintendent's reply.
3. To the editor of a newspaper or magazine drawing attention to an error
   in an article dealing with a subject of which you have some knowledge;
   and the editor's reply.

Exercise G

Write a tactful letter of adjustment in reply to the following letter. On
investigation you have found (1) that the bath panels order has been overlooked (2) that the foreman slabber had found he had not sufficient 25 mm
tiles to provide a border and decided on his own initiative to omit it. The
bath panels can be sent immediately, but you want if possible to discourage
the customer from demanding the removal of the present tiles and their
replacement to his original specification. You are authorised to offer a
5 per cent discount. Make a particular effort to suit your letter to the
personality of the Rx as revealed in his letter.

17 Duckham Drove,
Grange Green,
Herts.
HER42 5MA
17th October, 19..

J. Dodge & Co.,
High Street,
Ickfield, Herts.
HER44 3JB

Dear Sirs,

    I refer to the provision of wall tiling and
bath panels at my new house at this address.

Regarding the bath panels, I am at a loss to understand the cause of the delay in delivery. Your representative personally verified with me, on the occasion of my visit to your showroom on July 7th, that they could be supplied in a colour matching the selected tiles. This was later confirmed in a letter from you to myself, dated July 28th, stating that these panels were available for immediate delivery. This is now nine weeks ago; having occupied my house for nearly a month, I am still awaiting them. If you cannot supply them forthwith please cancel the order.

The wall tiling has not been carried out as directed by me and agreed to by you. The decorative 25 mm border has not been inserted, although this was specifically asked for, and later confirmed by telephone. On enquiring, I was told that the reason for not laying this border was that there were not enough of the 25 mm tiles to do the job. You must agree that this is a quite unsatisfactory way of doing business. I should at least have been informed so that a possible alternative arrangement could have been made. By the time I knew what had been done it was too late to make any alteration, short of having the whole wall tiling pulled away. The statement that there were insufficient tiles can only imply inefficiency in view of your earlier assurances.

I regard the whole business as thoroughly unsatisfactory and would be glad to learn what you propose to do about it.

Yours faithfully,

John Duff

Exercise H

You are employed as Sales Manager for a company manufacturing *Stabrite* liquid polishing wax. This product contains a high proportion of expensive carnauba wax and is therefore about 20 per cent dearer than its competitors. On the other hand it dries, without buffing, to an unusually long-lasting shine which improves on repolishing and with normal use. The finish is completely water-resistant and will not 'spot' when water is spilled on it.

Sales are to date through over 400 retail outlets regularly visited by a small team of salesmen. Your company now proposes a limited national advertising campaign aimed to increase sales by 25 per cent over six months. Write a letter to an advertising agency asking for first suggestions for such a campaign with indications of the cost involved.

Exercise I

A firm of builders whom you have employed to repair a section of the roof of an annexe to your place of business has submitted an estimate of £180 for the work. The structure of the roof is of bitumenised felt laid over slabs of a patent insulating material known as Strawtex, and the builder has stipulated that his estimate shall not take account of replacement of sections of this material, parts of which may have 'exploded' because of ingress of water through faulty waterproofing. The eventual bill comes to £278 and the itemised account includes a substantial amount of heavy timber and some £45 for lead flashing (not mentioned on the estimate or used on the original structure). Write a letter to the builder concerned querying the account as presented and requesting a fuller explanation of the 50 per cent addition to the estimate. Draft a reply from the builder justifying all or most of the increase in cost. Use suitable fictional addresses. Pay particular attention to layout and punctuation.

[*Royal Society of Arts and London Chamber of Commerce, Ordinary National Certificate in Business Studies*]

Exercise J

Mr and Mrs Beefy of 9 Paddock Close, Plumpminster, Devon, EX51 7BJ, purchased from Rassemblit Ltd of Dreverton, Somerset, BA46 6FA, a three-piece suite of the type that is despatched as packages of component parts that are to be assembled by the purchaser. On unpacking, Mr Beefy was pleased to find that all the necessary parts had been sent and the instructions were clear and easy to carry out. In less than an hour he had completed assembly; the suite looked in every way as good as the one they had seen in the showroom.

Three days later, when Mr and Mrs Beefy had been sitting on the settee for about two hours watching television, the sponge-rubber seat suddenly gave way and they fell through. As soon as he had freed himself from the resulting uncomfortable and ludicrous position, Mr Beefy examined the settee to see if he had made some error of assembly. It was, however, only too clear what had occurred. The seat was supported on eighteen ashwood slats about three inches wide, joined at their ends by strips of webbing so that they formed a ladder shape. On assembly, these were stretched along the settee, the ends of each slat resting on two angle bars which ran the length of the settee, one at the front and one at the back. These slats were now slightly bent and it was apparent that the combined weight of Mr and Mrs Beefy (who were well built but not enormous) had curved the slats so much that their ends could slip off the angle bars. It looked as if the seat would always collapse when they both sat on it for any length of time.

Mr Beefy reasoned that either there was a serious design fault (the settee would take only a limited load) or there was something wrong with the slats supplied. Although he was not unaware of the comic side of his predicament, he decided he must face writing to the firm and explaining what had happened.

A. Write Mr Beefy's letter

Rassemblit Ltd had in fact begun to suspect that one consignment of ashwood had been below standard and slats made from it were too flexible, because one or two letters of complaint similar to Mr Beefy's had already been received. Unfortunately the firm had no way of finding out which sets of slats had been made from that particular consignment. The firm's view was:

1. Mr Beefy must be sent a replacement set of slats.
2. They would like to examine the original slats supplied to Mr Beefy.
3. Mr Beefy should not be deprived of the use of his settee for any period or put to any expense.

The firm had no delivery service of its own.

B. Having decided on an appropriate adjustment procedure in accordance with the indications above, write the firm's reply to Mr Beefy's letter

Exercise K

Make a précis of the following correspondence in approximately 120 words, excluding title.

THE MARKET PRESERVING CO.
Kingsborough   Lincolnshire   LIN26 5BQ

OUR REF: JD/AH/W.1   12th May, 19..

Hollick, Timms, Bradfoot & Co.,
112 Highfields Lane,
Worcester, Worcestershire.
WR9 3JC

Dear Sirs,

       Our company is interested in establishing a
cannery in Worcestershire. For this purpose we
shall require an area, where we shall be able to
obtain permission to build, of approximately
150 hectares of good fertile land, well
irrigated, and suitable for growing soft fruits
and green peas. We shall want to build the
cannery on a small part of this area; the
remainder will be kept under cultivation.

       If you have knowledge of such a tract of
land, with easy access to a main road, for sale
or rent, we shall be pleased to hear from you.

                     Yours faithfully,
                     Market Preserving Co.

                          J. Duncannon

                     Manager

             HOLLICK, TIMMS, BRADFOOT & CO.
                  Estate Agents and Valuers
                     112 Highfields Lane
                     Worcester WR9 3JC

YOUR REF: JD/AH/W.1   14th May, 19..
OUR REF: T/A HJ

The Manager,
The Market Preserving Co.,
Kingsborough, Lincolnshire.
LIN26 5BQ

Dear Sir,

       Thank you for your letter of 12th May. We
think we may be able to offer you just the kind
of site you are looking for. A tract of land

measuring 158 hectares at Compton Deverill has
recently come into the market. Unfortunately
40 hectares are at present on short lease to a
market gardener but the site is fertile, well-
drained, and has a small spring-fed stream
running through it. It is situated only 120
metres from the A.38 to which it is connected by
a minor road quite suitable for lorries.

We fear you may have some initial
difficulty over permission to build in this
predominantly agricultural area but since you
are intending to keep most of the land for
agricultural purposes this should not prove an
insurmountable problem.

The vendor is prepared to accept £950 per
hectare for a quick sale. We hope therefore to
hear from you further without delay, when we
shall be willing to arrange for you to visit the
site if you are interested.

> Yours faithfully,
> for Hollick, Timms, Bradfoot & Co.
>
> *James Timms*

THE MARKET PRESERVING CO.
Kingsborough Lincolnshire LIN26 5BQ

YOUR REF: T/A HJ   17th May, 19..
OUR REF: JD/AH/W.2

Hollick, Timms, Bradfoot & Co.,
112 Highfields Lane,
Worcester, Worcestershire.
WR9 3JC

Dear Sirs,

Thank you for your letter of 14th May,
19.. We are interested in the tract of land at
Compton Deverill you describe but need further
information on one or two points.

First we must know how much longer the
lease of that part of the property that is out
for rent has to run. Second we should like your
opinion of our chances of recruiting local

labour to the extent of probably 40 male and 150
female workers in this rather remote rural area.
Subject to you being able to give satisfactory
answers on these points we are interested in
this proposition and would appreciate a detailed
large-scale plan of the site. There does not
seem much point in arranging a visit at this
early stage.

Yours faithfully,
Market Preserving Co.

J. Duncannon

Manager

Exercise K

Read through the following correspondence carefully. Then (*a*) write
Emmanuel Bodger's reply to Mr Fore's letter of 16th May; (*b*) make a
précis of the correspondence, including the letter you have written, in
about 130 words.

5 Hallan Way,
Grange Green, Kent.
BR65 4BE
11th May, 19..

Bodger & Bodger Ltd,
Brick Lane,
Ickfield, Kent.
BR61 5AC

Dear Sirs,

Plot 10, Mill Pond Estate, Ickfield

Progress on my new house at Ickfield does
not appear to be very satisfactory. It is now
seven months since I completed the contract.
Your building manager gave the figure of
"fifteen weeks" for completing the house but it
has only reached the rafter stage by now. How
much longer will I have to wait before I can
take over the house and live in it?

Yours faithfully,

John Fore

BODGER AND BODGER

Builders and Decorators

Brick Lane,
Ickfield, Kent.
BR61 5AC

YOUR REF:
OUR REF: EB/JHF

13th May, 19..

J. Fore, Esq.,
5 Hallan Way,
Grange Green, Kent.
BR65 4BE

Dear Sir,

Plot 10, Mill Pond Estate, Ickfield

Thank you for your letter of 11th May. We
are aware of slow progress with your house, but
would ask you to bear in mind the following
points. (1) Our building manager quoted you a
figure for completion which is perfectly
possible in favourable conditions, but quite
impossible in the heavy snows of the past
winter. (2) There has been a nation-wide shortage of bricks and bricklayers and this caused
further delay, as the outer skin of your
proposed house is entirely brick-built.

We are now experiencing a further hold-up,
as we are unable to obtain delivery of the
special 'Cotswold' tiles you required. Would you
consider accepting 'Antique Red' as substitutes
as we hold ample stocks of these? It is
desirable to complete the tiling as soon as
possible as heavy rain would penetrate the felt
roofing at present covering the rafters and wet
the structural timber of the house.

Yours faithfully,

Emmanuel Bodger

5 Hallan Way,
Grange Green, Kent.
BR65 4BE

EB/JHF   16th May, 19..

Bodger & Bodger Ltd,
Brick Lane,
Ickfield, Kent.
BR61 5AC

Dear Sirs,

Plot 10, Mill Pond Estate, Ickfield

I was very disappointed to be informed, by
your letter of 13th May, that you are unable to
obtain 'Cotswold' tiles for my house. This seems
a very unsatisfactory state of affairs in view
of the fact that I specified these tiles more
than seven months ago. However, I seem to have
no alternative but to accept 'Antique Red'. This
will necessitate a complete change of colour
scheme for the exterior painting of the house,
and I should be grateful for the return of the
scheme now lodged with you.

You still do not tell me when I can hope to
occupy the house. Will you please repair this
omission in your next letter?

Yours faithfully,

John Fore

Chapter 9

Reports

I. TYPES OF REPORT CLASSIFIED

A. *Definition*

In this chapter the word *report* is used (in accordance with general business usage) to refer to a document providing an account of something witnessed or examined, or of work carried out, or of an investigation together with conclusions arrived at as a result of the investigation.

B. *Classification by content*

Reports may be classified by content as follows:

1.   **EYE-WITNESS REPORTS**

2.   **WORK REPORTS**

a. **PROGRESS REPORTS**
Periodic reports on work as it goes on

b. **COMPLETION REPORTS**
Final progress reports

c. **SINGLE WORK REPORTS**
On work of limited scope or duration

3.   **INVESTIGATION REPORTS**

a. **INFORMATION REPORTS**
Detailing and analysing findings and showing significance only

b. **RECOMMENDATION REPORTS**
Advising on action to be taken as well

Fig. 6

C. Oral reports

Although this chapter deals only with written reports it must be remembered that ORAL REPORTS (see Chapter 13) are quite common, especially for categories 1 and 2a. Reports made at meetings of societies or committees are also usually oral.

D. Routine and special reports

ROUTINE REPORTS are reports for which there is a precedent; their purpose and form will have been decided when they were first instituted and their presentation therefore offers no problem. Most routine reports (or returns) are in fact submitted on predesigned forms which reduce the use of language to a minimum.

SPECIAL REPORTS in business are once-only reports called for by a superior, a colleague, or a customer, under special circumstances. Special reports from individuals may also be called for by an organisation (for example a club that you belong to) and committees are frequently required to produce such reports for the consideration of the organisation that set up the committee. Previous experience in dealing with similar reports may be useful, but each special report poses its own questions; the best pattern for that particular subject will have to be sought from scratch.

It is the special report which is the subject of this chapter.

EYE-WITNESS REPORTS, called for most often in cases of accident, constitute simple narrative writing with a straightforward chronological order. Provided *What? Who? Where? When?* are solidly established in the opening sentences, little difficulty is likely to be met. Diagrams are often useful for clarifying the physical relationships of the people and objects essential to the account. Practice work is provided on page 146.

The majority of WORK REPORTS are routine reports, and even SINGLE WORK REPORTS tend to follow a well established pattern. Some of these, however – especially those dealing with planning and reorganisation (which is, of course, a type of work) – are as without precedent as any other special report and the advice in this chapter will be relevant.

Although some INVESTIGATION REPORTS, such as EQUIPMENT REPORTS, are of routine type and can be filled in on a set form, it is into this category that the majority of special reports fall and it is with the SPECIAL INVESTIGATION REPORT that this chapter, therefore, particularly deals.

E. Classification by length

Reports may be further classified by length. SHORT (or SUMMARY)

REPORTS give their findings in a summarised form throughout. Some firms specify a length (such as one sheet of foolscap typescript) which must not be exceeded. FULL (or DETAILED) REPORTS give full details of findings and a summary as well.

F. *Classification by form*

Reports may finally be classified by form. Apart from routine reports and eye-witness accounts, the following are the three variants possible:

    1. LETTER FORM. This is suitable where:

    a. the subject matter is simple and limited

    b. only one viewpoint is involved

    c. there is an obvious (probably chronological) order of presentation.

It does not differ in layout from any other formal business letter.

    2. SCHEMATIC PRESENTATION (see Example B). The great disadvantage of the letter form is that it must all be read, and in the author's order. It is frequently difficult for the reader to see the connection between various parts of the report and he cannot easily select parts only, for close study or to weigh against each other. In short, it is difficult for the reader to find his way through complex material arranged in letter form. A schematic presentation aims to make this easy for him by classifying, analysing, and labelling the material (see Chapter 2). The subject matter is divided into major sections and then subdivided. If the material lends itself to it, further subdivisions are made and suitable headings for the sections devised. The sections are placed in a logical order of maximum convenience for the reader.

Headings of equal importance should be:

    1. the same part of speech

    2. similarly displayed (this refers to: use of capitals; underlining; spacing; and whether centred, at left-hand margin, or indented).

These points may be illustrated by the following, which represents the HEADINGS ONLY of part of a detailed report on the breakdown of office appliances suffered by a company over a certain period.

III CAUSES OF BREAKDOWN

A.   Electrical

    1.   Insulation failures

    2.   Continuity failures

        a. Dry joints

        b. Dirty contacts

```
        c. Defective wiring
            (i)   Input leads
            (ii)  Internal circuitry
    3.  Component failures
        a. Capacitors
        b. Resistors
B.  Mechanical
```

Notice how the more subordinate the heading is, the more indented it is. Principal section headings are usually centred in a long report. The system of numbering used here is useful when five degrees of importance are to be indicated; letters and numerals are alternated, upper case Roman numerals being used for the most important, and lower case Roman for the least important, divisions. For four degrees of importance the lower case Roman numerals are dropped, and for three all Roman numerals. Other similar systems are in use; it does not really matter how you indicate the relative importance of the headings, provided you have a consistent method maintained throughout the report.

Not all material lends itself to this sort of treatment. Sometimes, especially with very long reports, it is better simply to number all the paragraphs of the report and to interpose headings indicating how the subject matter falls into groups of paragraphs. A refinement of this method is to number the first paragraph of the first section 1.1 and subsequent paragraphs 1.2, 1.3, 1.4, etc., until a change is made to what is considered a new section of the subject matter (whether a heading is used or not) when numbering changes to 2.1, 2.2, 2.3, etc.; when the third section is reached the next paragraph will be numbered 3.1. This system is useful when the report is likely to be discussed by a group because reference to a particular section is quick and accurate, but it is not so convenient for the single reader as a system of headings and numbered subsections, which is recommended whenever the material permits.

Detailed reports with schematic presentations are usually accompanied by a *covering letter* (or *letter of transmittal*) but this is unnecessary with a short report (see Example C).

3. MIXED FORM (see Example A). Here the report starts like a letter but changes to a simple schematic presentation when the findings are reached. The scheme will probably involve no more than a numbering of the items, which will be typed on separate lines, with, perhaps, subheadings. The letter style is returned to at the end of the report. This form is suitable where the material is too brief to look well if laid out entirely schematically but is a little too complex to fulfil the conditions for normal letter form.

G. Memoranda

Reports are *called for*. Sometimes an executive submits an unsolicited work report or investigation report to draw attention to some matter to which he has devoted time. It is more satisfactory to use the word MEMORANDUM (plural MEMORANDA) to refer to such documents. They are usually formal in style, employing schematic presentation and headed:

From: To:

Subject:

A short introductory section should follow this heading, making clear the circumstances under which the memorandum came to be written; this replaces the 'Term of Reference' section of a report. Apart from these preliminaries, the instructions on report writing that follow will be found to be also appropriate to memoranda of this kind.

II. REPORTS IN EXAMINATIONS

These are bound to be of the short or summary kind, although if the report is an alternative to an essay, or a principal question (as in London Chamber of Commerce Private Secretary's Diploma) a length of at least 350 words will be expected, and schematic presentation is essential. In examinations where a much shorter time allocation is made for a report, a very short one is obviously required, and the mixed form may provide the neatest solution.

You will be expected to invent sufficient detail to make the report (1) convincing and (2) long enough to show that you can organise material effectively. The examining bodies requiring fairly long reports supply background material to start you off, but you are still expected to supply additional material from your imagination.

In the sections that follow you will be taken through the various stages of practical report writing, including the preparation of detailed reports. This will not only help you when you come to write your own real reports, but will also assist in stimulating your imagination when it comes to inventing fictitious material for exercises and examination answers in report writing.

III. TERMS OF REFERENCE

The first step when you are instructed to prepare a report is to decide exactly what the report is to be about. This is *defining your terms of reference*. If the man instructing you is good communicator he will take pains to define them for you, but often instructions are vaguely formulated.

The degree of formality in defining the terms of reference is often in direct ratio to the gap in rank between the man issuing the instruction and the man preparing the report. 'I say, Tom, you remember that reorganisation scheme you were talking about last week? Get something down on paper and I'll put it up to the Board next week.' This sort of thing – very friendly and very vague – over the telephone may be the start of an important report where the gap in rank between the two men involved is slight.

At the other extreme, a much more junior manager may receive from the same man who was speaking to Tom a memo like this:

Please submit a detailed report on our sales in the Andover sector over the period 1st April–1st December 19... Special attention should be paid to house-to-house trading compared with our normal retail outlets in that area, and to seasonal effects on both. No recommendations. Required before December 20th next.

Probably the boss here is a good communicator who is aware in the first example that the groundwork has been well covered orally and that Tom knows well enough what he is to include, but in the second that if he is not given tight terms of reference the junior manager will include unwanted material.

The terms of reference should be quoted or otherwise made clear at the start of a well planned report. For example, the instructions[1] by the Minister of Education in March 1956 that led in 1959 to the very influential report on 15–18 year-old education known as the Crowther Report were 'to consider, in relation to the changing social and industrial needs of our society, and the needs of its individual citizens, the education of boys and girls between 15 and 18, and in particular to consider the balance at various levels of general and specialised studies between these ages and to examine the inter-relationship of the various stages of education'. These terms of reference are quoted in the first paragraph of the preface to the report. Simpler terms of reference can often be incorporated in the title of the report: '*Report on the Breakdown of Five Maddison Electric Typewriters during the week January 10th–January 17th 19. .*' is self-explanatory.

With the more important types of report, it is usual to state your authority for preparing it along with the terms of reference. Typical authorisations are: resolutions passed by committees, letters of authorisation, and other forms of written instruction, such as internal memos. Frequently the authorisation appears in the report in no more precise form than *on the instruction of . . .* , the gap being filled by the rank or formal title of the man issuing the instruction.

[1] To the Central Advisory Council for Education.

Often you will need to feed back enquiries, to complete the defining of your terms of reference. You should not proceed until you are clear (1) precisely what is to be included in, and what excluded from, your report, (2) whether it is to be summary or detailed and, approximately, what length is expected if the latter, (3) how long you have for preparing it.

IV. ASSEMBLING THE DATA

Having made sure exactly what it is you have to report on, you then proceed to assemble your data. You will decide upon certain lines of enquiry, and perhaps action, which will supply information. Your sources of information will be threefold:

1. written (is there a previous report on this; what is there on your files; is there a relevant magazine article or book?)
2. personal (who can you write to, phone, speak to, with first-hand experience?)
3. direct (look, ask, for yourself; conduct experiments, tests).

Thus if you were a personnel officer instructed to report on apprentice unrest in a factory you might:

1. check your files to see if there was any previous history of this sort of dissatisfaction in the firm
2. phone up shop superintendents and foremen to hear their versions of what has been happening
3. go down on the shop floor and question apprentices about their grievances.

At each step you would make notes and try to check the accuracy of the information obtained, taking care to distinguish fact from opinion.

V. ORGANISING THE DATA

Having collected what you consider to be sufficient data you then seek to collate it. Which are the significant facts; which bear on each other; do any contradict each other? What is the tendency of the facts; to what conclusions are they leading you? Only when you have answers to these questions can you start testing for relevance. Be careful not to jump to conclusions or to suppress facts which do not fit in with your theory. You may now find some of your data have to be rejected as unnecessary, some reduced in bulk as of limited importance, some perhaps expanded.

The next step is to group your findings into sections under defining headings and decide on the best order of presentation. You will have to decide if your conclusions are going to be given at the end of each section or held back to form a separately headed section near the end of the report. The second method is more frequently used, though with a very long report a combination of the two methods can be effective. You will decide on your recommendations, if these are called for by your terms of reference, and assemble them as a further section.

VI. DRAFTING THE REPORT

SHORT REPORTS, whether schematic or in letter form, tend to follow a set order:

1. Terms of reference
2. Procedure, i.e. methods used to collect data, tests carried out etc.
3. Findings
4. Conclusions
5. Recommendations (if required).

The report should be dated, and signed by the person who submits it.

Fig. 7

THE DETAILED REPORT, by virtue of its length, requires more organisation if the reader is to find his way through it easily. He will want to be able to SKIM quickly through to obtain a general picture of what the report covers but also to DIP to get a detailed view of what particularly interests him (see Fig. 7). To facilitate skimming and dipping, your layout of a detailed report should include:

1. A title-page showing about what, by whom (see page 145)
2. A table of contents
3. A synopsis of findings, conclusions, and recommendations (see page 146)
4. Clearly headed subdivisions of the main text with cross-reference to appendices
5. Appendices to which are transferred detailed information which would prevent the reader's quick assimilation of the main facts (e.g. charts, tables of figures, verbatim statements, sub-reports, definitions of terms etc.).

VII. WRITING THE REPORT

The aim of the report writer can thus be seen to be diametrically opposed to the aim of the fiction writer. The latter, by holding back, by the device of suspense, tries to keep his reader reading to the last word; the former brings the gist of his findings forward so that the reader can decide as soon as possible how little he needs to read to find out what he requires.

The emphasis in the report is on the facts, and interpretation of the facts will be logical not emotional. The language throughout will be strictly objective. The author will need to be self-effacing and, apparently at least, neutral.

Except in the more informal reports, this will require impersonal constructions and a loss of that person-to-person contact which is so valuable in other forms of business communication. The other principles of good communication stressed in earlier chapters, however, have in reports one of their most important applications and they should be kept in mind at all times when writing the final version. The temptation to impress must be resisted sternly; reports are for the benefit of the man who reads them, not the man who writes them.

A report to management is probably the most formal piece of writing the young man working in an office will ever be called upon to produce. Dignity of language and extremely high standards of correctness are expected; but this does not mean inflation of the subject matter, wordiness, and pomposity. Conciseness is a merit in such a report more than anywhere; so many verbose reports (unread) block the drawers of the manager's desk.

If such a report is schematically presented the personal is best avoided, either by the author's use of the third person to refer to himself (*The Fire Officer checked the condition of the fire-fighting appliances in the office block*, when the writer *is* the Fire Officer) or by passive impersonal constructions (*The condition of the fire-fighting appliances was checked*).

Reports going out of the firm (to customers, for example) demand a similar dignity of tone. They often present an additional communication problem – how to suit the language and treatment to an Rx of whom you know much less than you do about your seniors in your own firm. Further, you cannot assume a common stock of knowledge and will probably have to devote space to clarification of fundamentals and explanation of terms that are taken for granted in internal reports. Broadly speaking it is true to say that you must make a greater effort to simplify your subject matter to prepare the way for each stage than you need to with a report inside your own organisation.

Reports across to colleagues need not be so formal in tone or style. In fact, schematic presentation and impersonal constructions may seem humourless or ostentatious in reporting to somebody of the same rank, whom you know quite well. Unless the material is very complex, the mixed form is the most satisfactory, with an informal introduction. The language of such a report, while still maintaining high standards of accuracy and clarity, can to good effect be allowed to become a little more relaxed and unbuttoned.

It is a matter of opinion whether reports should be written in sentence form throughout or whether some sections can be in note form or mere listings of points. The latter method has the attraction of brevity but many departmental heads and senior officers maintain that a report in sentence form is quicker to read although it is longer, because of the gain in smoothness and continuity; this is probably a valid argument. Certainly for examinations it would be safest to keep to sentence form, except for very compelling reasons. You should under no circumstances alternate between sentence form and non-sentence form *within the same section of the report*. For demonstration purposes, both styles are used in Example B, sections I and V being in non-sentence form.

VIII. EXAMPLES

Example A

MIXED FORM. A maintenance engineer reports to a firm about discoloured tap-water at branch premises.

BARLOW AND BARING LTD
Broadway
Helmstead   HEL2 5PB

12th April, 19..

The Office Manager,
Barlow and Baring Ltd.

Dear Sir,

Hot water supply, 53 Long Lane

You instructed me, on the 9th April, 19..,
to investigate the cause of the discoloured
draw-off from the hot water supply at the
firm's branch premises at 53 Long Lane,
Helmstead. I accordingly visited the property on
11th April and made the following observations:

1. Draw-off from the cold water supply is
   clear
2. The hot water system is of the direct
   kind and includes three radiators
3. All piping, together with the hot-
   water cylinder, is of copper
4. The radiators are of pressed steel
5. The Long Lane area of Helmstead is an
   acid ('soft') water area.

I am of the opinion therefore that the
discoloration is caused by reaction between the
acid water supply and the steel radiators and
recommend that these radiators be replaced by
others, of non-ferrous material.

Yours faithfully,

J. F. Jimpson
Maintenance Engineer

NOTE 1. the language, dignified, yet not pretentious 2. the logical
arrangement of the findings 3. the standard order – terms of reference,
proceedings, findings, conclusions, recommendations.

Example B

SUMMARY REPORT (schematic presentation). The personnel officer of a
factory reports on apprentice unrest.

REPORT ON APPRENTICE UNREST AT ADPRESS
ENGINEERING

I. Terms of reference

   On the instructions of the Works Manager
(2nd May, 19..) to report on apprentice
unrest and make recommendations.

II. Procedure

   A. All supervisory grades concerned with
   apprentices were interviewed.
   B. Twenty apprentices, selected at
   random, were interviewed in the works.

III. Findings

   A. Extent of unrest

   The comments of the Apprentice
Supervisor and foremen revealed a widespread malaise and resentment amongst
apprentices. Although manifestations of
this in individual breaches of discipline
and a general uncooperative attitude were
considered only minor, several foremen
expressed the view that the situation was
deteriorating and serious outbreaks of
misbehaviour might result.

   B. Causes of unrest

   Resentment is felt by apprentices over
the following matters:-
      1. Training. Complaints were made
      that:
         (a) supervision was inadequate
         (b) apprentices were kept too long
             in one section
         (c) apprentices were being used on
             production lines
         (d) skilled men intent on bonus
             earnings were unwilling to
             spend time explaining what they
             were doing.

2. Conditions. Complaints were made that:

   (a) machines were left dirty by skilled men

   (b) safety precautions were ignored particularly by operation of machines with guards removed.

3. Pay. The belief was widespread that rates paid to apprentices were the lowest in the area.

IV. Conclusions

A. Extent of unrest

   On matters of justified complaint, immediate action must be taken to prevent further disturbances.

B. Cause of unrest

1. Training. There is evidence that all complaints were well-founded.

2. Conditions. Complaint 2(a) above is unimportant but removal of safety guards is an offence against the Factories Act and must be stopped.

3. Pay. Our rates compare favourably with those paid to apprentices in other factories of this area, and complaints on this score would cease if apprentices were made aware of this.

V. Recommendations

A. A training officer to be appointed and instructed to draw up a training scheme which will ensure balanced experience in the works and adequate supervision.

B. All supervisory grades to be reminded of the importance of keeping machinery guarded when in operation.

C. The Personnel Officer to address a meeting of apprentices and explain the favourable rates of pay enjoyed in this factory.

9th May, 19..

                          John Smith
                         Personnel Officer.

NOTES
1. The language is formal and impersonal; the author refers to himself in the third person in the final recommendation.
2. Items similarly numbered and lettered within the one section are grammatically parallel. Note particularly in this respect the *Recommendations*. These could have been shown in several other ways: (1) each prefixed by *that*, (2) introduced by a clause (*It is recommended that:*), (3) *as sentences* (*A training officer should be appointed* etc.). Any of the four methods is acceptable; but not a mixture.

Example C

SELECTIONS FROM A DETAILED REPORT

  a. The letter of transmittal

BARLOW AND BARING LTD
Broadway
Helmstead   HEL2 5PB

19th December, 19..

The Sales Manager,
Barlow and Baring Ltd.

Dear Sir,
        You instructed me on the 10th April, 19.. to prepare a detailed report on our trading in the Andover sector over the period 1st April, 19..-1st December, 19.. and I now have pleasure in submitting this report.

Yours faithfully,

P. J. Churt

NOTE: Such a letter may well replace the terms of reference section in a long report.

  b. The title-page

BARLOW AND BARING LTD

Trading, Andover sector,
1st April 19..-1st December 19..

Report to Sales Manager
by P. J. Churt

19th December, 19..

c. The synopsis

Between 1st April and 1st December 19.. the overall value of the company's turnover in the Andover sector rose by 72.2 per cent. Records of trading with all our normal retail outlets show a slight rise (4.9 per cent) when compared with the same period in the preceding year, negligible seasonal variation, and only minor differences between branches. Door-to-door direct trading, however, apart from a sharp seasonal drop in sales during the months of October and November, developed rapidly over the period, and accounted for 80.6 per cent of the overall sales increase.

IX. EXERCISES

Exercise A: Eye-witness reports

1. Write a clear account, in chronological order, of a football or cricket match (or similar event), or of an accident you have witnessed recently. You should keep within the margin 150–180 words.
2. An accident prevention group's survey recently contained the following story:

   A young steelworker risked his life to save a pay packet. He was leaning against a guard rail when his packet slipped on to a conveyor belt. Ignoring shouts from colleagues and a factory inspector, he vaulted the rail, climbed on to ventilation pipes, and leaped 10 feet to another conveyor belt carrying iron ore. He scrabbled 25 yards up the conveyor, grabbed the packet, and jumped on to a gangway just in time to avoid being toppled into a storage tank where he would have been crushed.

   Rewrite this, in letter form, as a formal eye-witness account, imagining you were the factory inspector and had been told to report to the works manager. Invent supporting details (including names and dates) necessary for your report.

Exercise B: Summary report with supplied subject matter

As sales manager of British Knitwear Ltd of Beeston Road, Nottingham, you have just returned from a fact-finding tour of West Germany. German wholesalers criticised your firm's products for women on the following grounds: too many pastel shades; sizing English not Continental; conservative styling; poor finishing; lack of 'chic'; clumsy turn-out; poor shaping; restricted size range; lack of strong colours.

Organise this material in the form of a summary report approximately 200 words long.

Exercise C: Report practice with known subject matter

Reports 1 and 2 should be about 200 words long and one of these should be attempted first.

1. Compare a ball-point pen with a conventional fountain pen and with a pencil, for convenience, price, efficiency etc. Try to think of as many points of comparison as possible. Write out your findings under headings in schematic presentation form.
2. Make a report on some possession of your own, comparing it with other types on the market and showing where it is better, where inferior.

Reports 3–8 inclusive should be about 350 words long.

3. Prepare a recommendatory report on sports facilities at your technical college. You can assume it has been asked for by the principal.
4. Prepare a short information report on the street you live in that would be helpful to a man of 40 and his wife (with two children aged 7 and 10, both boys) contemplating moving into the same street.
5. Prepare a short information report on the parks and recreation grounds of the town in which you attend college. Your information is to be the basis of a section in the town guide. Such points as size, situation, buildings, facilities for games, and special amenities should be borne in mind.
6. Prepare a short information report on the library of your college. You can assume your report is for the use of new students.
7. Report on any recent college function, estimating its success and making recommendations for improving similar future functions.
8. Prepare a summary report on what you have been taught about the use of English this year.

Exercise D: Report practice with fictitious subject matter

In these exercises you will have to invent sufficient imaginary detail to make the report seem convincing. Little points, like dates, times, addresses, names of people and firms, are very important for this. The object is to give you practice in laying out and organising material in report form; it does not matter, therefore, if some of your 'facts' are wrong, or even downright impossible.

You will need a length of at least 350 words if you are going to be able to practise schematic presentation properly; but if you are preparing for an examination where only very short reports are called for you will probably want to try some of these exercises at about 200 words, using the mixed form. Do not forget to define your terms of reference, even though you have made them up yourself.

1. As secretary to a youth club, report on unoccupied premises which have been offered to the club by a local business man at a very low rental but for three years only. At the end of this period, the premises are to be pulled down to make room for an extension of his offices.

2. Prepare an equipment report on any piece of equipment of which you have some knowledge. You must assume the equipment has been severely damaged – how and to what extent, you can decide.

3. Your firm makes *either* sports equipment *or* cosmetics. Report on the space available for your company at the Milan trade fair and make recommendations as to the most effective form of display.

4. You have been instructed by your firm to prepare a report on a newly-invented portable appliance for converting salt water to potable water, and its potential uses and commercial possibilities. You can assume technical investigation of this device has been completed already, and a favourable report has been received from the laboratories.

5. You have attended a trade fair on behalf of your firm. Prepare a short report on your visit, drawing attention to new products of importance to your firm.

6. You are the area supervisor for the firm of Hamm and Egg, multiple grocers. Most Hamm and Egg branches have been converted to self-service. Prepare a recommendatory report on the Hamm and Egg shop in Helmstead, which has not been so converted.

7. You are employed in the office of a medium-sized manufacturing firm (product of your choice). Prepare an information report on the effects of unusually severe snow during January.

8. You have been instructed to investigate the possibilities of staggering working hours in the large concern for which you work and to submit a recommendatory report. Write this report.

Exercise E: Practice memoranda

1. As a member of the staff of a small office, prepare a memorandum on office reorganisation (see page 19 for some ideas on how to tackle this).

2. Prepare *one* of the following memoranda:

 a. To the secretary of your students' association suggesting new directions in which student leisure activity can develop.

 b. To the college librarian suggesting useful expansion of the services provided.

 c. To the management of the firm in which you are a commercial apprentice, suggesting improvements in the apprentice training scheme.

Chapter 10

Advertising Writing

I. COMMUNICATION AND ADVERTISING

To be able to sell we have to let the consumer know what goods we are offering. Less commonly, when we wish to buy we may have to make our requirements widely known if we are to obtain exactly what we want. Thus public communication, or advertising, is an inevitable part of the business world.

A useful distinction may be made between advertising that seeks to inform, and advertising that seeks to persuade. Without the former, commerce could not continue; and it is to the consumer's advantage as well as the seller's to know what is available on the market. It is understandable, however, that the seller will not be content merely to announce his goods; he will also want to praise them and to persuade the public to buy from him, not his rival. As soon as persuasion starts it will accelerate steadily, for every seller has the same idea and each finds himself forced to shout louder and louder to draw attention; to make more and more claims for his product; and to seek continuously new ways of influencing the consumer in his choice. During this century advertising has developed from the naïve puffery natural to a manufacturer talking about his product to a highly sophisticated technique of directing the public's spending into accurately preplanned channels. Advertising of this kind is still communication; but it is communication not so much of information about the product as of an attitude towards the product.

This is something very different from the factual communication in words which is the subject of this book, and something which the ordinary business man no longer attempts himself on any scale. For this the specialists exist – the advertising agent and his copywriters. The reader of this book is not likely to be called upon to write copy for his company's national campaigns and major selling drives, and it would be a waste of his time to attempt to learn the specialised skills of persuasion.

There are, however, simpler forms of advertising that may come his way – for example, leaflets publicising small retail businesses; classified advertisements and small display advertisements in the local press and trade journals; public notices; 'hand-outs' which are to be the basis of a publicity story in the press. The smaller the firm, the more such tasks are left to one of the company's own men, with no specialised training.

With small firms much of the wording of its advertising may still be in the hands of members of its sales staff. Probably the most important kind of advertising still frequently written by a firm's own men is the unsolicited sales letter, or 'circular', distributed either at random from door to door or selectively as, for instance, to previous customers, or to potential customers selected by sex, occupation, geographical location, age, income etc. In the following section, detailed attention is given to the unsolicited sales letter. It is hoped that this will be valuable not only in itself, but also as an illustration of the kind of approach necessary in all simple advertising copy of the kind the reader may be expected to write for a firm.

II. THE UNSOLICITED SALES LETTER

A. The eye-catcher

When the householder opens what appears to be a personal letter (and increasingly firms are using good quality envelopes for their sales letters so that they do not too obviously proclaim what they are) and finds inside a piece of advertising in the form of a letter his natural reaction is one of disappointment, even annoyance. He may very well feel inclined to throw it unread into the waste-paper basket. The reaction of the business man who finds you are selling, not buying will be similar. It is necessary, therefore, to provide a striking opening that will catch his eye and start him reading.

A common device is to start with a challenging question:

Are you certain your cold water pipes are not going to freeze this winter?
How well did you sleep last night?

Imperatives are sometimes used:

Don't risk your life using worn tyres!
Read this now! It will change your ideas of battery performance.

Care must be exercised to avoid letting a hectoring note creep into imperatives. Your letter is already forcing its way into the Rx's house or office; do not let it bully him as well. An audacious trick is to make reference to what you most of all wish to avoid:

THROW THIS AWAY UNREAD – if you want to throw away a chance of increasing your business.

Challenging statements of a statistical kind (*It takes 100 bees ONE YEAR to make the wax for ONE TIN of BEEWACK polish*) or quotations from the famous that can subsequently be shown to have a bearing on the goods to be sold are two other useful openers. Most successful of all eye-catchers is something bizarre and unexpected:

> *HELP! That is what we are bringing you news of – help in the home!*

The language of these eye-catchers must be vigorous and sinewy. The Beewack eye-catcher would have much less effect in the form:

> *The average beeswax content of a tin of BEEWACK polish may be approximately represented as the annual output of one hundred bees.*

Well-tried literary devices help to punch home the message – in the Beewack advertisement, repetition – in the *HELP!* eye-catcher, alliteration – in every example, rhythm.

B. Persuasion

Having secured your reader, you must now start to sell. The first stage of this is to make him want what you have to offer – you must make it attractive to him by appeal to his desire for pleasure, health, success, love, the high opinion of others, comfort, increased money, or increased leisure. Ask yourself in what way the service or product you are offering can aid your Rx's achievement of any of these aims for himself or his family, and emphasise this.

Having thus given sales appeal to your product you then bring forward those selling points which will carry most conviction. At this stage ask yourself what your product has that its rivals have not got and emphasise this. This may be: its novelty; its high efficiency; its ease of use; its durability; its low price (though increasingly the last is becoming of doubtful value as a selling point as it is often associated with low quality in the mind of the Rx). The best advertising persuades not by unsupported affirmation but by bringing forward evidence – laboratory tests, statistics, specifications, testimonials from users or, better, from acknowledged authorities.

C. The final appeal

Having put your arguments and persuasions before the reader and, you hope, made his attitude towards your product favourable and receptive, you should at the end of the letter try to provide something which the Rx can do, or offer to do something yourself which will take the Rx a stage nearer to purchasing.

For action, you can provide a tear-off section to be addressed and returned which is either an order-form or, with expensive goods, a request for further information or a demonstration. Better still, send a prepaid card. If your product does not lend itself to this method, invite your potential customer to write, phone, or call at your showrooms.

Offers by the firm have been made so often as an additional inducement that something of this kind is virtually expected by the potential customer now. These offers may take many forms. Free samples, goods sent on approval, even a price reduction for a sale within a certain period, are all frequently offered. On a more modest scale, booklets, catalogues, colour guides, patterns, specimens, may be available on return of a card. If you can offer nothing else, at least conclude by expressing your willingness to advise or send further information on request.

D. Example

Dear Sir,

Are you judging this letter by the paper it is written on?

You probably are. Most people do. Letters on high quality paper gain dignity, are treated with extra respect - even a sales letter like this.

This one is on BUSINESS BOND, today's finest business paper. BUSINESS BOND is snowy white, smooth-surfaced, and of good opacity. You can see this for yourself.

What you are not able to see is that BUSINESS BOND is manufactured in British mills to very high standards of quality control. It prints superbly on small offset machines and by letterpress and die-stamping processes. It can be supplied by all paper merchants from stock without delay.

BUSINESS BOND means business. If you want to try before you buy, fill in the prepaid card. A trial pad will be on your desk within forty-eight hours of your posting it.

Yours faithfully,
BUSINESS BOND SALES LTD

III. PRESS ADVERTISING

A. Introduction

Display advertising in the national Press is a very expensive matter. If a company pays several thousands of pounds for half a page, it will employ experts to write the copy as well as to prepare the layout. You, as a non-specialist member of a firm, may, however, be called upon to write copy for routine newspaper advertisements, especially in local papers. These will consist principally of classified advertisements, public announcements, and small displays.

B. Classified advertisements

Classified advertisements have no display (i.e. no special layout, large-type headings etc.). They are printed in columns under headings such as 'Business for Sale' or 'Situations Vacant' and this general heading is what is relied on by the advertiser to draw the attention of those who will be interested. They are charged at a rate per line, and there is a premium therefore on brevity, especially as this form of advertising is normally used by firms only when economy is an important consideration. Abbreviations are used sometimes to reduce the number of lines, but these also reduce the effectiveness of the communication. Here are two typical classified advertisements:

1. (under the section-heading 'Re-upholstering'):
   Appledons of Pidderminster. Craftsmen Upholsterers. Workman-ship guaranteed. Estimates free. Wide selection of patterns available. Market Place. Tel: Pidderminster 79.
2. (under the section-heading 'Auctioneers, Valuers, and Surveyors'):
   Negotiations for rating. Survey reports and valuations. Sales by auction and private treaty. Mortgages. Harvey Drewitt & Co., Market Place, Pidderminster. Tel.: Pidderminster 84 and 617.

C. Public announcements and small display advertising

Public announcements may be made exactly like a classified advertisement under a section-heading 'Public Announcements'; but as they are usually of some importance they are frequently treated similarly to a small display advertisement. Some public announcements are to fulfil legal obligations and the wording is circumscribed by legal requirements. Others are of a kind that comes very close to being advertising (announcements of lecture courses by the local education authority, for example) and the boundary between the two is not easily defined.

Small displays are achieved most convincingly in local papers by paying for two or three columns in the classified advertisements pages to a certain depth using the resultant space for the advertisement. Simple devices of layout, headings, varying typefaces and sizes, can be used to increase the impact on the newspaper reader.

Here is an example of such a small display advertisement. It is in a dignified style – using sentences not just headlines – that would also suit a public announcement. A similar style could be used for publicity leaflets.

J. HARDY & SONS LTD
have vacancies in the counties of Wiltshire and Gloucestershire
for
SALES REPRESENTATIVES
Applicants should be between the ages of 22 and 32 years, and have proved selling ability. A background knowledge of agriculture would be an advantage.

Good salary and commission. Training given. Car provided with expenses paid.

The post offers outstanding opportunity to the right man in a highly competitive, but interesting, field, selling direct to farmers.

Write, in first instance, in confidence, to:

THE REGIONAL SALES MANAGER

J. HARDY & SONS LTD

BRISTOL ROAD, DELLWATER, GLOUCESTERSHIRE

GL33 2MS

Many small display advertisements are, of course, very different from this and shriek at the reader with disjointed headlines and ugly, or haphazardly mixed, typefaces. There seems no point in illustrating these – you will be able to see a large number of them by glancing at your local newspaper – and no point in learning to write them.

IV. EXERCISES

Exercise A

1. Criticise the following unsolicited sales letter.
2. Rewrite it, so that it will have greater selling power. Invent details that you think should have been included.

Dear Madam,

May we trespass upon your time to draw your attention for a moment to the GNOME High Speed Gas Kettle? Your time is what this kettle will save for you - and your money wasted on unnecessary gas. The kettle is manufactured from heavy gauge aluminium and the special system of flutings on the base ensures rapid and symmetrical distribution of heat from a gas-burner so that water boils faster. Laboratory tests have shown this kettle will boil 2 litres of water in 3.7 minutes.

With normal use the GNOME High Speed Gas Kettle should pay for itself within a few months of purchase and subsequently, a considerable reduction in gas bills should be a recurrent advantage.

The kettle is made in the 2 litre size only and the price is £2.25 net, including tax. If you wish to purchase one of these you should be able to get it from your local Gas Showrooms, or if they have not received a supply perhaps you will be good enough to notify us and we will post one to you direct. If you would like to order direct from us kindly send a Postal Order for £2.25 and state what colour handle and knob you require. Your kettle will then be despatched to you by return, post free.

Yours truly,

GNOME KETTLES LTD

Exercise B

Prepare an unsolicited sales letter for HOUSE-HOT Oil-Fired Boilers from the following notes:

Three models – outputs 8, 10 and 15 kW – priced £75, £85, £120 respectively.

Silent, odourless. Easy installation by our engineers. Attractive design and vitreous finish in white, cream, red, or royal blue to harmonise with kitchen. Technical representative will call to advise on installation free.

Exercise C

Prepare an unsolicited sales letter to advertise Oxbridge Encyclopedia. Use the following notes. You do not have to employ all the material supplied – appropriate selection is part of the exercise.

10 volumes. Total of 4 600 pages. Illustrated with 295 black and white photographs (full-page). Price £38, Rexine binding; £52, half-leather binding. Many drawings and diagrams in text. Last volume consists of detailed index. Articles in alphabetical order. Revised throughout, this year. Intended for children aged 11–14. 125 separate contributors. All contributions edited by a board to ensure vocabulary and sentence structure suitable to children, and all illustrations clearly drawn and easy to understand.

Payment by monthly instalments available – £10 initially with 24 instalments of £1·25 (Rexine binding): £15 initially with 24 instalments of £1·65 (half-leather binding).

Exercise D

Prepare an unsolicited sales letter to be addressed to sales managers of companies employing travelling sales representatives. It is to introduce the REGENT Business Card Service. Selling points are: genuine copper-plate engraving; fast delivery; advisory service for designs; special express service for new members of your organisation; packed in 20s in special slide-out packs – convenient and preventing soiling or damage.

Exercise E

Prepare an unsolicited sales letter to Managing Directors of production companies to introduce READICHEF Refreshment Machines. Selling points: fresh hot drinks 24 hours a day; time spent in 'brew-up' eliminated; queuing reduced; reduction of time and labour for canteen staff. Will serve tea (with or without sugar), coffee (with or without milk and/or sugar), hot chocolate, and soup (i.e. 8 hot drinks). Will hold 800 cupfuls and delivers in 6 seconds into a non-tainting throw-away cup.

Exercise F

Prepare classified advertisements for *two* of the following situations. Do not exceed 30 words for each. Aim to include the maximum amount of material, but be careful not to make the advertisement unreadable. Do not omit information that would be essential in the real-life situation.
1. Selling a house.
2. Selling a second-hand car.

3. Advertising a situation vacant.
4. Advertising a small grocery shop.

Exercise G

Prepare a small display advertisement for *one* of the following purposes. Indicate your layout.

1. Seeking suitable lodgings for 400 workers coming into the area as a result of expansion of your plant.
2. Advertising a service for supplying foreign magazines – current subscriptions and individual back-numbers.

Exercise H

Prepare copy for one of the following:

1. A leaflet to be distributed from a supermarket to notify customers that it is now licensed for the sale of wines and spirits.
2. A leaflet to supply outline information about a weekend course at a residential college of adult education.
3. A leaflet for distribution to students, pointing out the facilities available to members of the students' association and appealing for their active support.

Exercise I

Below are given two advertisements, A and B, taken, respectively, from a 'quality newspaper' (QN) and a 'popular daily' (PD). (In both, the names of the advertisers and of their products have been suppressed.)

You are required to rewrite both advertisements, A in a form in which it might appear in PD, and B in a form in which it might appear in QN.

A

Agriculturally, many relatively small seeds are used to produce amazingly heavy crops; a ley, for example, can be produced by sowing as little as twenty pounds of seed per acre, but the crop grown from it may well yield twenty to thirty tons of greenstuff per year and, furthermore, continues to do so for several years.

To be completely successful in the field, seed rates as low as this demand an extremely high standard of analytical purity and germination. By scientific methods of seed production and seed cleaning, we are able to offer seed quality of the standard required. . . .

Wherever you see a fine field of corn or lush pastures, it is usually a sign that a wise farmer has been sowing X's seeds.

B

Budgies! Someone's doing right by us at last! They've found out what it takes to make us Budgies *bounce* with health. Result? A new food! Proper balanced food at last! Canary seed and millet, of course. But with extras. *Three* extras. Listen!

1st Extra: Concentrated Protein. Puts feathers on your chest, pal!
2nd Extra: Vitamins A and D. That 'A' is good for your tubes. The 'D' makes strong bones. Saves them adding cod-liver oil, too.
3rd Extra: Special Seeds against Enteritis. About time, too!
Clean? As a whistle! Budgies! You're entitled to it. Spread the word!

[*Royal Society of Arts, English Language Stage III*]

Chapter 11

Special Applications of Communication Principles

I. INSTRUCTIONS

A. *What or how?*

So far we have considered only the information-passing, or information-seeking, function of communication. Instructions, however, may tell the Rx what he is to do (or what he must not do). This involves the action-producing (or action-stopping) function of communication.

Instructions may, on the other hand, merely tell somebody how to do something (how to reach the College; how to write a report; how to take off the lid of a tin) when they are no more than information-passing. It might be thought that it would be convenient if we made a clear-cut linguistic distinction here, perhaps reserving *instructions* for the 'how' and using *orders* or *directives* for the 'what'. In practice we do not do this; and in fact the ambiguity in the meaning of *instructions* is not without its usefulness since we frequently have to tell people not only what they are to do but also how they are to do it.

There is a danger to good communication in this ambiguity, though – that the Tx (and, sometimes, the Rx) may forget whether the instructions are 'how' or 'what' instructions. This is particularly liable to occur since the same style can be used for both. For example *Insert a coin in the groove at the corner of the tin, and turn to release the vacuum* and *Check these figures by Friday next* are both imperatives; but their intention is very different. The first aims to help the Rx to achieve something he is attempting to do; the second orders the Rx to do something. It is easy for the Tx to slip into an inappropriately mandatory tone when explaining how to do something. Similarly, the imperative, *Change the oil-filter every* 20 000 *km* in a user handbook looks rather like an order to the Rx, although it is intended as advice by the Tx. It would be better rephrased as *It is advisable to change the oil-filter every* 20 000 *km* or *Changing the oil-filter every* 20 000 *km is recommended.*

B. *Style*

The imperative is only one of many styles which can be used for instructions. When we are giving 'how' instructions orally we use the second person present indicative (*You turn to the right past the bus-stop and go on to the end of the road*) but this is not considered suitable for formal writing. All other styles are suitable for both speech or writing; which is the most suitable will depend on: the subject matter; the Tx and Rx; whether 'how' or 'what'; and the circumstances in which the instructions are given.

Here are the principal styles we can choose between:

You are to report this matter immediately
You must report this matter immediately
You will report this matter immediately
You should report this matter immediately
This is to be reported immediately
This will be reported immediately
This must be reported immediately
This should be reported immediately
The Supervisor[1] is to report this immediately
The Supervisor[1] must report this immediately
The Supervisor[1] will report this immediately
The Supervisor[1] should report this immediately
Report this immediately.

The first task then in conveying instructions is to decide on the style that will best suit your purpose. Second person forms are direct and vigorous. They establish a bond between Rx and Tx. More distant and dignified are the impersonal forms; and the third person styles are the most formal of all (suitable for printed rule-books, standing orders etc.). The style employing the verb 'to be' and an infinitive is suitable only for directives; it is smoothly mandatory, firm but not aggressive. 'Must' forms are not often used for 'how' instructions; they are strongly mandatory but a little overbearing. 'Will' forms are curious. By using the ordinary future in a context which is one of instructions the effect is produced of an exceedingly firm imperative. Their firmness is, in fact, often resented by the Rx. They are suitable only for directives in a situation where orders can be backed by disciplinary measures (as in the Forces). 'Should' forms, suitable for both 'what' and 'how', are more friendly than the last two styles but introduce a moral note of what *ought* to be done that some people find irrelevant and distracting.

Most direct and certain for orders is the imperative. It is also the shortest form always. It does not disguise at all that orders are being given and sometimes this is a disadvantage. As we have seen, when used for 'how' instructions it can sometimes appear to bully rather than help.

---

[1] Where the Rx *is* 'The Supervisor'.

However, its advantages of clarity and brevity are not easily outweighed. It is particularly valuable when dealing with a rather lengthy procedure which is capable of being broken down into a series of comparatively simple actions.

It is, of course, possible to combine these styles, and over a sustained series of written instruction (as in a textbook) it is essential to do so, as circumstances change and to give variety. Fairly short self-contained passages of written instruction are, however, more effective if written in one style throughout.

C. Sequence

Instructions, more than any other form of communication, require accurate arrangement in logical – usually chronological – sequence. The intimate connection between mandate and sequence is revealed by the double meaning of *order* as a noun. The verb *to order* originally meant 'to regulate, to arrange'. 'How' instructions equally require to be given in the correct sequence if they are to fulfil their purpose. Nothing is more confusing to the Rx than to be told halfway through a series of instructions that he should already have made certain preparations that he is now hearing of for the first time. This kind of sequence error – some vital stage has been temporarily forgotten by the Tx – is understandable enough in speech; unfortunately it is also common in written instructions, where it can only be a result of careless preparation.

D. Example

Here are two good ways of expressing the same set of instructions. Would you prefer one to the other if you were the Rx? Can you think of any circumstances (*a*) when 1. would be better to use than 2.; (*b*) when 2. would be better to use than 1.?

1. *Duties of staff responsible for opening incoming mail*

Registered letters should be recorded in the registered letter register and a note made of the person to whom the letter is passed for attention. Envelopes of other letters should be torn completely open to ensure that no enclosure is overlooked. All letters should be date-stamped as soon as opened and placed with enclosures in the appropriate departmental tray. All cheques and drafts should be crossed with the name of the Company's bankers immediately on extraction from the envelope, a note of the amount made on the covering letter, and the remittance passed to the cash department.

2. *Procedure to be adopted when opening letters*
a. Record all registered letters in the registered letter register. Enter the name of the person to whom the letter is to be passed in the column provided.
b. Tear open all envelopes completely. Check that no enclosure is overlooked.
c. Date-stamp all letters immediately on opening.
d. Place letters and enclosures in the appropriate departmental tray.
e. Cross all cheques and drafts with the name of the Company's bankers immediately. Make a note of the amount on the covering letter. Pass the remittance to the cashier's department.

E. *Personal instructions*

The preceding sections apply principally to instructions which are being issued generally or to a number of staff. Instructions which are intended for an individual can be more closely tailored for that person. His intelligence, his vocabulary level, his previous experience of this type of instruction, his personality and previous relations with the Tx – all these should be borne in mind in deciding the wording of the instructions.

Personal directives are often best worded as requests:

Will you check these figures and let me have your final estimate by Tuesday? Would you please investigate the cause of this excessive paper consumption?

or favours:

I should be obliged if you would let me have full details of your departmental requirements before 31st March.

Even the imperative can be softened by the use of 'please':

Please arrange lunch and a tour of the works for Mr Thomas Jackson (British Manganese) for Friday 10th March.

These less direct ways of giving orders to individuals do not disguise from the Rx that they are orders, and that he has to do what is asked. But people do prefer being asked to being told; and the Rx is more likely to carry out instructions accurately, and with a good grace, as a result of a polite approach by his superior. Such touches do much to boost morale in an organisation.

II. INTERNAL MEMORANDA

A. The original meaning of *memorandum* was 'a note to help the memory' and the word is still often used in that way. It is, however, also applied in business to various types of written communication – nearly always internal – which do in fact provide an aid to memory in that they provide a written record, but whose primary function is to convey information or instructions, or to make proposals for the future.

B. The longest and most formal memorandum is a document resembling a report. A junior manager may see a new way of increasing sales or an opportunity to improve office efficiency; as a vehicle for his ideas he prepares a memorandum to be submitted – unsolicited – to his superior. Memoranda of this kind have already been described in Chapter 9 (page 136) and practice work provided on pages 148–149.

C. The term is also used to refer to a much simpler type of document which is sent to those concerned to remind of, or introduce, certain arrangements. Instructions, for example, of the kind discussed in the previous section may be circulated in this manner.

Such a memorandum is normally headed *Memorandum* or *Internal Memorandum* with the words *To* and *From* followed respectively by the name of the sender and the names of the recipients. In practice, the nominal sender – who may of course not be the person who actually writes the memorandum – is usually referred to by his rank or position, rather than his name.

Here is an example of a memorandum of this type:

FROM: Training and Education Officer

TO: Managing Director
Works Manager
Course members (as under)
Mr Mayhew, Main Gate
Mrs Paulson, 'D' Mess
The Principal, Bromhill Technical
College
The Head of Department of Languages,
Bromhill Technical College
Miss M. Harcourt, B.A.

Foreign Language Course - French

Arrangements have been made with the Principal, Bromhill Technical College, and the Head of Department of Languages, to provide an intensive French course for executives of this company on company premises. The course is to be conducted by Miss M. Harcourt, B.A.

Enrolment forms will be available and should be completed on the first day of the course. Details are as follows:

Courses will be held in 'D' Mess, Kentish Street, on Tuesdays and Thursdays 17.30-18.30 hours, commencing Tuesday, 16th March 19..

The following have indicated their intention to attend:

Mr J. Aylett	Mr T. Jackson
Mr F. Baker	Mr L. M. Kneightly-Smith
Mr D. Coombes	Mr F. J. Lansdown
Mr L. F. Griffin	Mr T. Smithson
Mr J. P. Hollies	Mr I. Zarottini

D. A very large number of brief internal communications between individuals are exchanged daily in most organisations. Although many of these will be informal and improvised (a message scribbled on a page torn from a diary and pinned to a man's desk in his absence, for example) it is desirable that as many as possible of these messages be conveyed on a standard message form, this marking them out instantly as official.

Most organisations provide pads (often interleaved with blank sheets for carbon copies) of headed message forms for this purpose. Such messages too are sometimes called 'memoranda' – or more often 'memos' – especially when written on printed standard message forms.

The printed section of the form will normally consist of the name of the organisation, a space for indication of department, the words *To* and *From*, and a space for the date. Here is a typical layout:

COLLINGBOURNE AND THOMAS LTD

Department.....................

From.................... To..................... Date.....................

The memo form is deliberately kept small so that wording will be held to a minimum. Good memos must be brief, unambiguous, without irrelevancies, yet friendly.

They ask for, or transmit, information; they convey personal instructions. Much of the day-to-day working of an organisation depends on them.

They represent a field in which communication principles can be applied to particularly good effect.

Such memos should not be signed. The longer type of memorandum (as the one about the French course) is, on the other hand, often signed by the sender.

III. NOTICES

Instructions, announcements, appeals for cooperation etc. are best directed to those concerned by means of memoranda. It sometimes happens, however, that too many people are involved for this to be practicable. To find a wholly satisfactory method of mass communication within an organisation is virtually impossible, but certainly the most widely used is the notice board.

To be effective a notice board must be:

1. well sited (large numbers must pass it daily)
2. big and attractively painted (so that it draws attention)
3. kept up to date (staff soon learn to ignore a notice board covered with old notices).

Even then, a large number of people will walk straight past it – this is its great defect as a communication medium. For notices of special importance, attention may be attracted by such devices as coloured tapes radiating outwards from the significant notice or a printed hand with pointing finger (of the type used as direction indicators in corridors) pinned beside it. Such devices lose their effect, however, if used frequently.

The quality of the notice itself is of great importance, not only in ensuring good communication on that particular occasion but also in encouraging staff in the habit of stopping to look at the notice board. Dull or incomprehensible notices will soon discourage even the most conscientious.

When a manager receives a memorandum, (or other written instruction) that he considers affects his whole command, he is not usually doing his communication job properly if he merely pins it to the notice board. The memorandum will be one intended for *his* level of intelligence and experience in reading, and for quiet perusal in his office. For the notice board simpler and bolder presentation is necessary, and the message must be so worded as to be comprehensible to the lowest common denominator of intelligence and vocabulary amongst those likely to read it. The language should be vigorous and direct – aimed straight from Tx to Rx. Thus

NOT *The attention of management has recently been drawn to the increased use of motor vehicles by employees, which is causing progressive overloading of our already strained parking facilities.*

BUT *More and more of you are using cars to come to work. As a result, we are rapidly approaching a stage where we shall not have parking space for everybody who requires it.*

The message should be kept as brief as possible. This will involve not only concise wording, but also rigorous selection – only material that it is essential that everybody reads should be in the notice.

There is no harm in borrowing some of the milder devices of the advertiser. People who are screamed at all the time they are away from work by newspaper headlines, posters, and television commercials, are going to take very little heed of a notice which consists of just a page of close typescript.

At least the heading and/or opening sentence should be of eye-catcher kind. An announcement of voluntary French classes sponsored by management is going to attract more attention if headed: *You can learn French free* than if headed *Voluntary French classes*.

Some element of display (such as the use of a felt pen) would make it more likely that the heading would attract attention.

There is no need for a notice couched in vigorous and lively language to be undignified or vulgar. It is simply a matter of remembering that: (1) you have got to start the Rx reading, and keep him reading, (2) on a notice board only simple clear-cut sentences will carry much weight, (3) the Rx may be less intelligent, less knowledgeable, less used to reading, than you are; and it is your job to allow for that, (4) your notice is a waste of time for everybody if it does not produce the result you intended when you put it up.

EXAMPLE

<u>You can learn French free</u>

There is no catch in it. If you would like to
start learning French next week, just hand in
your name to the Personnel Officer before
Friday. We will do the rest.
Classes will be held immediately after work in
'D' Canteen on Tuesdays and Thursdays. They will
last one hour.

Remember 1.   You have nothing to pay.
         2.   If you do not enjoy learning
              French, you can drop out whenever
              you like.

Places will be limited. Be one of the first on
the list - hand in your name to Mr Lawton NOW.

NOTES

1. Material is whittled down to the minimum – further details such as

precise times of meetings can be conveyed to those interested after names have been handed in.

2. Vocabulary is simple; sentences and paragraphs are kept short. Layout makes for easy reading.

3. Two advertising devices are used – the eye-catcher headline and the appeal to action at the end.

4. The Personnel Officer, Mr Lawton, appears both by name and by title, in case some know him only by name and to reinforce who is the right person to go to.

Of course, such an approach is not suitable for everything. Important policy announcements, standing instructions, notices drawing attention to breaches of discipline – these require a more formal presentation. But they too will be more likely to be read and understood if the writer has taken some trouble to use a layout that will command attention and language that is well within the range of all potential readers.

IV. FORMS AND QUESTIONNAIRES

A. Use of forms

An increasing amount of business communication is now carried out by means of 'forms' – that is to say ready prepared documents with blank spaces to be filled in by the Tx. They are sometimes used for action-producing (as order forms, applications for share warrants, job cards etc.) but are here considered chiefly in terms of information-passing.

Reference has already been made to routine reports (page 133) which are frequently submitted on forms; but the most interesting type of information-passing form is the one that is sent by an organisation that requires information, and which thus ensures that the information returned is exactly what is required, given in a standard order. A further refinement is so to arrange the wording on the form that the answers written in are of minimum length, thus making the task of both Tx and Rx easier. Forms may affect the young business man in two ways – 1. filling them in 2. designing his own.

B. Filling in forms

With a well designed form, filling it in is one of the easiest acts of communication. All the Tx has to do is to read the instructions and obey them.

It is advisable to leave no part unanswered. If sections do not apply to you, draw a line through or write 'not applicable'. Sections left blank are worrying to the recipient who is never certain why you did not fill them in. Answer fully. If details are asked for, such as full Christian names, or names of, and dates of attendance at, all schools, these must be supplied – not a selection.

Unfortunately many forms are badly designed, and worded without regard to communication principles. Such forms are difficult for everybody.

C. Designing forms

It is likely that the designing of only very simple forms, of a kind that can be duplicated in the office, is likely to come the way of the average young manager.

The arrangement of the form should be logical and it should be free from internal contradictions, or apparent contradictions.

RF.1A, the 'Application for Renewal of a Motor Vehicle Licence' has a question to be answered under 'Particulars of Vehicle':

Are the registration particulars as stated in the Registration Book (See instruction 4 in the Registration Book)? If not give details of any alterations (including change of colour, type of engine, and/or propelling fuel) which have been made since the last previous declaration.

Cross-referencing of this kind, to documents other than the form the Tx is filling in, is to be avoided. But in this example much more confusing to the Tx than the actual wording of the question is the fact that the first of the group of numbered instructions at the head of form RF.1A reads:

Do not use this form but a full declaration form if there has been any change in the particulars of the vehicle recorded in the Registration Book affecting taxation class or duty payable e.g. alteration to the vehicle or in its use.

Of course, it is possible to work out that these two instructions are not completely contradictory – that a distinction is being made between alteration 'affecting taxation class or duty payable' and other alterations. But why should the applicant be put to the effort of working this out; and will every applicant be able to?

Instructions and questions should be arranged, then, in a logical order. They should be expressed in clear, simple, and direct English. Reference to explanatory notes should be kept to a minimum but where such notes are unavoidable they should be part of the form. Where space is left for an answer it should be large enough for the kind of answer expected – it is extraordinary how many firms do not leave sufficient space for a country customer's full address, for example. Direct questions and instructions are better than headings.

Thus

What is your surname? Answer in BLOCK CAPITALS	
What are your full Christian names?	
What is your full postal address?	

is to be preferred to

NAME (Surname first in block capitals)
ADDRESS

If there are several general instructions they should be introduced by some such heading as:

Read these instructions carefully before completing this form.

D. Questionnaires

A questionnaire is a document, circulated in a sample of a group about which information is required, which is intended to obtain that information by a series of carefully designed questions. Such information is subsequently collated and permits deductions to be drawn about the group.

Originally such questionnaires were handed to the Tx to fill in himself, but increasingly today they are administered by a trained interviewer, who reads out the questions and fills in, or ticks off, the interviewee's replies. The compilation of questionnaires and the selecting of a true 'random sample' is skilled work that the ordinary business man is not likely to be called upon to carry out.

It is, however, interesting to note how far the modern questionnaire has gone in removing the necessity for the Tx to write anything at all. The need to use computers in analysing results has been the principal cause of this development, but it has the additional advantages of time saving and increasing objectivity. The designer of forms could well take a few lessons from the designer of questionnaires.

Here is an extract from a questionnaire designed for the magazine *Encounter* and sent to all readers. Its purpose was to enable the magazine to assess the characteristics of its readership. The questionnaire was introduced by a letter from the editors, and the questions headed by the general instruction: *Please put a cross in the box beside the most appropriate answer, leaving the other boxes blank.*

9. *Do you own any of the following?*
- ☐ Record-player/radiogram
- ☐ Tape recorder
- ☐ Camera
- ☐ Cine-camera
- ☐ Typewriter
- ☐ Musical instrument

10. *About how many* hard-back *books do you buy each year?*
- ☐ Less than 5
- ☐ 5–10
- ☐ 11–20
- ☐ 21–30
- ☐ Over 30
- ☐ None

11. *About how many* paper-back *books do you buy each year?*
- ☐ Less than 5
- ☐ 5–10
- ☐ 11–20
- ☐ 21–30
- ☐ Over 30
- ☐ None

12. *About how many gramophone records do you buy each year?*
- ☐ 1–3
- ☐ 4–6
- ☐ More than 6
- ☐ None

13. *About how often do you go to the cinema?*
- ☐ Once a week or more
- ☐ Once in two/three weeks
- ☐ Once a month
- ☐ Less frequently
- ☐ Never

14. *About how often do you go to the theatre, opera, ballet or concerts?*
- ☐ Once a week or more
- ☐ Once or twice a month
- ☐ Three/four times a year
- ☐ Less frequently
- ☐ Never

V. TELEGRAMS, CABLEGRAMS, TELEX MESSAGES

A. Telegrams, cablegrams, and messages for Telex present an identical problem – to produce a clear unambiguous message in the minimum number of words – and the same technique is used for all three. Telegrams will serve to exemplify the method.

B. Messages of this kind are usually sent to produce immediate action. Information-passing by these methods will be confined to extremely urgent material. Thus the first task for the Tx is to select from the material at his disposal relevant to the situation that which is essential to produce the correct action, or which must be transmitted to the Rx if the message is to be of any use.

C. The content of the message having first been reduced to its minimum in this way, the wording of the message is next reduced. All minor words (such as articles, personal pronouns, and prepositions) are removed and normal sentence division is ignored (except in very long messages, where the word 'STOP' is inserted between sentences).

D. EXAMPLE I. The situation is that the Tx's car has broken down and he will be late for a committee meeting as a result. He decides to send a telegram to a friend who is attending the same meeting, but will not yet have left home. If the Tx were writing this message, he would probably put something like this:

Dear Tom,

My car has broken down outside Luton and it will take at least an hour to get going again. I shall be unable to arrive at the committee meeting before eight o'clock at the earliest. Please apologise for me to the chairman.   Jack.

To reduce this message to its minimum, we would argue that all the Tx has to convey is: 1. what has happened (but not where) 2. that his friend is to apologise to the chairman – the action the telegram is being sent to produce 3. the time he hopes to get to the meeting. Reduced in this way the message would run something like this:

My car has broken down. Please apologise to the chairman. I hope to arrive at eight. Jack.

Reducing this to the minimum, by omission of minor words and concentration on verbs and nouns, we arrive at the following as the best telegram the Tx can send:

CAR BREAKDOWN PLEASE APOLOGISE CHAIRMAN HOPE ARRIVE
EIGHT JACK.

This is the best telegram because it is the minimum number of words that can produce the action required. It could be argued that the cause of the delay need not be mentioned, but it does enable the Rx to apologise more convincingly; however, if economy were very important it could be omitted. The 'please', on the other hand, cannot be omitted – politeness should not be sacrificed to economy.

E. Since such messages are highly compressed and are transmitted without punctuation and capitalisation it is very easy to produce ambiguities. There are many variants of the anecdote about the business man who instructed his broker to go on buying certain shares, and disappeared, far from telephones, into the grouse moors. In his absence, the price of the shares soared and the worried stockbroker sent a telegram, with a prepaid reply, that read:

SHARES NOW ABOVE SIX POUNDS DO I CONTINUE TO BUY

only to receive the baffling answer:

NO PRICE TOO HIGH.

Before the message is sent, the Tx must check that it contains all the information asked for, or all the information permitting intelligent action to be taken; and that there is no ambiguity in the wording. It is sound practice to write out messages of this kind in block capitals so that the Tx sees for himself how it will appear to the Rx.

F. Cablegrams are very expensive and those who use them frequently develop a somewhat bizarre English of their own in the constant attempt to keep costs down. Thus SEND SOONEST manages to say in two words what it is impossible to say with orthodox grammar in fewer than five.

G. EXAMPLE 2. The following is a typical exchange of Telex messages between firms. It will be noted that the wording is identical with that which would be used for a telegram or cable.

a   VELOX BROMHILL
      FURTHER DELIVERY DHP7 MOTORS URGENTLY
      REQUIRED PLEASE REPLY BY RETURN
      TOMPKINSONS

b   TOMPKINSONS BLEAK HILL WANNINGTON
      DELIVERIES DHP7 HELD PENDING CLEARANCE OF
      £396.24 ON OCTOBER ACCOUNT WHEN CLEARED
      WILL DESPATCH MOTORS IMMEDIATELY
      VELOX.

Notice too that in addressing and signing telegrams, cablegrams and Telex messages minimum wording is used – the firm's name without 'Ltd' or 'Messrs', a personal surname without Christian name or 'Mr', 'Mrs', or 'Miss' unless there is a real risk of confusion between members of a family. Frequently the simplest and friendliest way of signing is a Christian name only, provided the Tx is confident that the Rx will be able to identify from the message which of several people with the same Christian name is sending the message. Addresses and names are paid for by the word at the same rate as the message.

VI. EXERCISES

Exercise A

Write out instructions how to get to your home from your technical college 1. in colloquial style as you would tell a friend, 2. in formal written style.

Exercise B

In each of the following groups say which instruction seems to you the most appropriate in style for the subject matter and which the least, and why:

A.
1. You are to empty the contents of this can into a saucepan and heat to boiling point.
2. Empty the contents of this can into a saucepan and heat to boiling point.
3. The contents of this can should be emptied into a saucepan and heated to boiling point.

B.
1. Please complete this form in ink. Use block capitals. Use a typewriter for name, date of birth, and sex only.
2. You should complete this form in ink, using block capitals. You should use a typewriter for name, date of birth, and sex only.
3. This form should be completed in ink, using block capitals. A typewriter may be used for name, date of birth, and sex only.

C.
1. You are to arrange transport Leeds to Manchester for Mr Tompkins and book accommodation for him in Manchester for the night of 25th June.

2. Transport is to be arranged by you Leeds to Manchester for Mr Tompkins and accommodation booked for him in Manchester for the night of 25th June.
3. Please (1) arrange transport Leeds to Manchester for Mr Tompkins (2) book accommodation for him in Manchester for the night of 25th June.

Exercise C

Which of the following imperatives, in your opinion, (a) tells how to do something, (b) gives an order, (c) gives advice? Are there any where you are not sure – if so, why is that?

1. Catch the 10.10 from Liverpool Street. Bring the documents with you.
2. Remember that the 10.10 from Liverpool Street is usually ten minutes late at Ipswich. Don't forget the documents.
3. Check that there still is a 10.10 from Liverpool Street on Saturdays.
4. Let me have your detailed report by Monday next.
5. Please send me a copy of your illustrated brochure, as advertised.
6. Insert coin and slide the knob to the right.
7. Give to each telephone call, no matter how trivial, the same attention that you would give to the caller in person.
8. Do not lean out of the window.
9. Ask your chemist for NERVORITE.
10. Answer all the questions.

Exercise D

1. Make detailed comment on the following standing instructions to be posted in a room of a technical college.
2. Rewrite them.

FIRE PRECAUTIONS

In the event of a fire alarm all students are to observe the following instructions:

1. Follow the advice of your tutor as to whether to evacuate the room or not.
2. From this room the quickest exit route is via the east staircase rear exit to the yard.
3. Students leaving this room please assemble for checking at the rear yard.
If the east staircase is affected students are to proceed along the corridor to the west staircase.
Lifts must not be used.

Exercise E

Prepare *one* of the following memoranda:

1. to office staff on answering the telephone
2. to members of a tennis club on care of the (grass) courts
3. to new students outlining their responsibilities to the students' association.

Exercise F

Write the following messages for use on message forms ('memos'):

1. Notifying a junior member of staff that his holiday choice of July 26th–August 9th has been asked for by too many, and only March 15th–29th is available for him.
2. Asking another department whether a parcel of GPO pamphlets on the use of the telephone has been delivered to them by mistake.
3. Instructing a senior member of your staff to prepare a roster for overtime duty after consultation with other members of the office. Give a time limit for completion of this.

Exercise G

Write out notices, about 100 words in length, suitable for display on a notice board, for *two* of the following:

1. Drawing attention to the facilities of the college library.
2. Soliciting support for ONE of the following college activities – rambling group; chess club; wild life preservation society.
3. Announcing a distinguished visitor (specify) to works, office, or college and calling on all for support in making his visit a success.
4. Introducing a system of staggered tea-breaks for various departments of college or office.
5. Drawing attention to *either* health hazards *or* fire hazards caused by cigarette smoking.

Exercise H

Prepare a short questionnaire on one of the following topics, or one of your own choice.

The exercise can be made more realistic (and more interesting) if you are working in a group. You can then arrange amongst yourselves to choose different topics, duplicate your questionnaires, fill in each others, and analyse results. With a large group some will have to think of subjects of their own, similar to the following suggestions.

1. Newspapers
2. Reading
3. Motoring
4. Leisure activities
5. Careers and ambitions

6. Shopping habits
7. Holidays
8. Television viewing
9. Amenities of local town (or district of large city)
10. Communication in business.

Exercise I

Write telegrams for the following situations. Include name and address of the Rx each time. Invent necessary supporting detail. The aim is to produce a practical message with all detail the Rx would need. Use block capitals throughout and no punctuation marks.

1. The estate agent who is selling your house has notified you of an offer of £6500 and your immediate reply is required. Refuse this offer and give £6850 as the minimum you will consider.
2. You are secretary of the college or office football team. On the morning of an away match your centre-half phones you to tell you he sprained his ankle the previous evening. Your most useful substitute in this position is not on the phone but you would like him to play rather than the reserve.
3. You are on a walking tour, and have run short of cash. You will have to shorten your holiday if you cannot obtain a little more. Ask parents or a good friend to wire ten pounds to you at the next place you are stopping at.
4. You are expecting a firm to collect and replace a defective duplicating machine they have supplied, but they have not called. You wish the matter to be dealt with quickly but you have no telephone number for the firm.
5. You have written to a firm complaining of non-delivery of goods (specify) and within an hour of your posting the letter the goods arrive.

Exercise J

One alarming feature of the past decade has been the increase in damage done to property by apparently wanton acts of vandalism. Many of the most vulnerable targets are items of public property (e.g. public telephones) and a large proportion are the responsibility of local authorities. Recently, for example, almost all the movable fittings in a public park were destroyed or taken away in one night.

You have been asked to devise a short notice or advertisement for your Authority, *either* discouraging acts of vandalism in general, *or* discouraging vandalism against a particular public amenity or item of property.

(*a*) Design the notice/advertisement in whatever form you consider appropriate, and (*b*) write a passage (not more than 200 words) stating your view on vandalism as it affects local authorities. Consider how serious the problem is and what steps local authorities ought/can take to combat it. Write as far as possible in relation to your own experience and to the area in which you live.

[*Local Government Training Board –*
Clerical Examination]

Exercise K

Draft the memorandum referred to in the following transcript of instructions from a senior officer.

There have been far too many minor accidents recently in our offices. I'd like you to draft a memorandum on this subject to all members of staff.

Here are some examples of the sort of accidents I mean and the dangerous practices which can cause accidents.

Secretaries and other people tend to leave cabinet drawers and desk drawers open. This is not just a nuisance for those who have to shut the drawers; it's positively dangerous. And in this connection I was taught never to open more than one drawer of a filing cabinet at one time.

At least two members of the public have been involved in incidents which were the fault of our staff. In one case, someone was badly bruised when a swing door was pushed right into him, although the door was clearly marked PULL TO OPEN. The other incident involved an old lady who was knocked over by a member of staff who was running down one of the passages.

The other day, one of the staff fell down some stairs and broke an ankle because he didn't look where he was going while he was carrying a lot of files. And while we're on the subject of carrying things, I'm really worried whenever I see one of the girls carrying a typewriter or trying to lift something too heavy for her. Actually, it's the same for anyone. You shouldn't try to lift or carry anything on your own if it's too heavy or bulky for you to manage.

Last month we had a minor fire when someone dropped a cigarette end into a waste-paper basket. The excuse I was given was that it was a metal one. That doesn't matter. We work in offices in which there's always a lot of paper about. That's why there are plenty of ash-trays.

Still on the subject of fire hazards – people should not put materials on or against any sort of heating apparatus.

It might sound ridiculous; but some of us manage to injure ourselves even when we use pins and stapling machines. And of course there's the occasional mishap with other bits of office machinery, such as guillotines.

Lastly, I'm convinced that it's extremely important to be tidy in an office. Don't leave things lying about when you finish a job. And if you spill something or break something, clear it up straight away. If you want to get rid of broken glass or razor blades, don't leave them in the waste-paper receptacles. Wrap them up and label them clearly.

That's about all, though you may well think of something important that I've left out. If you do, then put it in.

The essential thing about your memorandum is that it should encourage *staff, in the friendliest way possible, to be genuinely safety-conscious. You should not just give them a list of accidents that have happened or might happen. And remember it's for all office staff, not just those in your own office.*

[*Local Government Training Board –
Intermediate Examination*]

Exercise L

1. Imagine you are employed in the Town Clerk's Department at Blenkinsop. The following letter has been received:

5 Pudding Rise,
Blenkinsop, Yorkshire.
YO53 7BM
15th April, 19..

The Town Clerk,
Civic Offices,
Blenkinsop, Yorkshire.
YO53 1AF

Dear Sir,

    The garden of my house, in this area of high rateable values, abuts upon the Gracing Green Corporation Allotments. Last year it became the practice of several allotment holders to bring their transistor radios on to their plots to provide music while they worked, to the considerable annoyance of those of us who wished to enjoy the peace of our gardens.

    This nuisance has already started again this year. Is it possible for you to write to these people pointing out the annoyance to others? Perhaps your powers can permit you to ban their use altogether on allotments.

Yours faithfully,
John Studwick

The Town Clerk's comment is: *I think we should do something about this. I don't know whether our present powers permit us to go so far as banning radios on allotments. It is an offence to play one in any park or open space under our bye-laws, but I'm not sure whether an allotment would be considered a park or open space. Better try Mr Studwick's letter approach with perhaps a vague threat of further action. Send the letter across to Mr Williamson, the Park Superintendent, with a memo as from me telling him to send a circular letter on those lines to all allotment holders.*

Write (*a*) this memo, (*b*) a reply to Mr Studwick for the Town Clerk's signature.

2. Now imagine you are on Mr Williamson's staff. Draft a suitable circular letter.

Chapter 12

Essays for Examinations

I. ESSAYS AND COMMUNICATION PRINCIPLES

This chapter need be studied only if you are using this book as a textbook in preparing for an examination in English. The essay is widely used in written examinations to test candidates' powers of communication.

Special difficulties arise from the unnatural circumstances of the piece of writing required. The Rx is faceless and unknown; unlike the Rx of everyday life he is not really interested in finding out what you have to tell him, but principally in how you tell it. Communication principles cannot, therefore, be fully applied, and the essay will be judged not only for its linguistic but also for its literary achievement. Further, under examination conditions you are frequently forced into writing about something you know little about, and this affects the kind of planning you can employ.

You will have met these problems before in previous English examinations. What follows is not, therefore, intended as a comprehensive guide to essay-writing but to draw your attention to particular points of importance concerning essay-writing at the post 'O' level stage.

II. ESSAYS IN POST 'O' LEVEL ENGLISH EXAMINATIONS

A. Choosing the topic

An essay may consist of (1) narrative, (2) description, (3) exposition, or (4) discussion.

Certain essay titles confine you to one of these treatments at a time – for example *The life of a notorious pirate* (narrative) *A walk in winter* (description) *Uneasy lies the head that wears the crown* (exposition) *A woman's place is in the home – discuss* (discussion). Those that limit you to narrative or description are not likely to be set at this level.

Other titles leave you to select your treatment or to blend several treatments. Thus the title *Advertising* leaves you free to handle it as narrative (history of advertising) description (the forms advertising takes, with examples) exposition (the various media of advertising, with their relative effectiveness), or discussion (do the advantages to the customer outweigh the addition to the cost of the product and the extent to which our lives are dominated by advertising?). Or a combination of two or more treatments is possible – thus a brief history of advertising or a brief survey of the forms advertising takes may lead into a discussion of its advantages and disadvantages to consumer, retailer, and manufacturer.

Exposition and discussion are more difficult to handle than narrative and description, but they give you much more opportunity to show that you are capable of logical thought. At this stage, that is what an examiner is looking for, and a very high level of writing indeed would be necessary to compensate for the comparative simplicity of narrative or descriptive treatments. Topics should, therefore, be chosen which permit predominantly exposition or discussion treatment.

B. Timing the essay

Timing is very important in English examinations. You are always working against the clock and if you fall behind you may have to leave a question out – almost the only way of scoring nought for a question in a conventional English paper. The essay must therefore take not a minute more than is provided for it. On the other hand, an essay that occupies less than the allocated time, or is short of the required length, is bound to be marked down.

Some examining bodies indicate essay length by time, others by the number of words required. It is useful to have a conversion formula for these and the following will give an approximate indication of what is required.

1. TIME TO WORDS. Allow one-sixth total time for plan – then assume 10 words written per minute of remaining time. Thus a one-hour essay works out to 10 minutes planning and 500 words written.

2. WORDS TO TIME. Allow 10 words per minute and add one-fifth of this time as planning time. Thus a 300 words essay requires 30 minutes writing and 6 minutes planning.

C. Planning the essay

A plan – that is to say brief notes of the points to be made with an indication of the order in which you propose to make them – is essential to success. A plan serves you in three ways:

1. It prevents 'drying up'. Time spent staring at the ceiling is time wasted. When you start again there is inevitably a hiatus at that point which shows to the examiner. Often you go off at a complete tangent.

2. It enables you to check your timing. If you have a plan, you know

if you are going too slowly or using up your material too fast; and you know early enough to be able to make adjustments that will not show in the final product.

3. It gives shape and development to your essay – the most important advantage. A good essay has form. It should lead the reader point by point to a predetermined conclusion. At the end the reader should feel he has arrived at a destination – not that the essay has suddenly expired because all the material has been used up.

Two types of plan are of use. These could be called the *Imposed Plan* and the *Organic Plan*.

THE IMPOSED PLAN can be used only when you are fortunate enough to have plenty of material to write about. It is a limiting plan whose chief purpose is to ensure that you provide a balanced coverage of your subject matter and do not try to squeeze a quart of material into a pint-size essay. Decided upon by the principles of logical organisation discussed in Chapter 2, this plan edits, selects, and arranges.

The best essays spring from the Imposed Plan but the examination candidate does not always have the necessary depth of material to draw upon. In such a situation the ORGANIC PLAN will help. The method is as follows:

1. Scribble down as quickly as possible all the ideas that come into your head as you decide your essay topic. These are got down without editing or arranging, before the stream (or trickle) dries up.

2. Read through the list of points and strike out any which are too weak to be of use or which do not fit in with the others.

3. Note points that are connected with each other (these will often be close to each other in the list because an association existed in your mind when you wrote them down). These can be looped round in pencil, and tails coming from the loops joined to show connection (see Fig. 8). These looped and joined points are to form your paragraphs, so it is worthwhile at this stage to try to produce one or two extra points that can be added to them.

4. Arrange these paragraphs in the most effective order by numbering the joined tails of the loops. You will probably find Chapter 2 useful in deciding order; but you must remember that, as the essay is a literary form, suspense and building to a climax are legitimate devices. Search hard for any tendency in your notes to point in a certain direction. If you can find a 'line' to take this will give development to the essay. Look too for bridging devices between your paragraphs so that one paragraph leads to another.

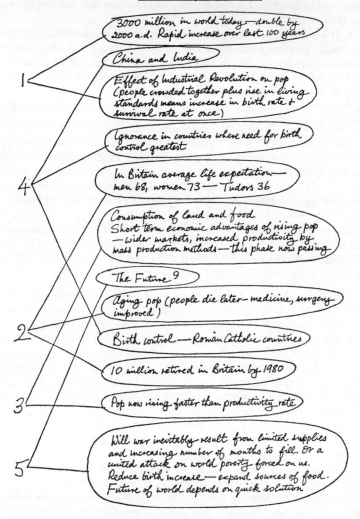

The World's Population Problem

1
- 3000 million in world today — double by 2000 a.d. Rapid increase over last 100 years
- China and India
- Effect of Industrial Revolution on pop (people crowded together plus rise in living standards means increase in birth rate & survival rate at once)

4
- Ignorance in countries where need for birth control greatest
- In Britain average life expectation — men 68, women 73 — Tudors 36

- Consumption of land and food Short term economic advantages of rising pop — wider markets, increased productivity by mass production methods — this phase now passing

2
- The Future 9
- Aging pop (people die later — medicine, surgery improved)
- Birth control — Roman Catholic countries
- 10 million retired in Britain by 1980

3
- Pop now rising faster than productivity rate

5
- Will war inevitably result from limited supplies and increasing number of mouths to fill. Or a united attack on world poverty forced on us. Reduce birth increase — expand sources of food. Future of world depends on quick solution

Fig. 8

5. There is no need to write out the plan again; it can be used as it now stands.

Essays of argument, and these are amongst the most common at this stage, are easy to arrange. You will probably have your own opinion on the matter under debate and will seek to move the reader to agree with you. Arguments are always arranged in ascending order of weight (since the effect of a weak argument coming after a strong one is to discredit the strong one). Thus in an essay of argument there is almost a stock plan:

a. Introduction establishing basis of argument and defining terms
b. Arguments against your viewpoint (in the weakest position)
c. Arguments for your viewpoint in ascending order of importance (probably a paragraph each, unless there are a large number of them)
d. Quick survey of arguments, and decision in favour of your viewpoint.

D. Some points of style

Personal experiences and recollections can be effectively introduced into some essays, and for these the first person singular should be used (any other method is clumsy and unnatural). Apart from this use, the first person singular should be avoided. Expressions such as *I believe, in my opinion, I think* not only obtrude the writer into a formal context (which is normally an impersonal context) but weaken the impact of the opinions so introduced.

Direct speech should be avoided and imaginary conversations of the kind: *People may ask, 'What is the point of all this expenditure on social services?'* Rhetorical questions (*What will the future bring? How are we to solve these problems?*) are also best avoided.

Vocabulary should be formal. Slang and colloquialisms must be avoided, and all abbreviated forms such as *don't, can't, won't*. Abbreviations generally should be introduced only when essential. A list of examples which trails off in a vague *etc.* produces a particularly slipshod effect.

Some attempt should be made to vary sentence length and sentence structure. If your vocabulary is wide you should demonstrate this fact provided this can be achieved with tact – thrusting unusual words at the reader is ostentatious and impolite in an essay, as in other forms of writing. Above all, you should aim at crispness and originality of expression.

E. Practice essays

The following groups of essay subjects are designed so that each gives a balanced representation of the types of topic set in post 'O' level English examinations. You should write for the time, or the length, prescribed in the examination you are preparing for. As a variant you can, especially in the early stages, prepare plans for, say, three essays in one group; then decide which is the most effective of your outlines and write an essay based on that one.

1. Professionalism in sport
   Early marriages
   Alcohol and the motorist
   The ideal companion
   'There are only two nations, East and West' – Napoleon.

2. Student protests
   The preservation of wild life
   Growing up
   Should the mothers of school-age children go out to work if this is not an economic necessity?
   'Amusement is the happiness of those that cannot think' – Pope.

3. The future of NATO
   Britain's steel industry
   Fashion
   Has Christmas become nothing more than a festival of commerce?
   'All men are created equal' – Thomas Jefferson.

4. Can national expenditure on space research be justified?
   Commercial apprenticeship
   The working materials of the contemporary world
   Making a house a home
   'Any man can make money if he has nothing else in his head' – Hazlitt.

5. In defence of pop music
   The effect of advertising on our daily lives
   The do-it-yourself movement
   Choosing a present
   'What is written without effort is in general read without pleasure' – Samuel Johnson.

6. Organ transplants
   Do we still have class distinction in Britain?
   Industry and the countryside
   The importance of a sense of humour
   'To be a good animal is the first requisite for success in life' – Herbert Spencer.

7. Is local government spending to support the Arts justifiable?
   The world's food problem

Examinations as a test of ability
The right to strike
'Educate a woman and you put a knife in the hands of a monkey' –
Indian proverb.

8. Teenage morality
Incentives
Should all tobacco advertising be made illegal?
Film societies
'The car is going to contribute very largely to wrecking our civili-
sation' – Sir Alex Issigonis.

9. Do local government elections matter?
Are we happier now than we would have been 100 years ago?
Consumer organisations
Worry
'The liberty of the Press is the birth right of a Briton' – John Wilkes.

10. Are English workers lazier than their continental equivalents?
The problems of new towns
Ambition
Is private charity an anachronism?
'Economy does not lie in sparing money, but in spending it wisely' –
T. H. Huxley.

III. THE EXTENDED ESSAY

A. Choosing the topic

Extended essays (i.e. essays of 3 000–5 000 words) on subjects relevant
to your business or professional interests are required if you are a candidate for the Ordinary National Certificate, or Ordinary National Diploma,
in Business Studies. You are not, therefore, free to choose just any topic
that interests you; it must be one that is recognisably connected with
business studies.

For the Ordinary National Certificate in Public Administration the
topic selected must be one that requires 'the acquisition or application
of some knowledge beyond what is specified in the subject syllabus of the
course'. It should occupy you throughout the second year of the course,
but preliminary work may be started in the first year.

A common mistake is to choose a topic that is too big; 3 000–5 000
words seems very long if you are used to essays only a tenth of that length,
and it is natural to want to make sure you have sufficient material to
last the distance. However, large general themes such as *Oil* or extended

historical treatments such as *The Development of the Merchant Navy* provide too much material and the essays inevitably become a breathless catalogue. *Recent Trends in Oil Marketing* or *The Development of Merchant Shipping during the Seventeenth Century*, at first more forbidding titles, will in practice serve the candidate much better, as the subject matter can be kept under control and sufficient space is available to permit something interesting to be said.

You should first decide upon your field of interest, and subsequently limit the area in this field which you are going to explore thoroughly. What you finally choose to write about should represent a still further reduction of this area, since the best extended essays are produced when you know more about the subject than the part you are selecting for your essay. It is sound policy to decide upon your detailed topic only when you have already carried out some investigation into the subject generally and are able to see what particular part or aspect of your material will make a self-contained and easily handled topic.

Local interests should not be neglected. A lively essay could, for example, arise from the study of some local industry about which little is known nationally. Commercial or industrial history limited to your own area will be more compact and controllable than similar themes treated nationally. Similarly, for an essay for the ONC in Public Administration, the investigation of some aspect of the work of your own authority or civil service department might provide admirable material not generally available.

B. Preparation

1. RESEARCH. You will not be expected to attempt much in the way of primary research (i.e. obtaining information firsthand or examining original documents) although some field work is recommended in the extended essay for the ONC in Public Administration. The bulk of your research will be secondary – you will be drawing your information from the writings of those who have carried out primary research or who have at least assembled conveniently the product of secondary research on a scale you could not hope to emulate. Your principal sources will be books, magazines, and newspapers. This is not to suggest that your essay will be a mere matter of copying or rehashing what others have written. Having obtained the information you require from your sources, you will then have to collate it (one source against another), assess it, and attempt to form your own opinions and viewpoint. The facts in your essay may come from your sources, but not the way those facts are expressed or the conclusions drawn from them.

For certain subjects you may be able to draw upon what you have been told (oral reports) if the source is a reliable one. Many firms and institutions are willing to cooperate by supplying pamphlets dealing with their work and will sometimes supply information that is not generally available if you explain your request in a courteous letter.

Your first task, then, is to prepare a reading list. Starting is difficult sometimes, as there are only a limited number of subjects for which libraries hold readymade bibliographies, and those they do have may be out of date. Your tutor will probably be able to make some suggestions to start you off; the college librarian or local public reference librarian will also be prepared to offer advice and direction. Once you have started, you begin to find out for yourself what you should read next. For example, a good start is often an encyclopedia article, which will not only outline your subject but also list books that you can then refer to. These books in turn will provide further bibliographies. The only danger about this way of assembling your reading list is that it tends to be out of date, as you are working backwards and no reference can be more up to date than your original encyclopedia article. Some subjects date more than others, but it is always important to note the date of publication of a book referred to – if it is an old one it may still be the best there is, but it may be one that has been superseded and much of the material in it discredited by a more recent work. It is best to avoid topical subjects because of the danger of some political change, for example, suddenly making your essay out of date just as you have completed the work on it.

The most topical source is the newspaper, but it is also the least reliable. Specialist periodicals include material that is normally more up to date than that in a book, since the delay in writing and publishing a book is considerable. Material sent by firms may be assumed to be as up to date as a magazine article, if in the form of printed pamphlets, and completely up to date if provided specially for you.

To find out what are the latest books dealing with your subject you should:

a. Check the subject catalogue of all libraries to which you have access.

b. Watch book reviews and switch on for TV and radio programmes relevant to your subject.

c. Study the annual volumes of the *British National Bibliography* for the last two or three years. This is arranged under subjects, but will, of course, show only works published in the year of that particular volume.

2. KEEPING NOTES. As you read you will make notes indicating the exact source, including page references, in case you wish later on to refer

to the original again. Material which you intend to quote must be copied out accurately with a full note of the source. Distinguish between facts and opinions. You are bound to have to draw your facts from your sources; but you should try to form your own opinions, or at least weigh one writer's opinion against another's.

It is useful to keep your notes on separate pieces of paper in a loose-leaf folder, so that they can be shuffled about and rearranged as necessary. If as you make the notes you try to arrange them under headings this will help you when you come to the planning stage.

3. PLANNING follows broadly the principles laid down in Chapter 2, and the hints on the imposed plan earlier in this chapter. Paragraphing alone does not usually provide sufficient organisation for an essay of this kind and you are recommended to divide the work also into sections or 'chapters' each with its own heading. It is then a matter of deciding the best order for these chapters and the best order for the paragraphs within the chapters.

Subjects which have a chronological sequence present few problems, but others may involve much thought before the best order reveals itself to you. Planning an essay of this length is not a ten-minute matter. You need to familiarise yourself with your material and live with it over a period – a weekend for example – continually returning to the problem of how best to order it. The recommended notes on separate sheets grouped under headings will save you much trouble at this stage. It is much easier to try over various arrangements by moving these notes about physically than it is to carry all the ideas in your head or to write out several experimental outline plans.

4. THE ROUGH DRAFT of your extended essay must be fully written out in the form that at that stage you intend as the final form. It must be legible, because your tutor will have to read it and discuss it with you. He will be able to draw your attention to errors of fact, unsubstantiated opinions, faults of arrangement, and imperfections of style. After discussion with your tutor you will either write out the final version correcting the flaws that have been pointed out to you, or prepare a modified rough draft for further discussion with him.

C. Presentation

You should try to make the final product as handsome as possible. If you can type, it should be typed. If it is handwritten, it should be neat and legible. You should supply a thin cover of some kind (heavy covers should be avoided as the essays may be posted) and a title-page. If the work is divided into chapters with headings, a table of contents listing these chapters and the pages on which they start should appear immediately after the title-page. The whole essay should be sewn or stapled together.

If you think it will improve your essay to include free-hand maps and sketches, or photographs, diagrams, and tables of statistics clipped from periodicals, these should be stuck into the text neatly at appropriate points, with captions to explain their relevance to the essay. The addition of illustrative material of this kind should be kept under control and always serve a purpose. You do not want your essay to look like a schoolboy's 'project'. Wording included in such material must not be counted as part of your 3 000–5 000 words.

You should not 'lift' passages from your sources, but must reexpress the material in your own words. Short quotations may be employed where you consider the original wording particularly striking or where it constitutes important evidence about a point you wish to make. Such quotations should be enclosed between inverted commas and the source of the quotation made clear. There are several ways of doing this. The simplest is to introduce the quotation by a form of words such as: *J. Hampshire in Advertising Today says:* . . . Alternatively, after the quotation you can add: (*J. Hampshire, Advertising Today*). A more scholarly way of referring to this work would be to add the date of publication: *J. Hampshire, Advertising Today, 1970*. Footnotes can also be used to indicate the source of a quotation. You should keep to one system throughout the essay.

If 'Advertising Today' was not a book but the title of an article in a periodical you should refer to it in this way: *J. Hampshire, 'Advertising Today', The Advertising World, January 1970*.

Quotations from talks and speeches may be indicated in this way:

J. Hampshire in a lecture to the Royal Society of Arts, 7 January 1970.

A modest number of such short quotations (say six to eight) may be counted towards your total of words.

You should make a similar reference to your source when you are not quoting but are nevertheless paraphrasing or summarising material pretty directly.

In short, the reader should be put in a position where he is able to distinguish what is your own original contribution – ideas and interpretations – from what you have extracted from the books, articles, and pamphlets you have been reading.

At the end of the essay all sources of information should be listed and your main sources incorporated in a bibliography (i.e. a list showing for each the author, name of work, and date of publication, as above). Where field work has been undertaken, brief details of this should be added.

Part III

Chapter 13

Oral Communication

I. DIFFERENCES BETWEEN SPOKEN AND WRITTEN ENGLISH

Some American communication consultants recommend, 'Write as you talk'. During recent years there has certainly been a considerable blurring of the boundary between speech and writing, but in England at least we are not yet in a position where we can assume that the spoken and the written forms of the language are completely interchangeable.

We have already seen (in Chapter 5) that some words and expressions are at any one time in the history of the language considered suitable for speech only (colloquialisms) although these may subsequently be accepted into the written language. The existence of colloquialisms constitutes an important vocabulary difference between speech and writing. On the other hand, there is a considerable vocabulary traditionally associated with the most formal kinds of writing that sounds strained and unnatural in speech. Of a man who uses this vocabulary when he is talking people say, 'He talks like a book' or 'He's swallowed a dictionary.'

As well as vocabulary differences between speech and writing, there are differences of syntax. In speech we have greater licence. We do not, for example, speak in perfect sentences. *Just going down the road for a bit*, we say – with no subject and no finite verb. *I am just going down the road for a bit* would sound a little pedantic in most situations. This is the kind of lesson that the tyro at playwriting has to learn. Dialogue – which has been written – sounds unnatural when spoken if the writer has failed to allow for the greater freedom of the spoken language, and often has to be altered by a producer before the actors can speak it effectively. The same lesson has to be learned by the manager preparing his speech or his oral report.

There are a number of minor grammatical imperfections which are accepted in the spoken language – partly because the difference between the forms is not easily detected by the ear. Thus *who* is widely used for *whom* and the accusative instead of the possessive before the verbal noun (*Do you mind me asking a question?*) Accusatives after the verb 'to be' are so well established in speech (*That's them!*) that the formally 'correct' version sounds wrong. In such examples, to follow the rules that apply to formal writing is to make our speech sound pedantic and to alienate our Rx.

In speech we can produce shades of meaning by stressing one word rather than another in a sentence. There is no satisfactory equivalent to this in writing, though in informal writing underlining of the stressed word is sometimes possible. Consider the words: *You might have known me better*. Probably the most usual stressing of this sentence is to put a slight emphasis on *known*. Variations on meaning arise with shift of stress, as follows:

1. Stress on *you:* 'You of all people might have been expected to have known me better.'

2. Stress on *me:* 'You might have known that I at least would not have done such a thing.'

3. Stress on *might:* 'It is possible that you could have known me better.'

4. Pause before, and slight stress on, *better:* 'You might have known me when I was a better person.'

Two important observations must be made about this example. 1. The written versions have to be longer than the spoken if they are to avoid ambiguity – stress emphasis permits greater economy of words in speech. 2. The six words written down might be capable of any of these interpretations. A prime cause of ambiguity is failing to notice that words written down, and thus deprived of the stressing you give them in dictating, or even just in your mind, may to a reader carry a meaning that you did not intend.

Similarly in speech we can convey, by gesture and facial expressions, a shade of meaning, an emphasis, a hint of mockery, humour, irony – a whole range of delicate modifications of our words denied to us when we write. This is something that must be remembered all the time when we are dictating material. It is to be borne in mind too when we are on the telephone, and therefore invisible to our Rx.

Finally, the separations of word from word, sentence from sentence, paragraph from paragraph, that are characteristic of writing, do not apply in speech. Words are run together into convenient speech groups: we do not necessarily pause at the end of a sentence: there is nothing in speech which is equivalent to division into paragraphs. The first of these three points affects the oral Tx. It is a mistake to believe that slowing up delivery by putting a pause after every word improves communication (adults frequently address children in this way). In fact the breaking up of the familiar speech groups that results is a source of confusion and irritation to the Rx, as will be quickly recognised by all who have ever listened to an old-fashioned headmistress addressing pupils and parents on Open Day.

That we do not normally divide spoken material into sentences and paragraphs affects the dictator – who has to do just this when he is dictating – and also the man who has to talk a great deal in his job but seldom writes. When such a man does have to write he tends to run his sentences into each other, with a comma between, and to forget about paragraphing until he has gone well past the place where he should have changed paragraph.

II. DICTATING LETTERS

Two special difficulties confront you when you have to dictate a letter or indeed any other material.

1. Although you are speaking, your Rx will read your communication and therefore consider it writing, and expect it to conform to writing standards. You are therefore 'writing' by speaking, an unnatural activity bound to produce problems since the spoken and written language are, as we have seen, not identical.

2. It is impossible to see what you are 'writing' or what you have 'written'.

The following recommendations will be of use to you when you dictate and will help you to meet these two special difficulties.

a. Prepare ahead. Have ready the letter you are answering and any other document you will need to refer to. Think before you start to speak, and rough out your letter in your mind. If the letter is likely to be at all complicated, jot down headings to remind you of the principal points. If it is likely to be very complicated, write out a full rough draft before you start to dictate (this is easier if you are using a dictating machine than if you have a shorthand-typist waiting for you to start).

b. Dictate slowly and clearly. Do not mumble, or speak with cigarette or pipe in your mouth. Spell out personal names, brand names, and obscure technical words that it is unreasonable to expect a typist to know.

c. Indicate sentence division by saying firmly, 'Period' or 'Full stop' at the end of every sentence. Indicate each change of paragraph by saying, 'Paragraph'. Less familiar punctuation (such as dashes to mark a parenthesis) should also be indicated – how far you go in dictating punctuation may depend upon your previous experience of a secretary's knowledge of punctuation, but it remains your responsibility to see that the letter is punctuated the way you want it to be.

d. Keep your sentences and paragraphs short.

e. If you do lose track of what you have 'written', do not hesitate to ask the shorthand-typist to read back (or play back to yourself, if using a machine). Do not hesitate to make corrections, though you should try to avoid dictating material that needs correction.

f. Remember all the time that your vocabulary and syntax must be that of writing, not speech.

g. Try to avoid emphasis by stressing.

h. Avoid facial expressions and gestures that modify meaning in a way that cannot be conveyed on the typed page.

i. With all but the most simple letters have a read-back or play-back at the end, to check that the letter is all that you wish it to be.

j. Remember to observe communication principles. The recommendations for business letters made in Chapter 8 apply just as much to dictated letters as to any other kind.

III. USING THE TELEPHONE

Some of the difficulties that confront the dictator are also relevant to the use of the telephone, particularly that gesture and facial expression are invisible to the Rx. Certain tones of voice, especially those conveying irony or humour, seem to get lost in transit; jokes misfire and flippancies are easily taken as serious comment.

Calls should always be kept short as this helps to clear the firm's lines. There has, however, been an additional demand for brevity since the introduction of STD. STD calls are charged on the basis of a very short time unit (at normal rates, twenty-four seconds for local calls; twelve seconds for distance if thirty-five to fifty miles; eight seconds for longer distances.) To obtain the maximum benefit from STD the greatest possible number of non-local calls should be confined to the minimum unit, and it should be looked upon as a rarity to exceed twenty-four seconds for any call. Even twenty-four seconds allows you and your Rx barely sixty words between you.

This permits no social chatter of digressions; every word must be a necessary one. To compensate for inevitable curtness it is necessary to cultivate warmth and friendliness in your voice. Although the seconds are ticking past (and there are no warning 'pips' for STD) you must seem to your Rx calm and assured. The key to success will be (as so often with communication problems) good preparation; know precisely what you have to ask before you dial the number.

When it is your turn to be the Rx, seek to aid the Tx in making his call

as economical as possible. When you answer, give your name and department (*Mrs* or *Miss* is added to the name by women, but there is never a
need for *Mr*). Give an answer if you possibly can; otherwise take a
message or offer to ring back. Do not ask unnecessary questions or waste
time trying to find out about something while your Tx is still on the line.
Be pleasant; keep calm; avoid waffle.

IV. SPEAKING IN PUBLIC

A. Preparation

Preparation is also the key to successful speaking in public. The surest
protection against nervousness is the consciousness of having good preparation behind you. The first consideration is the audience – how many are
there likely to be; what will their attitude be; how much will they know
already; how will they compare with you in education and intelligence?
As in all communication, know your Rx and plan accordingly.

Next the purpose of your talk must be considered. Is it to put the Rx
in the picture only; to supply detailed information, as in a lecture; to put
forward new ideas; to teach a skill; to introduce a new policy, or a new
line of action?

Finally you collect and assemble your material – from previous knowledge or experience, from discussion with others, from documents and
reference works – and set to work to organise it. The principles governing
organisation of material presented in Chapter 2 will assist you, but
remember that beginnings and endings are of particular importance in a
talk. Your beginning must arouse interest in your material or enlist
sympathetic attention to your viewpoint. Allow your own enthusiasm to
show from the start; if possible, show too that your subject is of personal
importance to the audience. Your ending must be carefully thought out.
Do not go on too long. Many a speaker, having made a number of points
effectively, has destroyed his impact on the audience because he felt that
he had not talked long enough. What comes last is best remembered by
the audience. Your natural ending is therefore either a rapid summary of
your principal points or a forceful presentation of the point that you
particularly wish the audience to carry away with it. The old dictum:
*Tell them what you are going to say; say it; then tell them what you have
said* has much to commend it. Repetition is an essential part of good
spoken communication; the Rx has no second opportunity to grasp what
you are saying unless you provide it.

Some speakers find it helpful to write out their opening and closing sentences in full and to have these with them. You should certainly not write more of your talk than that – a talk which is read, or is writing memorised, carries no conviction, unless you are exceedingly skilful in writing in such a way that it sounds like speech (as in broadcasting, for example).

Even full notes are more of a handicap than an aid. The speaker who is continually referring to his notes is speaking most of the time to his chest rather than to the audience, and presents the top of his head for inspection rather than his face. Ideal as a stand-by during a talk is a list of the principal topics of your discourse, clearly printed (so that you do not have to peer) on a half postcard held in the palm of the hand. If you have prepared thoroughly, these headings are all you will need.

B. Delivery

You are bound to feel a little nervous before you start, especially if you are a beginner. One or two very slow, very deep, breaths help to calm you down. Then go straight into your talk with something to interest your audience. Nervousness and selfconsciousness will soon disappear as you sense your hold on the audience tightening.

Speaking directly to the audience increases your hold over it. You should, however, avoid fixing your gaze on any particular face. Your eyes should focus just above the heads of the back row of your audience (assuming a level seating arrangement). You should keep still – not rigidly to attention but not walking up and down or twisting your fingers together, or turning one foot over and back continually. Mannerisms distract the audience from what you have to say – if you throw up the chalk almost the entire concentration of the audience is on whether you will catch it.

Speak clearly, with adequate volume for the size of room (but no more – audiences do not like being shouted at). Speak slowly enough for your points to have their full impact. Pauses between sentences are a better way of slowing your delivery than pauses between words. Regular pauses between sentences disguise too the moment when you have to pause a little longer than usual because you are not quite sure how to put the next point. If you remain calm, an audience will in fact accept your remaining silent for a considerable time while you think out what to say next – silences never seem so long to the audience as they do to you. Noises such as 'um' and 'eh', at moments when you are at a loss for a word, irritate the audience and should be eradicated from your delivery.

Make full use of the advantages of spoken communication over written. Use gesture, facial expression, stress emphasis, pauses, variations of pitch and speed of delivery, to draw attention to your main points and to avoid monotony. Many beginners deliver their talks in a dreary monotone as if they themselves were bored – you cannot hope to interest an audience if you do not even sound interested yourself.

C. Timing and feedback

There are two types of timing that affect the public speaker.

First he must ensure that his talk lasts for approximately the time expected of him. If he runs out of material considerably earlier than the organisers had expected he causes embarrassment to all, including himself. On the other hand, to go on after time throws a strain on the audience and is often resented. Accurate timing of this type comes only with experience but during preparation the time that the talk is to take must be borne in mind. Speeds of delivery vary considerably but as a very rough guide you can assume you will probably speak at about 150 words a minute. During the talk an eye should be kept on the time so that adjustment can be made as the talk goes on.

The second type of timing is a matter of adjusting your speed of delivery to the reception speed of the audience. If a second point is made before the first is fully absorbed, both points will be inadequately communicated. Long pauses between points when the audience is absorbing the points rapidly and easily lead to boredom and distracted concentration. Successful timing of this kind depends partly on previous experience and partly on rapid reception of feedback from the audience. The glazed eye, the restless movement of feet, even the way people are sitting on their chairs – these are the indicators that you are going too fast or too slow. They are more easily 'read' with a small group, but even with a very large audience the alert speaker is aware of feedback; he knows whether the audience is with him or not.

Lack of response from the audience may be caused by other faults than those of timing. Your vocabulary may be unsuitable; your assessment of their previous knowledge of the subject wrong; your manner·of delivery monotonous or infectiously sleepy; perhaps they just cannot hear you. It is part of your job as an oral communicator to try to find out the cause of an unfavourable feedback and correct this as your talk goes on. This will often be a matter of trial and error, and sometimes you will not succeed; but the attempt to amend what is displeasing the audience must always be made.

V. ORAL COMMUNICATION TO INDIVIDUALS AND SMALL GROUPS

A substantial amount of the day-to-day communication that goes on in any business is spoken communication between individuals (face-to-face communication) or between an individual and a small group (committee work, oral reporting to a board, instructions given to a group of subordinates, etc.).

Although it is written communication that is feared and avoided by the lower ranks of an organisation it is oral communication that is thus treated by those nearer the top. It is easier to dismiss a man in writing than face to face; a proposal can be turned down in a memo without giving the proposer a chance for last-minute arguments; unpopular decisions and rulings are more easily pinned to a notice board than told to the men concerned in person.

Writing has the advantages that it can be more easily kept unemotional and that a permanent record of the communication exists for future reference. Oral communication has the advantages of immediate feedback (you can see whether you have been understood) and that you can have no doubt that the communication has been made (how can you ever be sure that the Rx has read your written message?). Oral communication also allows much greater opportunity for friendliness and establishing good relations.

Where the communication chain consists of one Rx and one Tx only, the advantages of oral communication probably outweigh the disadvantages, though even with a line as short as this it is desirable to confirm the more important oral communications by memos. With longer lines distortions creep in as oral messages are conveyed down, or up, a communication chain. American experiments indicate that the greatest loss of detail in oral communication occurs at the second stage (i.e. when the first Rx becomes a Tx and passes the message on), and that false additions to the message and distortions of what remains of the original message become very marked by the fourth stage of a chain.

The principal problem in oral communication is ensuring that the Rx continues to listen. A brisk lively voice helps, and you should watch the face (or faces) of the Rx to detect first signs of misunderstanding or loss of concentration. Vigorous language with avoidance of clichés also helps.

Barriers between you and your Rx may include: your face, your clothes, your accent, your tone. Only the last of these is much within your control. If the Rx does not like your face this is a serious disadvantage to your power of communication; you can reduce it by at least trying to look friendly. Your clothes may mark you out as earning more money, doing a more sedentary job, or being of higher rank, than your Rx, and this may antagonise him (them). With some Rxs a sports jacket may not carry as much authority as a lounge suit. A beard, long hair, trendy clothes, not wearing a tie – such things may arouse quite sharp opposition in the Rx. You can do little about this but to avoid extremes, and to dress fairly conservatively. Your accent may mark you out as public-school educated or of working-class origin, and with certain Rxs either can be a handicap. It is difficult to eradicate class accents of this kind and attempts to do so often sound ridiculous.

Tone, however, you can control. An overbearing bullying tone, or a patronising one, is very harmful to communication. Friendliness, helpfulness, reasonableness, patience – these are what your tone should convey, and, above all, sincerity.

Small groups are in some ways more difficult to talk to than a large audience. The large audience is anonymous and develops a group response to you that is usually predominantly cooperative. With small groups, individuals stand out; a single antagonistic element in a small group can be very harmful. Differences between members of the group become apparent and are threatening all the time to break the group into a number of separate people difficult to communicate with equally at the same time. A blanket treatment for all will not work and you have to be alert for feedback from individuals and deal with this individually, while not allowing any one person to dominate the group that is your Rx. Usually a much more intimate and relaxed approach is possible than with a large audience, and some informality of manner and language is often helpful.

Face-to-face communication with individuals is the simplest form of oral communication. You have only one Rx to think about and the feedback indications from him are comparatively easy to read. Your Rx has also plenty of opportunity (provided you do not insist on talking all the time yourself) of becoming a Tx in his turn; complete two-way communication is possible as it never is with a group. When it is your turn to be the Rx do listen; do not merely wait for the other man to stop so that you can start again – that is the commonest cause of communication breakdown between individuals. When he is talking, continue to watch his facial expression, while concentrating also on the subject matter of what he has to say; do not spend so much time thinking how to reply to his first points that you do not even hear his subsequent ones. If he looks like bringing up more points than you can easily carry in your head, stop him for a moment while you deal with what he has said so far. This does not mean that you can feel at liberty to interrupt him whenever you like. If you do this, he will forget what he was going to say and your mutual communication will be that much the less complete.

VI. ORAL REPORTS

Oral reports should present little difficulty if the recommendations of the last two sections are borne in mind. The more formal oral report, such as the report of an officer at a meeting of an organisation, offers problems similar to those confronting the public speaker, and the problems are met in the same way. Fuller notes than for a speech are, however, necessary and this could be one occasion when the whole thing is written in advance and merely read out.

The less formal oral report (as when you are called in by the boss to give him your version of what happened or are required to report progress to a committee) should be treated as no more than a special example of oral communication to an individual or group.

VII. EXERCISES

Exercise A

1. Give as many meanings as you can to the following sentences by varying the stress emphasis.
2. Write out sentences which fully express these variations of meaning.
   a. What are you doing here?
   b. The complete sales figures will probably not be published this year.
   c. Your action has not been entirely justified by this letter.
   d. The whole course is not essential for men employed full-time in advertising agencies.

For Exercises B, C, and D the tutor or a member of the group should act as chairman and introduce you briefly. Start your talk with 'Mr Chairman, Gentlemen' or 'Mr Chairman, Ladies' or 'Mr Chairman, Ladies and Gentlemen' as appropriate.

Exercise B

Prepare and deliver a three-minute talk on the town or village you come from (or district, if a large town or city). Comment from group and tutor.

Exercise C

Prepare and deliver a four-minute talk on a hobby, sport, or similar activity that you are interested in. This should be tape-recorded and played back to you. Your own comments first, followed by those of group and tutor.

Exercise D

Prepare and deliver a six-minute talk on a subject of your choice. If you say 'um' or 'eh' your audience is to repeat this after you each time, or – if this is considered too noisy – raise their hands each time.

Exercise E

1. If you have a job, explain to the group what your duties are. Imagine the group are new members of the firm who will have to carry out the same duties. If you are a full-time student without a job, explain the rules of a game, or the rules of a club you belong to, as you might to those new to the game or club.
2. Answer questions from the group.

Exercise F

If you are working in a group, each member should produce a letter on some business topic requiring a reply. The subject matter should be simple and non-technical. These letters are then distributed at random through the group and replies 'dictated' by those who receive them. It is advantageous if replies are made onto dictating machines or tape recorders in a language laboratory, so that you can play your recording back to yourself, note your own faults, and rerecord to improve clarity of diction. If you are on your own, you should practise dictation into a tape recorder, so that you become aware of your own faults, and can check if you are correcting them.

Exercise G

The group should divide into pairs and perform the following telephone roles:
a. Student and registrar – enquiring what room a certain subject will be taught in that night.
b. Business man and hotel receptionist – booking a room for an overnight stay.
c. Customer and dry cleaners – enquiring why a suit for dry-cleaning (quote receipt number) promised for the previous Saturday has not been delivered.
d. Sales representative and sales manager – confirming a delivery date.
e. Two business men, Tompkins and Smethers – arranging for Tompkins to be met by Smethers off a certain train.
The member of the pair initiating the conversation should work out details such as times and dates in advance, but should not let his partner

know these before the conversation takes place. Members of each pair should take it in turns to initiate the dialogue. The aim is to complete the conversation in the shortest possible time without gabbling, or sounding impolite. It is desirable to have a third person time the pair (a watch with a good seconds hand is all that is needed). Alternatively dialogues can be recorded and timing worked out from the rev-counter of the tape recorder.

Chapter 14

Meetings

I. GROUP DECISIONS AND MANAGERIAL DECISIONS

Apart from face-to-face communication with individuals, the most important application of oral communication in business is the meeting.

The range of meetings that readers are likely to be concerned with (if not as organisers at least as amongst those present) extends from such extremely formal occasions as the annual general meeting of a company to the informal meeting called by a manager in order to discuss some aspect of their work with members of his command. This range may be divided into three principal categories – formal meetings, committee meetings, and command meetings.

Formal meetings and committee meetings have this in common – they are intended to produce group decisions, by some method of voting. The person controlling such meetings (usually called the 'chairman') is bound by prescribed or traditional rules of procedure. Command meetings on the other hand are called by managers as a communication device, to enable them to obtain information from their subordinates or convey information to them. Opinions may be sought but the manager alone is responsible for making decisions and there is no point therefore in taking a vote. The manager is free to devise his own procedure.

It is most important to distinguish clearly between the group-decision meetings and the command meetings that you attend. In the first the decision is a joint responsibility decided by a majority vote, and once the decision is made you must give it support even if you had previously voted against it, or cease to be a member of the organisation. In the second you may state facts or express opinions as required by your manager, but you are not able to influence the decision in any other way. The decision is binding on you not because it is a group responsibility, but simply because you are the subordinate of the man who makes the decision.

As for organising meetings, it will probably be several years before readers will be in managerial positions requiring them to communicate with subordinates by means of command meetings. Their immediate chances of experience in organising meetings are much more likely to be in connection with the formal or committee meetings of societies and clubs of which they are members – group-decision meetings. For this reason, although the command meeting plays such an important part in business communication, this chapter gives primary attention to the group-decision meeting.

II. FORMAL MEETINGS

Formal meetings follow set procedures which may be for public meetings those established by custom and precedent, or for private meetings those prescribed by standing orders of public authorities, by articles of association of bodies registered under the Companies Acts, or by the rules of organisations not trading for profit (i.e. social, educational, or recreational clubs and societies). 'Public' meetings are those on matters of public concern, or held in a public place, or to which the public or a section of the public is admitted (with or without payment). 'Private' meetings are ones which are of sectional concern only, or held on private premises, or to which admission is restricted.

By far the commonest type of formal meeting is the private meeting where attendance is limited to membership – this would include the meetings of registered bodies such as joint stock and other companies, or trade unions, and the business meetings of clubs and other special interest organisations.

Although some readers of this book doubtless aspire to becoming secretaries of registered bodies, it will be many years before they succeed. All readers are, however, quite likely to be able to obtain practice in the art of being a secretary by becoming secretary to an organisation not trading for profit (for example a college club) and are advised to seize such an opportunity if offered. It is for this reason that material in this chapter pertaining to formal meetings is illustrated rather from the meetings of such organisations than from those of registered bodies.

III. COMMITTEE MEETINGS

A committee may be defined as a small body of people appointed by a parent body to meet to discuss certain matters (defined by terms of reference) with a view to making group decisions on behalf of, or group recommendations to, the parent body. Such committees may be homogeneous – that is to say with all members of similar interests or perhaps similar status – mixed, or joint. The joint committee which represents both management and staff is of special value in improving communication within a firm.

IV. COMMAND MEETINGS

Within any firm or public authority where managers are aware of the importance of communication a large number of informal meetings will take place between managers and their subordinates (or *commands*). Such meetings have various names in various organisations – *staff meetings, conferences, manager's meetings* etc. – but in this book are called *command meetings*.

Two types of command meeting can be distinguished – the extended-command meeting, and the immediate-command meeting.

THE EXTENDED-COMMAND MEETING is a meeting called by a manager so that he can communicate orally to all those he has under his control. Except at the lowest levels of management, this will mean a large meeting where the manager can do no more than address all present and answer questions. It is therefore essentially public speaking that is required of him; considerable attention was devoted to this subject in the preceding chapter, and no more need be added here.

IMMEDIATE-COMMAND MEETINGS are between the manager and those directly responsible to him. These will be small meetings, permitting two-way communication. They will be called whenever a manager feels the need to explain, or to sound opinion, or to exchange information more rapidly than is possible by writing. In departments where there is a tradition of consultation and good communication, such meetings may, in fact, take place as a result of a request to a manager by his subordinates for clarification of certain points.

Before calling an immediate-command meeting a manager must be clear in his mind whether he is calling the meeting to tell, or to discuss and consult. It should, of course, as often as possible be for the latter purpose, to permit feedback, and the inclusion of staff suggestions in the final version of a project. Discussion and consultation must take place before the manager has reached his decision. To invite discussion, for example, of a scheme after he is fully committed to it, is to invite trouble. If the scheme meets with reasoned opposition, or hostility, he must either make a mockery of the whole concept of consultation by ignoring criticisms, or appear indecisive to his own manager by a reversal of his previous opinion – the latter being much the less harmful of the alternatives open to him.

Informal meetings of this kind are often not minuted and the agenda may well exist only in the mind of the convener. The latter should make every effort to produce a relaxed and friendly atmosphere where the difference of rank between himself and the group is not permitted to stifle the free airing of views. At the same time he should see that discussion is relevant and that it never moves outside the area in which he is the appropriate person to make decisions.

The higher the level of manager who is convening the immediate-command meeting, the more formal it tends to become. Meetings between the principal executive and his departmental managers, for example, will usually have a typed and circulated agenda, and be minuted by his secretary.

Minuting of command meetings is, in fact, desirable at all levels since it preserves a record of decisions reached. In recognition of the fact that such decisions are not group decisions a form of words such as *The Sales Manager decided that* . . . should be used rather than the styles shown in Section X of this chapter, which refers to minuting of group-decision meetings only.

V. NOTICE

For all meetings, adequate notice must be given to those who are to attend; the meetings of registered bodies, indeed, will normally be considered invalid if every member has not been notified.

Notice may be oral, written, or by public advertisement. For informal meetings oral notice is often sufficient, but for formal private meetings and committee meetings written notice is desirable. For public meetings advertisement, combined with oral and written notices to those thought to be interested, is usual.

The notice must state the date, time, and place of meeting. It is essential that it be given early enough for the recipient to have a reasonable chance of attending, and desirable that it should be early enough for him to be able to keep the occasion free of other engagements. Notice of formal private meetings must be sent to every person entitled to be present; the rules of the organisation usually specify how many clear days before the meeting.

The form of written notice ranges from a friendly 'memo' for an informal meeting to the strictly controlled legalistic language of the notices sent out by registered bodies. The notice for the annual general meeting of a large limited company (usually printed) will read something like this:

ADPRESS ENGINEERING LTD

Notice is hereby given that the Tenth Annual General Meeting of the Shareholders of the above named Company will be held at The Assembly Rooms, High Street, Bromhill, on the 19th day of August

19.. at 11.00 hours for the purpose of considering the Directors'
Report and Statement of Accounts for the year ending 31st March,
19..; of declaring a dividend; of electing Directors and appointing
Auditors; of transacting any other general business of the Company
requiring transaction. A member entitled to attend and vote is entitled
to appoint a proxy to vote instead of him; such proxy need not be a
member of the Company.

Dated this 27th day of July, 19..
By order of the Board,
James Harrington
Secretary

Social and recreational groups are less formal than this and the notice
usually takes the form of a letter:

BROMHILL DRAMA GROUP

10 Croft Road,
Bromhill, Kent.
BRO45 5TA
27th July, 19..

Dear . . .

The Annual General Meeting of the group
will take place at The Assembly Rooms, High
Street, Bromhill, on 19th August 19.. at
19.15 hours, and I hope you will find it
convenient to attend.

A copy of the agenda is attached.

Yours faithfully,
Sheila Lavington
Secretary

VI. AGENDA

An 'agenda' is simply a list of items to be considered during a meeting.
It is particularly associated with the formal private meeting, though the
more formal type of committee meeting or command meeting may also
have an agenda prepared in advance. For most informal meetings no
written agenda is prepared, though the convener is well advised to write
down for his own benefit a list of points he wishes to deal with. Agenda
for private meetings are prepared by the secretary of the organisation in
consultation with the chairman. Agenda for committees may be similarly

prepared by the clerk or secretary to the committee; or, for small committees, by the chairman himself.

The purpose of the agenda is to guide the chairman through the meeting and to give prior indication of what is to be discussed at the meeting to those attending. The agenda should therefore be circulated with the notice or incorporated with it. Even in the most informal circumstances the convener of a meeting should normally let those attending know what the meeting is about, so that they can prepare their ideas in advance.

In its simplest form the agenda will consist of a list of items, typed underneath each other, and numbered in the order in which they will be taken by the chairman. More elaborate agenda will include brief notes on the items. Items for discussion should, as often as possible, be already in the form of motions at the agenda stage and their proposers and seconders known.

Meetings vary greatly in character but the following is the most usual order of events at formal private meetings. Of course, not all these items will necessarily appear on every agenda.

1. Election of chairman (if necessary)
2. Reading of notice of meeting by secretary (optional)
3. Reading of minutes of previous meeting by secretary
4. Points arising from minutes
5. Reading of correspondence by secretary
6. Chairman's opening remarks
7. Business adjourned from last meeting (if any)
8. Financial matters (treasurer's report, circulation of accounts etc.)
9. Reports by committees
10. Election of officers (if necessary)
11. First motion moved and seconded (the wording of the motion should, if possible, appear on the agenda)
12. Further motions and points for discussion of which prior notice has been given (specified on the agenda)
13. Date of subsequent meeting
14. Any other business (this item is included to permit minor points to be raised; it is not intended for important matters of which prior notice should have been given)
15. Vote of thanks to chairman
16. Reply by chairman
17. Meeting declared closed by chairman.

The last three items do not always appear on the agenda sheet that is circulated, and in fact the chairman is not always formally thanked.

The agenda is sometimes worded as a series of titles for the stages of the business transacted (as above); sometimes as imperatives to the chairman (*Declare meeting closed*); sometimes as future tense constructions (*The chairman will declare the meeting closed*). The method used should be consistent within the one agenda.

VII. DRAFTING MOTIONS

In a formal meeting of group-decision type no matter should be debated that has not been proposed in the form of a motion. It is usual also for such a motion to be seconded; few chairman would permit the discussion of an unseconded motion, since it so clearly has no support.

For the meetings of large deliberative bodies it is necessary for all motions to be in writing, signed by the proposer, and submitted in advance. In less completely formal circumstances, such as the business meetings of social and recreational organisations, it is common for the wording of the motion to be submitted orally at the time of raising the matter. In the meetings of committees, matters are often discussed before a motion is formulated, the stimulus for discussion being a letter, a report, or simply the wish of a member to sound opinion on a certain point.

The wording of a motion is traditionally introduced by the word *That*. Thus a motion to a Joint Consultative Council might read:

> *That a committee be formed to consider methods of staggering working hours to avoid traffic congestion and overloading of public transport at 09.00 and 17.30 hours.*

It is very important that the wording should be clear and unambiguous so that nobody is in any doubt what he is voting about.

Proposals to amend the wording of motions before the meeting are drafted similarly. Thus if it was felt by a member that congestion at lunch-time was also important he might propose the amendment:

> *That the words '12.30, 13.30' be inserted between '09.00' and 'and 17.30 hours'.*

Amendments are voted on before the original motion. If the amendment is lost, the meeting proceeds to discuss the original motion. If it is carried, the modification in the wording suggested is made by the chairman and the meeting then considers the motion (now called 'the substantive motion') in its new form.

When a motion is carried it becomes a 'resolution'

VIII. MAKING NOTES

Undoubtedly the best way of making notes at a meeting is by shorthand. A verbatim note of the entire meeting is then possible, although rarely required; the note taken even by a skilled shorthand writer will usually be selective. Where it is necessary for an extensive note of proceedings to be taken at important meetings, a shorthand writer or shorthand-typist should be present to supply the secretary with a note.

Individuals present at the meeting and requiring notes normally have to make their own, and these will need to be highly selective if shorthand is not used. What is usually required is a note that will give the gist of what was said on matters having future reference. The note is to remind in the future. How much detail is required for the note to be an adequate reminder varies greatly with the individual. Many write very full notes, the composition of which prevents the writer from contributing fully to the meeting while he is there, and which are laborious to read through afterwards. Others scribble down cryptic one-word mnemonics that are of no help at all when the notebook is consulted later. What is right for the individual between these two unsatisfactory extremes will be found only by trial and error; but the aim should always be to take the minimum note that will serve the purpose.

Notes should be selective and systematic, material being broken down into logical subdivisions. Maximum use should be made of such aids to order as headings, underlinings, numbering, and lettering. In selecting and compressing material for notes, precisely the same skills are employed as in précis; practice at the one activity will improve performance in the other. Arrangement and organisation of notes will be according to the principles detailed in Chapter 2.

IX. REPORTS AND MINUTES DISTINGUISHED

When discussing meetings, it is important to distinguish between reports and minutes.

Reports in this context may be of three kinds:

1. A report by an individual (officer, official, expert witness etc.) to a meeting

2. The specific report by a committee to its parent body on the matter the committee has been required to investigate

3. A general account of what occurred at a meeting. This may be a verbatim report (as Hansard) or, more usually, a selective survey intended perhaps for the Press or for absent members who require more detail

than minutes provide, or one prepared by a representative for the benefit of those he represents at the meeting.

Minutes are primarily a record of decisions reached. Once signed by the chairman – at that or a subsequent meeting – minutes of formal meetings are legally binding, may not be altered, and may be submitted in court as evidence.

Essentially, minutes constitute a briefly worded record of the following:

1. Date and place of meeting
2. The names of those present (only number for a large meeting)
3. The items of business transacted, with the decisions reached – these will of course be in the same order as the agenda (unless the chairman sought the meeting's permission to vary the order); the agenda is therefore a most useful guide to the secretary in preparing minutes.

X. MINUTES OF GROUP-DECISION MEETINGS

Minutes must be 1. accurate, 2. clear and unambiguous, 3. brief, 4. self-explanatory. They should be in past tense reported speech (see Appendix II). It is recommended that each minute be numbered and, preferably, supplied with a title.

Although probably all who have experience in drafting minutes would agree with all these points, there is wide disagreement as to their precise interpretation, and minutes vary considerably from organisation to organisation and from secretary to secretary.

The most noticeable variation is in finding a point of balance between two requirements – to be brief but to ensure that the minute is self-explanatory. At one extreme, some secretaries maintain that only the decision itself need be minuted, and with a successful motion for instance will confine themselves to its wording, preceded by 'It was resolved' or 'Resolved'. At the other extreme, some – especially secretaries of social and recreational groups – will include not only such details as the names of the proposer and seconder (which is reasonable enough) but also details of the voting and a summary of the principal arguments put forward by speakers in the discussion. Legitimate versions of these extremes are exemplified by the following two methods of minuting a discussion, by an executive committee, leading to the selection of a suitable venue for an annual conference.

METHOD I
Annual Conference Venue

   It was resolved:

   1. *That the Royal Pavilion be adopted as conference centre for 19..*

    2. *That fifteen-minute adjournments for refreshments morning and afternoon be provided for in the conference programme.*

METHOD 2
Venue of annual conference

A further detailed discussion of the relative merits of the Royal Pavilion and the Palace Ballroom took place. It was generally agreed that the Royal Pavilion had better acoustics but that its refreshment facilities were inadequate. There was some disagreement over the suitability of seating accommodation provided for delegates at the Royal Pavilion. Mr. Carter proposed and Miss Branson seconded 'That the Royal Pavilion be adopted as conference venue for 19.., the refreshment difficulty being met by a fifteen-minute adjournment morning and afternoon'. The proposal was carried unanimously.

Both are sound minutes. It is a question of what the purpose of the minute is. In business, minutes serve only to provide a legally binding record of decisions for future action. The first form of minute serves this purpose. With clubs and societies, the aim often seems to be to provide through the minutes an outline history of the organisation, and a record of what took place for the benefit of future officers or members who missed a meeting. The second minute would fulfil this purpose.

Both minutes are, however, certainly on the extreme margins of what could be considered sound. Any attempt to compress the first further would make it less than self-explanatory. The second is rather wordy, in a style more appropriate to a report, and if a less summary treatment of the arguments leading to the resolution had been attempted would have laid the secretary open to possible attack on the grounds of misrepresentation of a member's viewpoint.

The most satisfactory minutes lie between these extremes. They consist of two parts:

1. A PREAMBLE. This makes clear the stimulus – motion, report, letter – and sometimes gives a broad indication of the principal argument leading to the resolution.

2. THE RESOLUTION. This makes clear for future action or reference what has been decided.

Various styles are used for drafting minutes on these lines. For example:

a. *On a motion by Mr —.*
It was resolved: or *Resolved:*
That etc.

b. *Mr — proposed, Mr — seconded and it was resolved:*
That etc.

c. *Mr — proposed and Mr — seconded: 'That* etc.' *The proposal was carried.*

Where the stimulus is not a motion but a letter or report, the preamble has to be more explanatory. For example, the following is not a satisfactory minute:

Shannon Gutters

On a report by the Borough Engineer.
Resolved: That the action referred to be adopted.

What is required if the minute is to be self-explanatory is something like this:

Shannon Gutters

The Borough Engineer reported that Shannon Ltd. had completed the first contract, for relining gutters of 100 dwellings; that they had submitted quotations (at the same rates as hitherto) for a further 100 dwellings; and that in order to provide continuity of work he recommended acceptance of this quotation.
Resolved: That the quotation referred to be accepted.

The wording of the preamble of the second version also avoids the curious non-sentence: *On a report by the Borough Engineer* – a form common in minutes but with nothing to be said in its favour.

The word *recommended* is sometimes substituted for *resolved* where the minute is that of a committee which on this matter can make only a recommendation to its parent body.

Not every item in minutes can be shown as a resolution or recommendation. Date and place of meeting are frequently incorporated in the heading:

Minutes of the Annual General Meeting of the Bromhill Drama Group held on 19th August 19.. at The Assembly Rooms, High Street, Bromhill.

The next item in minutes is to show those present.
They are shown by name, in a small meeting:

Present: J. Fitchins (in the Chair); Mesdames: Lavington; Miller; Thomas; Messrs: Adams; Freeman; James

or number, in a large meeting:

Two hundred and forty members were present. Mr. J. Fitchins was in the Chair.

It is not necessary to minute apologies for absence, unless these are the subject of a resolution (for example, to send condolences). The numbered items of the minutes start with the reading and signing of the previous minutes.

These may be minuted either descriptively:

Minutes of previous meeting

The Secretary read the minutes of the meeting held on . . . and these were thereupon signed by the Chairman

or as a resolution:

Minutes of previous meeting

Resolved: That the minutes of the meetings on . . . be signed as a correct record.

From this point onwards, items should be numbered in the order in which they occurred. The secretary should attempt to show as many items as possible as decisions. Even expressions of thanks, regret, congratulations etc. can be shown as resolutions:

Resolved: That the committee's regrets at the absence of Mr — owing to illness be conveyed to Mr — by the Secretary with the Committee's wishes for his speedy recovery.

Where reports, letters etc. are read out but it is decided to take no action (i.e. there is no resolution) they are minuted as 'received':

Proposed joint production

A letter from the Bromhill Barnstormers proposing a joint production for 19.. was received.

If it was intended to do something about this proposal, the minute would read:

Proposed joint production

The Secretary read a letter from the Bromhill Barnstormers proposing a joint production for 19...
Resolved: That the Secretary write to the Secretary of the Bromhill Barnstormers proposing the formation of a joint committee of four (two members from each society) to prepare detailed proposals.

In the attempt to reduce wording many secretaries write their minutes in semi-note style. Specifically they omit *the, and, a* etc. Thus:

Treasurer reported increased number of members had paid subscriptions in advance when the full form would read:

> *The Treasurer reported that an increased number of members had*
> *paid their subscriptions in advance.*

The improved readability of the full form would seem a greater advantage than the small saving of space resulting from semi-note style. Where minutes are of considerable bulk, however, and have to be printed (as local authority minutes) it is possible that this saving is worth while.

XI. EXERCISES

Exercise A. *Committee practice work with films*

Films of short committee meetings (lasting about twenty minutes) are available from the Commercial Educational Department of the London Chamber of Commerce. Originally intended as examinations in Meetings, for the Private Secretaries' Diploma Examination, they can be used to provide practice in note-taking, minuting, or reporting. If the examination papers for the year of the film hired (the films are classified by year) are also obtained these will provide a memorandum and instructions for a secretarial task to be carried out for that particular filmed meeting. Instructions are intended for shorthand-typists but can be readily adapted for use with longhand.

Exercise B. *Committee practice work without films*

Committee work can be simulated in class:

1. By choosing a topic of general current interest to discuss and attempting a group decision.
2. By selecting an agenda of debatable topics within the college (e.g. staggering of breaks, increasing number of books on loan to students from the library at one time). Motions can be prepared in advance or formulated during discussion.

For both the above methods at least one student should be allocated the task of minuting the meeting.

It may be necessary for the class tutor to act as chairman initially, but this role should be taken over by students, in turn, as soon as possible.

Correct meeting discipline must be maintained and all remarks addressed to the Chair.

Exercise C. *Command meeting practice work*

This can be simulated by role-playing, one member of a group being selected as convening manager and the others taking roles as his immediate command. For example, the convening manager can be the Managing

Director, and his subordinates the Office Manager, Chief Accountant, Personnel Manager, Sales Manager, Research and Development Manager, Chief Engineer etc. Or the meeting can be at a lower managerial level – e.g. between one of these departmental managers (for example the Chief Accountant) and his immediate command. Topics, or one topic, appropriate to the level of managerial decision selected are chosen, within the limits of the knowledge of the group (some reading-up for the occasion will be necessary) and information and recommendations made to the convening manager who then makes his decision based on this. Either the convening manager or one of the group selected as his secretary should keep minutes of decisions reached.

Exercise D. Consideration of actual minutes

The group obtains copies of current minutes of the local authority (probably the most accessible of professionally competent minutes). Selected minutes are then discussed from the following viewpoints:
1. Is it self-explanatory?
2. Is it unambiguous?
3. Is there a preamble? If not, why not?
4. What kind of language is used (tone, clarity etc.)?
5. Is it in semi-note style?

Exercise E

1. As P. F. Sellars of 13 Granville Street, Bromhill, Kent, BRO45 7AL, write to the Borough Engineer requesting renumbering of your house to 12A Granville Street.
2. This letter is put before the Highways Committee which agrees to the request. Write the relevant minute (including a title).

Exercise F

Imagine you are the secretary of a college club or other similar social or recreational group. The organisation can be real or fictitious, but choose an activity of which you have some knowledge. The annual general meeting is about to take place.
Draft 1. The notice of meeting to be sent to members
      2. The agenda
      3. The minutes
      4. A short report of the meeting for the Press.
You should include one motion of which prior notice has been given; one letter which leads to a resolution at the meeting; one letter about which no action is to be taken.

Part IV

I. STATISTICS FOR INTERPRETATION

Statistics 1

All-Industries Index of Production
(1958 = 100)

	Unadjusted		Seasonally adjusted	
	1967	1968	1967	1968
January	131	135	132	136
February	137	142	132	137
March	134	146	132	138
April	137	136	133	137
May	134	143	132	139
June	136	140	133	139
July	124	130	133	140
August	115	125	133	141
September	134	140	133	139
October	138	146	134	141
November	142	150	135	143
December	138	142	138	143

Source: Central Statistical Office

1. What do you assume 'seasonally adjusted' to mean?
   What sort of adjustments would have to be made?
2. Give a brief account (about 150 words) of production tendencies in 1968 making comparisons with 1967 and 1958.

Statistics 2

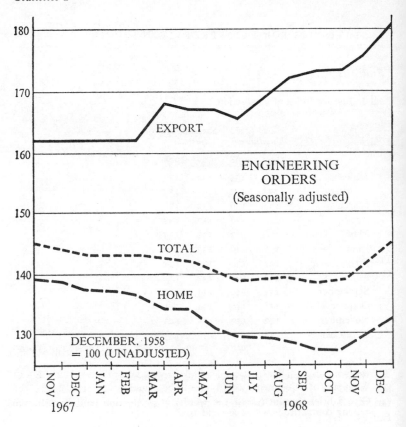

In about 150 words attempt a verbal interpretation of the information graphically represented above. You should make specific reference to:

1. Comparison between 1968 and 1958 performance;
2. The general pattern of total and home orders during 1968;
3. Differences between this and the trend of export orders – remember 1968 was a year in which Great Britain was struggling to reduce an unfavourable trade gap between exports and imports.

Statistics 3

Continental areas	Population millions	Teachers millions	Teachers per cent of population	Teacher shortage from 0·86 per cent norm millions
Africa	288	0·69	0·24	1·79
N. and C. America	291	2·94	1·01	—0·44
S. America	165	0·98	0·59	0·44
Asia (less USSR)	1 742	4·48	0·26	10·52
Europe (less USSR)	442	2·95	0·67	0·85
USSR	231	1·90	0·82	0·09
Australasia	14	0·13	0·93	—0·01
	3 173	14·07	0·44	13·69
				—0·45
				13·24
Country				
Sweden	7·7	0·075	0·98	
France	50	0·460	0·92	
Canada	20	0·239	1·19	
UK	54	0·464	0·86	
USA	195	2·393	1·23	

Statistics derived from figures published by the Bureau International d'Education (Geneva)

Reprinted from *Journal of the Royal Society of Arts*

The above table shows the ratio of teachers to population throughout the world as divided into seven continental areas. It also shows the ratios in five countries (including the UK) within one continental area, Europe (less USSR).

1. 0·86 per cent is shown as the 'norm'.
   a. What does *norm* mean?
   b. By what standard is 0·86 per cent the norm?
   c. Express 0·86 *per cent of population* in another way
2. What is the significance of the negative percentages shown in the last column?
3. Write an article (about 150 words) entitled 'World Teacher Shortage'. You should pay particular attention to: (a) the overall situation, (b) comparison between the various continental areas, (c) comparison between those European countries about which statistics are supplied.

Statistics 4

The following table provides statistical information about road casualties in Great Britain during 1968. Write a brief account of these (200 words) stressing tendencies, and suggesting explanations of marked variations in the figures from month to month.

	TOTAL CASUALTIES		NATURE OF CASUALTY			CLASS OF ROAD USER			
	All ages	Under 15 years	Killed	Seriously injured	Slightly injured	Pedestrians	Pedal cyclists	Motor cyclists and their passengers[1]	Other drivers and their passengers
January	23 885	3 357	498	6 251	17 136	6 030	1 761	3 389	12 705
February	24 679	4 092	506	6 119	18 054	6 193	1 730	3 446	13 310
March	27 493	5 337	549	6 930	20 014	7 298	1 899	4 483	13 813
April	26 715	5 919	449	6 572	19 694	6 880	2 261	4 501	13 073
May	28 747	6 139	514	7 192	21 041	7 394	2 366	5 147	13 840
June	30 272	6 113	535	7 519	22 218	6 733	2 358	5 518	15 663
July	31 253	6 235	568	7 957	22 728	6 917	2 674	5 826	15 836
August	32 139	6 358	620	8 222	23 297	6 871	2 521	5 985	16 762
September	31 228	5 950	620	7 966	22 642	7 131	2 304	5 518	16 275
October	31 377	5 962	629	8 086	22 662	8 017	2 397	5 546	15 417
November	30 783	4 593	658	7 952	22 173	7 475	2 163	4 982	14 711
December	30 637	3 907	664	7 797	22 176	6 712	1 796	3 838	18 291

[1] Including moped riders, motor scooter riders and passengers.

Source: Ministry of Transport and Scottish Development Department

Passage 1

I have never enjoyed making a fuss about defective goods or poor
service. I loathed it when I lived in the safe anonymity of a large
city, but living as I do now in a small rural community I hesitate
before taking action. It is so easy to be noticed here and word
travels around the neighbourhood if you do anything untoward.   5
I soon became labelled 'anti-bomb', and to this was added 'anti-
fox-hunting' after an unlooked-for fracas with the local hunt. So
it was with a good deal of diffidence that I became involved in yet
another field and thus risked becoming known as 'anti-everything'!

However, so many of my purchases have developed defects   10
recently and I have had so many examples of poor and uninterested
service from a variety of sources that it has been necessary to waste
a good deal of time attempting to have matters put right. I wonder
if I have been unusually unlucky or whether the following experiences are common.   15

The first issue on which I really took a stand was over a minor
repair to my typewriter. It needed a small roller replacing on the
back so I sent it off to a firm specialising in typewriter repairs to
have it replaced, expecting to have the machine back within a few
days. It was away for six weeks. I was nearly frantic as I cannot   20
write easily without it, but eventually it was returned with a new
small roller – and a bill for £3·90. Utterly amazed, I queried
this and asked for details of how such a sum could be justified but
I did not receive any satisfactory answer. During the next few weeks
I made several further attempts, all to no avail; so, after talking it 25
over with my husband, I refused to pay the bill.

The matter was then put into the hands of the firm's solicitors
and eventually a bailiff arrived at my door to serve me with a summons. By this time I had cold feet but my husband filled in the
'defence' section of the summons form with a statement to the   30
effect that we would ask the court how they thought the replacement
of a small rubber roller could cost £3·90, and then see what
happened. By return of post we had a letter from the solicitors of
the firm concerned asking us what price we would be prepared to

pay for the job. We sent a cheque for the amount we thought   35
sufficient and heard no more of the matter.

The two other most flagrant examples concerned a new refrigerator and a new vacuum cleaner. The refrigerator was a major buy
embarked on because shopping is so difficult. Within three months
the inside lining of the door (which holds butter, milk bottles, etc.)   40
had begun to break away from the door itself. I went along to the
local showroom of the nationalised industry from which I had
purchased the fridge and asked them to do something about it. To
my astonishment I was told that nothing could be done; in effect, it
was my bad luck. As I was buying on a hire-purchase agreement   45
I refused to pay any more payments until the matter was put right.
The day after I had written explaining what I intended to do a man
arrived with a new lining which he fixed inside the door for me, but
he seemed to think that I had 'got one over' the supplier in some
crafty way. 'Other people with this trouble,' he said, 'have paid for   50
a new lining themselves.'

Shortly after this a representative from the firm who made the
refrigerator came to see me and told me that the lining should have
been replaced at once. But he also added the astonishing information
that my fridge was one of a batch which had been sent out with the   55
wrong sort of plastic used in the door. This plastic was found to
crack at low temperatures but he offered no explanation as to why
the plastic had not been tested before being used in such a way. I
was left to ruminate on those people who had paid for their own
replacements.   60

When the new vacuum cleaner packed up when we were in the
midst of a building job which caused a great deal of dirt I began to
think there really were such things as gremlins. Once more I re-
paired to the same local showroom from which I had been mis-
guided enough to purchase my vacuum cleaner and implored them   65
to send up a mechanic as soon as possible to see what was the
matter. Nothing happened. Ten days later I asked again, to be told
that they had passed on my message to the representative of the
firm which made the cleaner who had 'given the impression' he
might be up soon.   70

Another week passed. Again I asked what was happening but
by this time no one had any record of any complaint; but nevertheless, I was promised action shortly. A week later I rang in fury
to be told that there was no trace of any complaint made by me but
that they would see that a mechanic came up before the weekend.   75

On the Wednesday of the following week I spoke to the manager explaining the whole story. He told me not to be 'hasty' and promised that someone would come and put the matter right the following morning. I told him civilly that if I was let down again I would ring the head office of the firm in Middlesex which made the cleaner and also his own area manager to inform them of how I felt. I waited in throughout most of the next day but when it became obvious that nothing was going to happen I did what I had threatened to do and made my telephone calls. Then, of course, there was action. First the manager of the local showroom rang me up and told me through clenched teeth that someone would be up directly, and during the following day we received a slow stream of mechanics and representatives of the vacuum cleaner firm. Again I wonder what happens to people less persistent than I am.

There are countless other smaller examples such as the parcel dispatched per British Road Services from Exeter (a distance of 180 km) which took eleven days to get here, and the wood sent from London by the same quaint method of transport which, after eight days, has still not arrived. It could hardly have taken longer by ox wagon in the Middle Ages.

Goodness knows what the answer is. The Consumer's Association and the various local consumer groups help the customer, but the fault lies deeper than this. How can a man making, say, a vacuum cleaner in a huge concern, who spends every hour of every day of his working week doing a simple, repetitive task in the course of the mass production of the article, feel anything at all for the customer who will receive it? He probably does not even see the finished product and is only interested – and who can blame him? – in getting home to his family at the end of the day and the amount in his pay packet.

Employees in branches of large concerns, either private or nationalised, rarely feel the interest in the customer that a small family business would have. If my vacuum cleaner goes wrong within weeks of its being purchased it does not really matter much to them whether or not I am satisfied as there will be no lack of customers if I never cross the threshold again.

It seems to be assumed that in this affluent society we are all so rich that we can afford to buy expensive pieces of household equipment without caring how long they will last, be prepared to do without them for weeks if they show a defect, and be happy to throw them away within a year or two for a later model.

I have little energy to spare and feel that there are bigger issues
to fight than whether or not my refrigerator falls to pieces, but as a
housewife on a very limited budget I cannot afford to pay for other
people's mistakes. Am I taking it all too seriously?   120

Judith Cook in the *Guardian*, 28 October 1963
(decimalised and metricated version)

1. What impression of the writer have you formed after reading this article?
2. What answer would you give to the rhetorical question she asks in
her last sentence?
3. In lines 96–116 the author attempts a common fundamental explanation for all her experiences. Do you consider (*a*) that such a common
explanation is probable or (*b*) that each experience requires its own
separate explanation?
If (*a*) do you consider hers a fully satisfactory explanation? Discuss.
If (*b*) what explanation would you offer for each episode?
4. Do you detect any points in these episodes where communication failure
may have (*a*) caused the unsatisfactory service (*b*) aggravated the situation?
5. Do you consider that in any of these episodes the author would
have been treated differently if she had been a man?
6. (*a*) What is the meaning of 'safe anonymity' in the second sentence?
(*b*) Can you detect an ambiguity in this sentence?
7. What is the precise force of (*a*) *fracas* (l. 7), (*b*) *quaint* (l. 93)?
8. Comment on the following expressions (*a*) *cold feet* (l. 29), (*b*) *major
buy* (l. 38), (*c*) *fridge* (l. 43), (*d*) *packed up* (l. 61).
Do you consider these appropriate in tone? What do you assume to be
the author's motive in using them?
9. Supply a title for the passage.

Passage 2

In considering the art of teaching, the first point is the actual
teaching process, the skill of passing on to the student the benefit of
the teacher's own experience. As a definition this is too simple.
The teaching process is a two-way one which involves the student
as a learner, as well as the teacher as a teacher. The teacher's function   5
is to guide the student's learning along effective and economic lines
and to teach the student how to learn a subject rather than to teach
the subject itself. One of the objects of technical teacher training
is to make the teacher aware that effective teaching does not just
happen; it is the consequence of careful preparation along specific   10
lines.

The teacher must appreciate that education and instruction are not synonymous. A study of effective learning in classroom and other situations, treated in a practical and realistic way, must therefore be given some degree of priority in a training scheme. The function of technical education is, however, education and not simply instruction, and more subtle factors are therefore involved.

It is essential that a teacher should develop an inquiring attitude of mind and a wide outlook to enable him to make use of every opportunity, however it may arise, to widen the educational horizons and develop the understanding of his students. Such an attitude of mind, if not already in existence, must be encouraged and nurtured during training. Discussions and seminars yield good results in this field.

All too frequently the teacher considers himself as a passer-on of information, a middleman between the recognised authorities and the student. His teaching is too often no more than the provision of pre-digested text-book material for his class. This is at once not enough and too much. The student only learns by active participation. To sit and listen to a lecturer while taking an occasional note does not constitute efficient learning. The most important function of the teacher is to make the student think. The teacher who, in an effort to save the student's time, does his thinking for him, is doing the student a grave disservice.

The teacher must therefore be shown how best to prepare and present his lessons so that the student shall most effectively learn. He must be made aware of the many teaching aids now available in addition to the blackboard, whether they be the simple home-made ones or the more sophisticated commercial products. He must learn to recognise their value in raising teaching efficiency by involving more than one sensory experience.

He must also be aware that he is doing more than producing technicians, technologists or craftsmen. He must have a sufficiently wide outlook to see his subject in the broader perspective of the course generally and of the culture in which we live. The specialist teacher has a tendency to consider his own subject as the most important in the curriculum and any course of teacher training should lead him to see his subject as part of a whole. To this end the history of education and allied subjects should be studied during the training as an aid to the creation of a sense of social purpose and as a means of obtaining a deeper understanding on the part of the students.

Assuming the teacher has learnt how to prepare and present his lessons and make full use of all suitable aids, he must also be made aware of his own personal influence on the teaching process. He 55 must be shown that even good teaching methods can be enhanced if presented with interest and developed with enthusiasm, and if the subject can be suitably related to current practice via the teacher's familiarity with industry. The effect of the teacher's attitude to his work cannot be over-emphasised. Too many teachers tend to base 60 their teaching on their memories of being taught at the final stages of their own courses.

A further function of teacher training is to enable the teacher to develop the student's ability for rational thinking. This can only be achieved by means of feedback from his students. The teacher 65 must therefore be shown how to adapt his presentation in such a way as to involve the students actively. The teacher then functions as a guide rather than a dictator. His leadership of the class is more acceptable and disciplinary problems are minimised. He must be made to appreciate that his job is to teach and that in order to do 70 this he must make his teaching acceptable. To say that a class is bored or will not work is in reality a reflection on the teacher rather than the class. It is the teacher's duty to present his material in such a way that the class will be interested and consequently learn. He must set an example of logical clear thinking and of neat orderly 75 presentation which the class can emulate.

It may seem superfluous to suggest that a teacher should be able to express himself clearly and logically. This unfortunately is not so. A new entrant to the profession may never have addressed more than two or three people at a time; he may be unaware of the differ- 80 ent techniques required to speak to a group of 20 or 30 people. Too many teachers unconsciously involve themselves in nervous mannerisms or make use of stereotyped phrases and dreary monotones. A tape recorder to enable the teacher trainee to hear himself as his classes will hear him, often has a salutary effect. A further 85 failing, particularly with the specialist teacher, is to indulge in the 'jargon' of his subject on the assumption, frequently incorrect, that his students know the language. Training can help to eradicate these undesirable tendencies.

Technical Teacher Training,
The Association of Teachers in
Technical Institutions, 1963

1. What is the meaning of the following words as used in the passage: *economic* (l. 6) *specific* (l. 10) *factors* (l. 17) *nurtured* (l. 22) *seminars* (l. 23) *sophisticated* (l. 39) *curriculum* (l. 47) *stereotyped* (l. 83)?
2. Do you consider this policy statement justified in referring to teaching as an 'art' in l. 1?
3. In what ways is the gloss of the words *actual teaching process* in the first sentence too simple for a definition?
4. In what ways are *education* and *instruction* not synonymous? (l. 12)
5. In what ways is *the provision of pre-digested material* an inadequate conception of teaching? (l. 27)
6. What types of *sensory experience* can be provided during a class? (l. 41)
7. In what ways can there be feedback from a class? (l. 65)
8. What differences of technique are required for addressing 20 or 30 people as distinct from two or three?
9. List all the functions of a teacher mentioned in the passage.
10. Supply a title for the passage.

Passage 3

Metals can not only be kept with as little loss as any other commodity, scarce anything being less perishable than they are, but they can likewise, without any loss, be divided into any number of parts, as by fusion those parts can easily be reunited again; a quality which no other equally durable commodities possess, and which   5 more than any other quality renders them fit to be the instruments of commerce and circulation. The man who wanted to buy salt, for example, and had nothing but cattle to give in exchange for it, must have been obliged to buy salt to the value of a whole ox, or a whole sheep at a time. He could seldom buy less than this, because   10 what he was to give for it could seldom be divided without loss; and if he had a mind to buy more, he must, for the same reasons, have been obliged to buy double or triple the quantity, the value, to wit, of two or three oxen, or of two or three sheep. If, on the contrary, instead of sheep or oxen, he had metals to give in exchange for it,   15 he could easily proportion the quantity of the metal to the precise quantity of the commodity which he had immediate occasion for.

Different metals have been made use of by different nations for this purpose. Iron was the common instrument of commerce among the ancient Spartans; copper among the ancient Romans; gold and   20 silver among all rich and commercial nations.

Those metals seem originally to have been made use of for this purpose in rude bars, without any stamp or coinage. Thus we are told by Pliny, upon the authority of Timaeus, an ancient historian, that, till the time of Servius Tullius, the Romans had no coined money, but made use of unstamped bars of copper, to purchase whatever they had occasion for. These rude bars, therefore, performed at this time the function of money.

The use of metals in this rude state was attended with two very considerable inconveniences; first, with the trouble of weighing; and, secondly, with that of assaying them. In the precious metals, where a small difference in the quantity makes a great difference in the value, even the business of weighing, with proper exactness, requires at least very accurate weights and scales. The weighing of gold in particular is an operation of some nicety. In the coarser metals, indeed, where a small error would be of little consequence, less accuracy would, no doubt, be necessary. Yet we should find it excessively troublesome, if every time a poor man had occasion either to buy or sell a farthing's worth of goods, he was obliged to weigh the farthing. The operation of assaying is still more difficult, still more tedious, and, unless a part of the metal is fairly melted in the crucible, with proper dissolvents, any conclusion that can be drawn from it, is extremely uncertain. Before the institution of coined money, however, unless they went through this tedious and difficult operation, people must always have been liable to the grossest frauds and impositions, and instead of a pound weight of silver, or pure copper, might receive in exchange for their goods an adulterated composition of the coarsest and cheapest materials, which had, however, in their outward appearance, been made to resemble those metals. To prevent such abuses, to facilitate exchanges, and thereby to encourage all sorts of industry and commerce, it has been found necessary, in all countries that have made any considerable advances towards improvement, to affix a public stamp upon certain quantities of such particular metals as were in those countries commonly made use of to purchase goods. Hence the origin of coined money, and of those public offices called mints; institutions exactly of the same nature with those of the aulnagers and stampmasters of woollen and linen cloth. All of them are equally meant to ascertain, by means of a public stamp, the quantity and uniform goodness of those different commodities when brought to market.

Adam Smith, *The Wealth of Nations*, 1776–78

1. What is the meaning of the following words as used in the passage:
perishable (l. 2)   *fusion* (l. 4)   *durable* (l. 5)   *rude* (l. 23)
stamp (l. 23)   *function* (l. 28)   *nicety* (l. 35)   *consequence* (l. 36)
assaying (l. 40)   *crucible* (l. 42)   *adulterated* (l. 48)   *facilitate*
(l. 50)?
2. By reference to dictionaries ascertain the meaning of *aulnager*. (l. 57)
3. What does the author mean by *dissolvents* (l. 42)? What is the usual
present-day word?
4. Can you distinguish between *frauds* and *impositions*? (l. 46)
5. By today's standards there is a fault of syntax and a punctuation
error in the first sentence of this passage. Identify these.
6. What argument against barter does Adam Smith put forward?
7. What is shown to be the origin of mints?
8. Much of the punctuation of this passage is not in accordance with
modern practice. Detail the changes that would have to be made to
modernise its punctuation.
9. Make a précis of the passage in not more than (*a*) 180 words (one-
quarter) (*b*) 70 words (one-tenth). Supply a title.

Passage 4

Under some conditions, people will hold money, not simply for
early use, but as a convenient way of storing wealth for future
needs. In some of its forms, money provides a store of wealth
which is easily protected against theft or destruction – while
remaining 'liquid', that is usable at any moment. The liquidity is   5
something valuable, and can itself be 'sold'; in most societies, a man
who gives up control over a stock of money for a period (by lending
it to someone else) will expect to be repaid 'with interest', that is to
say, with a percentage added. The interest is not only a recompense
for running a risk, for it is still paid when the risk is negligible; it is   10
a recompense for the disadvantage of giving up liquidity. The
existence of an organised system of money loans is itself a great
convenience to a complex community; it makes it possible (for
instance) for a man who has a good use for money (say, to build a
new factory) to get ahead without waiting for the tedious process of   15
saving up the money from his own income.

But, after all this, what is money? There have been so many
different forms of money that it is not easy to find a consistent
definition; but I shall here define money as anything which is
widely accepted in payment for goods and services, or in discharge   20

of other business obligations. Some kinds of money not only *are*, but by law, *must be*, accepted for payment. Such money is called *legal tender*, but for my definition acceptance in fact will suffice, whether or not the acceptance is required by law.

Some kinds of money have a value apart from their value in use as money. For instance, the old gold sovereign was valuable as gold; you could melt it down, and still have something which men prized highly. The paper of a bank-note, on the other hand, is useless, and the note acquires its value simply from what is printed on it. The various coins which we use in Britain are the metal equivalents of bank-notes. The value of their metal content is much below their face value, and so they retain their face value simply because a Government has said 'It shall be so', and the people have agreed to accept the coins so certified.

It can be seen from this that it is a very important function of the State – and one which must be carefully protected against the imitations of coiners and forgers – to issue and certify money. It is convenient to have a single trustworthy central authority, producing money in forms appropriate for the carrying out of everyday transactions. Nevertheless, it sometimes happens that people accept, and even prefer, money which is actually or apparently certified by some authority other than the State. Throughout Ireland, British and Irish notes and coins circulate side by side; and the gold sovereign, dropped from our currency a generation ago, still circulates in some areas abroad.

The state-certified notes and coin are, however, really only small change. In Britain and the United States, much the largest part of the stock of money is bank money, whose visible evidence is the figures in the account books of banks of amounts standing to the credit of depositors. About £2 500 million of notes and coin are outstanding in the United Kingdom, including £185 million of coins; the notes and coin actually in circulation with the public amount to £2 000 million. But bank deposits are of the order of £7 000 million. It is true that a bank cheque is not universally accepted as money; a great many shopkeepers would refuse a cheque, on the grounds that they have no assurance that there is money to meet it in the bank. But cheques are nevertheless so widely accepted (especially for the larger transactions) that they have a dominant position in the total of money transactions.

The room for manoeuvre in making purchases, which is given by the existence of money, can be expressed another way. Money breaks the link between income and spending; it makes it possible to spend in a year less than a year's income (holding back the rest as a money stock) or to spend more than a year's income (running down a money stock). But this is potentially dangerous; for if it is possible 65 to create or destroy money, adding or subtracting it from people's store of wealth, it is possible to create inconvenient fluctuations in demand (and therefore in prices). Thus it has come to be regarded as necessary for a strong central authority, not merely to issue and certify the small change, but to control the size of the whole stock of 70 money.

C. F. Carter, *The Science of Wealth*, 1960

1. What is the meaning of the following words as used in the passage: *negligible* ((l. 10) *complex* (l. 13) *obligations* (l. 21) *dominant* (l. 58) *manoeuvre* (l. 60)?

2. How does the author establish the meaning his Rx is to assign to (a) *liquidity* (b) *money*?

3. What is meant by *Some kinds of money have a value apart from their value in use as money* (ll. 25–26)? Have the two uses of (a) *value* and (b) *money* the same area of meaning?

4. What is the force of *actually or apparently* in *money which is actually or apparently certified by some authority other than the State* (ll. 41–42)?

5. In what sense are state-certified notes and coin 'small change'?

6. What is meant by *Money breaks the link between income and spending* (ll. 61–62)?

7. Make a précis of the passage in approximately 210 words (one-quarter), and supply a title.

Passage 5

Money began in nonliterate cultures as a commodity, such as whales' teeth on Fiji; or rats on Easter Island, which were considered a delicacy, were valued as a luxury, and thus became a means of mediation or barter. When the Spaniards were besieging Leyden in 1574, leather money was issued, but as hardship increased the popu-   5
lation boiled and ate the new currency.

In literate cultures, circumstances may reintroduce commodity money. The Dutch, after the German occupation of World War II, were avid for tobacco. Since the supply was small, objects of high value such as jewels, precision instruments, and even houses were   10
sold for small quantities of cigarettes. *The Reader's Digest* recorded an episode from the early occupation of Europe in 1945, describing

how an unopened pack of cigarettes served as currency, passing
from hand to hand, translating the skill of one worker into the skill
of another as long as no one broke the seal.   15

Money always retains something of its commodity and community character. In the beginning, its function of extending
the grasp of men from their nearest staples and commodities to
more distant ones is very slight. Increased mobility of grasp and
trading is small at first. So it is with the emergence of language   20
in the child. In the first months grasping is reflexive, and the
power to make voluntary release comes only toward the end of the
first year. Speech comes with the development of the power to
let go of objects. It gives the power of detachment from the
environment that is also the power of great mobility in knowledge   25
of the environment. So it is with the growth of the idea of money
as currency rather than commodity. Currency is a way of letting
go of the immediate staples and commodities that at first serve
as money, in order to extend trading to the whole social complex.
Trading by currency is based on the principle of grasping and   30
letting go in an oscillating cycle. The one hand retains the article
with which it tempts the other party. The other hand is extended
in demand toward the object which is desired in exchange. The
first hand lets go as soon as the second object is touched, somewhat in the manner of a trapeze artist exchanging one bar for   35
another. In fact, Elias Canetti in *Crowds and Power* argues that
the trader is involved in one of the most ancient of all pastimes,
namely that of climbing trees and swinging from limb to limb.
The primitive grasping, calculating, and timing of the greater
arboreal apes he sees as a translation into financial terms of one   40
of the oldest movement patterns. Just as the hand among the
branches of the trees learned a pattern of grasping that was
quite removed from the moving of food to mouth, so the trader
and the financier have developed enthralling abstract activities
that are extensions of the avid climbing and mobility of the greater 45
apes.

Like any other medium, it is a staple, a natural resource. As an
outward and visible form of the urge to change and to exchange,
it is a corporate image, depending on society for its institutional
status. Apart from communal participation, money is meaningless,   50
as Robinson Crusoe discovered when he found the coins in the
wrecked ship.

Marshall McLuhan, *Understanding Media*, 1964

1. What is the meaning of the following words as used in the passage:
mediation (l. 4)   *avid* (ll. 9 and 45)   *staple/s* (ll. 18, 28, and 47)
mobility (l. 19)   *reflexive* (l. 21)   *environment* (l. 25)   *arboreal* (l. 40)
enthralling (l. 44)   *status* (l. 50)?

2. What is the difference between a *literate culture* (l. 7) and a nonliterate one?

3. How is the 'pack of cigarettes' in l. 13 acting as currency until the seal is broken? In what sense does it translate the skill of one worker into the skill of another at each transaction?

4. Substitute your own words for:
   a. the sentence (l. 24) that starts: *It gives the power of detachment* . . .
   b. the sentence (l. 30) that starts: *Trading by currency is based* . . .

5. In what way can trading be likened to swinging from limb to limb of a tree (l. 38)?

6. Show how the trader and financier have developed 'abstract activities' from commodity trading (l. 44).

7. How is money meaningless 'apart from communal participation' (l. 50)? How is it a 'corporate image' (l. 49)?

8. What is the essential difference between commodity money and modern money?

9. Make a précis of the passage in approximately 140 words (one-quarter) and supply a title.

10. In 200–250 words outline the differences in attitude towards money of the authors of passages 3, 4, and 5.

Passage 6

Psychologists are interested in the meaning of symbols, specifically as triggers of behaviour. In this context we may distinguish between two kinds of meaning, 'denotative' and 'connotative'. Denotative symbols refer to specific objects or directions, and the things that they symbolise can be 'pointed to'. The meaning of such a symbol   5
will be the same to all who comprehend it. Most symbols in practice, however, carry both denotative and connotative meaning. Connotative meanings are essentially subjective, often rather emotional, and they evaluate. Thus the symbol 'black-legging' does more than describe a certain kind of behaviour. It evaluates and condemns such   10
behaviour.

The American psychologist, Osgood, established three main dimensions of connotative meaning – an evaluative dimension (good – bad, clean – dirty), a strength dimension (strong – weak, large – small), and an activity dimension (fast – slow, active – passive), the evaluative dimension carrying most weight. A phrase like 'planned redundancy' will carry many connotations, which are likely to vary considerably with the organisational status of the person hearing the phrase.   15

Communication occurs in the context of a whole range of organisational behaviour. When we receive a message from someone, our understanding may be affected by his dress, his accent, and so forth. His role in the organisation may be equally important. The same words may be interpreted differently if they are uttered by the managing director on the one hand or a shop steward on the other, for the 'who' is an important non-verbal symbol in the message.   20 ... 25

When we examine a sample of industrial behaviour which involves communication, we are confronted with evidence of all kinds of organisational characteristics, such as power, authority, conflict, leadership, control. When an executive communicates an order to his subordinate, their relationship might be complicated by the subordinate's experience of the executive's indifferent leadership, or by his resentment of what he thinks is a petty-minded control system, or by his own inability to make a certain type of decision. This incapacity itself might be a product of the particular organisational structure of the firm. The American Lyman Bryson, having defined executives as 'all members of an organisation who have access to the chief executive for purposes of policy discussion', points to some of the structural problems to which we refer. Where there is a choice between different courses of action, all executives are likely to be quite heavily committed to a point of view. In most cases they will express their honest conviction, but they are equally likely to have something in mind beyond the intrinsic worth of these opinions. They will be concerned for example with their own prestige, and they will want to make sure that they will be allowed to help in further decisions. 'In policy discussions,' says Bryson, 'it is a man and not an opinion who wins. Every member of staff wants to be that man, or associated with him.'   30 ... 35 ... 40 ... 45

N. C. Bowker and M. F. Hall in *The Manager*, November 1963

1. Express in other words: *specifically as triggers of behaviour* (ll. 1–2).
2. Distinguish between *denotative* and *connotative* meanings (cf. *objective* and *subjective*, page 65).
3. To illustrate each of the three 'dimensions' of connotative meaning

supply two pairs of antonyms other than those used in the article (ll. 12–16).

4. What connotations would you expect *planned redundancy* to carry for (*a*) the works manager, (*b*) a shop steward, (*c*) a newly appointed machine operator?

5. Consider the sentence *When . . . so forth* (ll. 21–33). What further examples may be added in place of the words *and so forth*?

6. How satisfactory do you consider Lyman Bryson's definition of *executives* (ll. 37–38)?

7. What meaning did you assign to *cases* in line 41 when you read the passage? Can you now see a possible different meaning for this word in this context? Is the author's use of *cases* here justified?

8. Make a précis of the passage in not more than 150 words (one-third), and supply a title.

Passage 7

The importance of speech as an indicator of social class is not likely to be underestimated by anyone who has lived in England. Our reactions to speech are in any case fundamentally important, for certain sounds, certain words, certain rhythms carry for most of us a very deep change of feeling and memory. The feeling that we should speak as other members of our group speak is also very strong. Indeed it is in just this imitative desire and capacity that the possibility of language, with its vital communication of our humanity, is centred. At the same time, this imitative process is dynamic, for no living language is ever fixed. There are variations of speech habit within the simplest group, and the complication of experience and of contacts with other groups is constantly modifying the very thing that we are imitating. Since it is both a confirmation and a discovery of our changing experience of reality, language must change if it is to live. Yet within any human lifetime, and within any society, our attachment to known ways will remain significant, and our important sense of belonging, to a family, to a group, to a people, will be vitally interwoven with the making and hearing of certain sounds – the making and hearing being a very large part of our social sense.

There is then a necessary tension in language, between powerful impulses to imitation and to change. This tension is part of our basic processes of growth and learning. In the general history of language, we can see two quite opposite tendencies: an extraordinary evolution

of separate languages, and a remarkable growth, in certain con-   25
ditions, of common languages. Almost all modern European
languages, from Welsh and English to Italian and Russian, together
with such Asian languages as Hindustani and Persian, have developed
and separated, through history, from a common root. And still, in
simple societies, there is an almost incredible variation, within tiny   30
regions, so that villages six or eight miles apart can often hardly
understand one another, or on an island of 100 000 people there can
be as many as forty dialects, often mutually incomprehensible. As
a group develops its own way of life, which may extend over a few
miles or over half a continent, it will, as part of this development,   35
create its own forms of language. The very factor which gives the
group its social cohesion can become the factor cutting it off, to an
important extent, from similar groups elsewhere. But on the other
hand, and especially now as communities become larger and
develop greatly improved communication systems, certain languages   40
(of which English is notably one) expand and flourish, serving as a
common basis for many different groups. Even within these common languages, however, and alongside the powerful tendencies to
expanded community of speech, the processes of growth and variation will continue, in different ways in different groups speaking   45
the common tongue. The variations may be of a regional or of a
class kind, and the case of class speech is particularly important, for
here the tension between community and variations may be seen at
its most sensitive.

A class is a group within a geographical community, and not a   50
community in its own right. In certain extreme cases, a class will
so emphasise its distinction from the community of which it is a
part that it will in fact use a separate language: either one of the
various hieratic languages, such as Sanskrit, or, as in nineteenth-
century Russia, a foreign language, French, which is thought of as a   55
mark of cultural superiority. More usually, however, class speech
will be a form of the ordinary speech of the region, and the relations
between the class dialect and the ordinary speech of the region
(which will usually itself be further sub-regionally varied) form a
complex of great importance in the development of a language. In   60
the case of English, the sensitivity of this complex is very high: a
very large number of Englishmen have become tense and anxious
about the way in which they speak their own language. This problem has a deep bearing on the development of English society, but
it is still not very clearly understood. There is commonly a lack of   65

historical perspective, and there are also many prejudices, both theoretic and practical.

Raymond Williams, *The Long Revolution*, 1961

1. What is the meaning of the following words as used in the passage:
reactions (l. 3)   *dynamic* (l. 9)   *significant* (l. 16)
tension (l. 21 and l. 48)   *evolution* (l. 24)   *mutually* (l. 33)
hieratic (l. 54)?
2. What is the difference between the use of *complex* in ll. 60 and 61 and the use of it in line 13 of Passage 4?
3. What is meant by:
social cohesion (l. 37)   *expanded community of speech* (l. 44)
a mark of cultural superiority (l. 56)
further sub-regionally varied (l. 59)   *historical perspective* (l. 66)?
4. Do you agree with the first sentence of this passage? Give reasons for your answer.
5. Why must language *change if it is to live* (l. 15)?
6. The author refers in the compass of a few lines (ll. 24–30) to *extraordinary* evolution, *remarkable* growth, *almost incredible* variation. What does the passage gain by these adjectives?
7. What is the force of *notably* in the parenthesis *of which English is notably one* (l. 41)?
8. Is the author's use of *case* in line 47 justifiable? Are the further uses at line 51 and line 61 equally justifiable? What about the use in l. 3?
9. Distinguish *theoretic* from *practical* prejudices in English speech (l. 67). What examples of prejudices of either kind can you think of?
10. Make a précis of the passage in not more than 190 words (one-quarter), and supply a title.

Passage 8

This flood of paper which now threatens to submerge the world is something peculiar to this century. The Hellenistic scribes who wrote on papyrus, the Chinese bureaucrats who exercised their penmanship on silk, and even the eighteenth century clerks who inscribed their civilities on rag paper with a quill pen, were guiltless   5
of anything that could be called mass production. It is our own age that has developed the swiftness of communication, the abundance of paper, the multiplication of copies and the widespread semi-literacy which are the immediate causes of the paper flood. Ease of communication has also made practicable such a degree of   10

centralised control as was never known before. Until a century ago
every large-scale and scattered organisation or empire was engaged
in a ceaseless struggle to make its distant units conform with central
policy. For reference to headquarters there was neither the inclin-
ation nor the time. Those in positions of theoretical responsibility   15
read with helpless dismay of provinces annexed, officials sacked,
branches opened and ships sold, their bleating protests coming
perpetually too late. With the laying of transoceanic cables they felt
for the first time that they had their agents on the leash. From about
1875 began, therefore, that tightening of the chain that has finally   20
destroyed the effectiveness of (among other things) colonialism and
diplomacy. The professional bargaining of plenipotentiaries has
given place to the bickering of impotent office boys, each tied to the
apron-strings of a government which has never even heard the
persuasions of the other side. Diplomatically, administratively,   25
commercially, the process of centralisation has been carried to its
logical conclusion with all authority vested too often in a single
man; and he, from overwork, quite obviously off his head.

It was inevitable that the central administration would make full
use of the tools that had suddenly become available. After centuries   30
of frustration those in authority could at last impose their policy
upon the whole organisation, not merely from day to day but from
hour to hour. They could exact the fullest information, collate the
most detailed returns, draw up the most voluminous directives and
issue the most peremptory commands. Of these opportunities they   35
have made the fullest use. But for all this they have had to pay the
price. The penalty has been that correspondence pours on them in
the present flood. Surrounding themselves with executives, they
battle with a rising tide of paper. Ordinarily waist-deep in letters
and memoranda, a week's illness will bring the high-water mark   40
up to their chin. Rather than drown, the key man prefers to suppress
his symptoms and stay at his desk; often with the worst results for
all concerned.

C. Northcote Parkinson, In-laws and Outlaws, 1962

1. What is the connection between the references in the second sentence
of this passage to *papyrus, silk, rag paper, quill pen*, and the first sentence?
2. *a.* Reexpress 'inscribed their civilities' (l. 5) in simpler language.
   b. What loss does the passage suffer if your words are substituted
   for the author's?
3. *a.* In what way is 'semi-literacy' a cause of the 'paper flood' (ll. 6–9)?

    b. Is 'semi-literacy' here contrasted with literacy or with illiteracy?

    c. Is this normal usage?

4. *a.* Why are the positions of those who 'read with helpless dismay' (l. 16) described as 'of theoretical responsibility'?

    b. Why are their protests described as 'bleating'?

5. What is the essential antithesis between *plenipotentiaries* and *impotent office boys* (ll. 22, 23)?

6. While retaining the full meaning, reexpress the following so that none of the author's original words are used:

> They could exact the fullest information, collate the most detailed returns, draw up most voluminous directives and issue the most peremptory commands (ll. 33–35).

7. The syntax of the penultimate sentence of this passage is open to two criticisms. What are they?

8. Make a précis of the passage in not more than 150 words (one-third) taking particular care to avoid all figurative language, and supply a title.

Passage 9

Although we naturally regard a *word* as a very important linguistic unit, we should realise that scientifically it is not a fixed and definite division like the *morpheme*. A word is merely a conventional or arbitrary segment of utterance, a minimum free form, consisting of one or more morphemes. A morpheme is the smallest significant   5 or meaningful unit, and it may be either *bound* or *free*.

    Take, for instance, the word *home*. Clearly this is a minimum free form consisting of one and only one morpheme, since it cannot be broken down into smaller elements. If, however, I use this word in its plural form and say *homes*, I then employ two morphemes, the   10 free form *home* and the bound form *-s* (bound because it cannot be used independently or in isolation) which happens to be one of the marks of plural number in English and is called an *inflexion*. The word *homely* also comprises two morphemes, the free *home* and the bound form *-ly*, which here serves as an adjective-forming suffix.   15 So, too, the word *homeward* likewise consists of two morphemes, the free form *home* and the bound form *-ward*, which obviously has nothing to do with its homonym *ward* meaning 'guard, custody', but which here serves as an adverb-forming suffix. The words *homestead* and *homework* also contain two morphemes each, but   20 both are free.

    The inflected form *homes*, the derivatives *homely* and *homeward*,

and the compounds *homestead* and *homework* exemplify the morpho-
logical processes known as *inflexion* (or simply *flexion*), *derivation*
(or *affixation*), and *composition* (or *compounding*) respectively.   25
Home is a simple word, *homely* and *homeward* are complex words,
whereas *homestead* and *homework* are compound words.

Since *home* is a simple word of one morpheme, it may be said to
contain only one *root* or radical element. This is true of thousands
of words like *man, wife, boy, son, house, room, roof, door, tree, ash,*   30
oak, beech, elm, flower, hedge, field, and *moor.* Of some words, like
barn and *nest,* it is true *synchronically* (descriptively for the language
as it now is) but not true *diachronically* (or historically). If we go
back far enough, we find that *barn* comes from two words meaning
'barley hall' and *nest* from two words meaning 'nether sit, place   35
where a bird sits down'. *Barn* and *nest* may therefore be described
as *obscured* or *latent* compounds.

Simeon Potter, *Language in the Modern World*, 1960

1. Express in other words 'a conventional or arbitrary segment of
utterance' (ll. 3–4).
2. Answer the following questions without using the words of the
passage:
   a. What is a *morpheme*?
   b. What is a *bound* morpheme?
3. What is *an adverb-forming suffix*?
4. What is the difference between *derivation* and *composition*?
5. What is the difference between a *morpheme* and a *root*?
6. What is the difference between something being true *synchronically*
and its being true *diachronically*?
7. *a.* What is the meaning of *latent*?
   b. Show that *nest* is correctly described as a *latent compound*.
8. Comment on the author's use of italics in this passage.
9. Supply a title for the passage.

Passage 10

In order that speech might be evolved, the nervous system had to
become capable of the complicated arrangements which underlie
its anatomy and physiology, though, of course, speech could have
developed only in a creature which possessed a suitable anatomical
structure in the mouth, lips, tongue, palate and larynx. The chim-   5
panzee certainly possesses the necessary organs of articulation. Its

inability to speak must therefore be due to lack of the appropriate
neural organisation.

One of the most puzzling questions in the neurology of speech is
the connexion between speech and handedness. Why is it that the   10
majority of people are right-handed, and in almost all of those the
nervous activities underlying speech are localized in the left
cerebral hemisphere? And which came first, speech or handedness?
We speak of the left cerebral hemisphere in right-handed people
as the dominant hemisphere, but is it dominant because it houses   15
the speech centres, and do people become right-handed because it is
the dominant hemisphere, or is it dominant because they are right-
handed and is that why the speech centres are localised in it?
Incidentally the opposite is not always true, for, although it had
generally been believed that in left-handed people the speech   20
centres are situated in the right cerebral hemisphere, recent work
suggests that in at least some left-handed people speech may be
represented in both hemispheres.

These questions are by no means easy to answer. One thing
which is clear, however, is that the acquisition of speech was not   25
the cause of handedness, for many animals, including chimpanzees,
exhibit a preference for one hand or the other, and it is said that
among chimpanzees right-handers and left-handers are almost
equally distributed. There are obvious advantages in the location
of the neurological arrangements underlying speech in one cerebral   30
hemisphere rather than in both, since it would seem that co-
ordination and control can best be exercised from one centre, and it
is perhaps natural that if the speech centres are to be localised in
one cerebral hemisphere, it should be the dominant hemisphere in
relation to handedness, for in a right-handed individual the right   35
hand would be used for gesticulation, for the manipulation of
objects and for the exercise of skills, all activities which become
closely linked with speech. So it would seem that handedness came
first, and determined the dominant hemisphere with which speech
became associated, and we are left with the question, why in the   40
majority of human beings, the left cerebral hemisphere should be the
dominant one? There seems no doubt that cerebral dominance is in-
herited, and we can only conclude that some evolutionary advantage
has tended to favour right-handed people as opposed to left-handed,
or at least to bring about a state of affairs in which right-handedness 45
is dominant in the Mendelian as well as in the cerebral sense.

Failure to develop a dominant hemisphere is often linked with disorder of speech. Stuttering has some association with left-handedness in the patient or his family, and may be precipitated by compelling a naturally left-handed person to write with the right 50 hand. And certain types of backwardness in speech, reading, writing, and spelling may be associated with lack of hemisphere dominance. If it is of clinical importance to know which is the dominant hemisphere this can now be discovered by observing the effect upon speech of injecting a barbiturate into either internal carotid artery. 55 On the side on which the speech centres are situated it produces temporary aphasia.

Sir Russell Brain,
Some Reflections on Genius and other Essays, 1960

1. What is meant by the following expressions as used in the passage:
   its anatomy and physiology (l. 3)
   lack of the appropriate neural organisation (l. 7)
   handedness (passim)
   dominant in the Mendelian as well as in the cerebral sense (l. 46)
   of clinical importance (l. 53)?
2. If *carotid* (l. 55) and *aphasia* (l. 57) are new words to you, deduce their meaning from their contexts.
3. What answer does the author give to the question he asks in ll. 10–13?
4. Is it always true (*a*) that speech is located exclusively in the left cerebral hemisphere for right-handed people? (*b*) that speech is located exclusively in the right cerebral hemisphere for left-handed people?
5. *a.* Why is it advantageous to have the neurological arrangement underlying speech in one cerebral hemisphere only?
   b. Why is it natural that this should be the hemisphere dominant in relation to handedness?
6. Arrange in logical order the sequence of arguments that would show why it is that the majority of people have the neurological arrangement underlying speech in the left cerebral hemisphere.
7. Make a précis of the passage in approximately 150 words (one-quarter), and supply a title.

Passage 11

What is the present state of explicit conceptual knowledge about administration in general? There is no general theory, and a great paucity of concepts and hypotheses about managerial processes. The meaning of many of the words which we use in discussing our

problems has no established or widely accepted content. No words   5
exist at all for many ideas and situations which occur daily in the
lives of managers. Such ideas can only be discussed in terms of
lengthy and often inconsistent description. Many of the words which
are used with great frequency, such as 'manager', 'supervisor',
'specialist', 'policy', 'subordinate', 'authority', have no generally   10
accepted and precise meaning. How then can we use them in discussing industrial problems? In fact, we spend most of our time
arguing about the meaning of the words we are using, instead of
discussing the problems themselves. In the absence of a language,
such as, for instance, the physicist has had to evolve, it is extremely   15
difficult to start substituting intuition by explicit knowledge.

The universities realise the need to equip graduates with as
much knowledge as possible about management. They have been
under pressure from various quarters in industry, and from the
British Institute of Management, to set up Chairs of Administration.   20
There is, however, *no body of knowledge* available of the appropriate
level of abstraction on which a degree course could be founded.
There are as yet no 'laws of management'. The first concern of a
university department of management would be with research in
order that the required body of knowledge could then be estab-   25
lished.

Here again, however, difficulty arises. University departments
can function only in so far as they produce concepts having an
integral connection with the real industrial situation. This would
seem to involve much deeper relations with industry than at   30
present exist where administration is concerned. Is there as yet any
real acceptance in the universities of the need for deep and pro-
longed study of this subject by the best brains available? Moreover,
when concepts emerge they will have to be tested in industrial
situations. If the engineering department of a university produces   35
new ideas on, say, some aspect of production technology and wish
to have these ideas tested by a particular company, they then would
need to make contact with that company's production engineers who
are responsible for advising its management on production techniques and for implementing changes. But in the field which I am   40
discussing, no such specialist branch yet exists. Great difficulty
would arise, therefore, in getting new notions tested.

A theory of industrial administration cannot be developed in
isolation within the laboratories of a university. Unlike the physical
sciences, it is not possible to import samples of the 'materials'   45

which interact in social processes or to build models of the processes which require analysis. These things exist only in the work
setting; their transplantation to a laboratory disrupts their reality.
Picture what would happen if universities and other bodies were to
turn seriously to research in this field and industrial companies were   50
to set up groups of specialists responsible for implementing the
results. Interchange of ideas about principles and concepts between
research workers and industrial specialists would lead to the emergence of ideas that were of general validity for industry as a whole.
It would gradually become possible to teach administration. A   55
manager's task would be greatly helped by the existence of accepted
laws of administration, for his field of choice in making almost daily
decisions would be narrowed by his knowledge of principles. The
engineer who knows his fundamentals can, by reference to them,
reject many choices which an untrained man, dependent on his   60
intuition alone, might accept – to his own and his company's later
discomfiture.

Wilfred Brown, *Exploration in Management*, 1960

1. What do you consider to be the exact meaning of the following
expressions:
explicit conceptual knowledge (l. 1)
a great paucity of concepts and hypotheses (l. 3)
no established or widely accepted content (l. 5)
the appropriate level of abstraction (ll. 21–22)
an integral connection with the real industrial situation (l. 29)?
2. What do you consider to be the meaning of *manager; supervisor;
specialist; policy; subordinate; authority?* What different meanings can
you see others might give to these words?
3. Distinguish between *intuition* and *explicit knowledge* (l. 16). Why
is exact language an essential for the latter?
4. Why, according to the author, is it not yet possible to found a degree
course in Administration? Do not use the expression *body of knowledge*
in your answer.
5. Why would a university department of administration find it difficult
to have new notions tested out in firms?
6. Why is it impossible to devise laboratories within a university where
theories of industrial administration could be developed?
7. From the point of view of the author of this article (*a*) what is the
most important similarity between the tasks of engineer and manager in
Industry (*b*) what is the most important difference?

8. Can you give any examples of ideas or situations which are part of
the lives of managers but for which no words exist (ll. 5–7)?
9. Make a précis of the passage in not more than 160 words (one-quarter),
and supply a title.

Passage 12

For the great body of the people in any modern community, the
proximate ground of expenditure in excess of what is required for
physical comfort is not a conscious effort to excel in the expensive-
ness of their visible consumption, so much as it is a desire to live
up to the conventional standard of decency in the amount and grade   5
of goods consumed. This desire is not guided by a rigidly invariable
standard, which must be lived up to, and beyond which there is no
incentive to go. The standard is flexible; and especially it is indefinitely extensible, if only time is allowed for habituation to any
increase in pecuniary ability and for acquiring facility in the new and   10
larger scale of expenditure that follows such an increase. It is much
more difficult to recede from a scale of expenditure once adopted
than it is to extend the accustomed scale in response to an accession
of wealth. Many items of customary expenditure prove on analysis
to be almost purely wasteful, and they are therefore honorific only,   15
but after they have once been incorporated into the scale of decent
consumption, and so have become an integral part of one's scheme
of life, it is quite as hard to give up these as it is to give up many
items that conduce directly to one's physical comfort, or even that
may be necessary to life and health. That is to say, the conspic-   20
uously wasteful honorific expenditure that confers spiritual well-
being may become more indispensable than much of that expenditure which ministers to the 'lower' wants of physical well-being or
sustenance only. It is notoriously just as difficult to recede from a
'high' standard of living as it is to lower a standard which is already   25
relatively low; although in the former case the difficulty is a moral
one, while in the latter it may involve a material deduction from the
physical comforts of life.

But while retrogression is difficult, a fresh advance in conspicuous
expenditure is relatively easy; indeed, it takes place almost as a   30
matter of course. In the rare cases where it occurs, a failure to
increase one's visible consumption when the means for an increase
are at hand is felt in popular apprehensions to call for explanation,
and unworthy motives of miserliness are imputed to those who fall

short in this respect. A prompt response to the stimulus, on the   35
other hand, is accepted as the normal effect. This suggests that the
standard of expenditure which commonly guides our efforts is not
the average, ordinary expenditure already achieved; it is an ideal of
consumption that lies just beyond our reach, or to reach which
requires some strain. The motive is emulation – the stimulus of an   40
invidious comparison which prompts us to outdo those with whom
we are in the habit of classing ourselves. Substantially the same
proposition is expressed in the commonplace remark that each class
envies and emulates the class next above it in the social scale, while
it rarely compares itself with those below or with those who are   45
considerably in advance. That is to say, in other words, our standard of decency in expenditure, as in other ends of emulation, is set
by the usage of those next above us in reputability; until, in this
way, especially in any community where class distinctions are
somewhat vague, all canons of reputability and decency, and all   50
standards of consumption, are traced back by insensible gradations
to the usages and habits of thought of the highest social and pecuniary class – the wealthy leisure class.

Thorstein Veblen, *The Theory of the Leisure Class*, 1925

1. What is the meaning, in the passage, of the following words:
    incentive (l. 8)   *extensible* (l. 9)   *honorific* (l. 15)
    conduce (l. 19)   *retrogression* (l. 29)   *imputed* (l. 34)
    emulation (l. 47)   *canons* (l. 50)?
2. Reexpress the following in simpler language:
    proximate ground of expenditure (l. 2)
    the conventional standard of decency (l. 5)
    habituation to any increase in pecuniary ability (ll. 9–10)
    the stimulus of an invidious comparison (ll. 40–41)
    the usage of those next above us in reputability (l. 48)
    insensible gradations (l. 51)
3. What colloquial expression, current after the time of Veblen's book,
puts the attitude towards consumption expressed in his opening sentence
into five words?
4. *a.* In what sense is it a moral difficulty that is experienced in attempt-
    ing to reduce a 'high' standard of living?
  b. Why is *high* in this context placed between inverted commas by
    Veblen?
5. *a.* How does Veblen suggest people expect us to respond to an
    increase in wealth?

    b. What motives are imputed to us if we fail to respond in the expected manner?

6. *a.* What standard of expenditure does Veblen suggest we all aim at?

    b. What do we hope to achieve by this?

7. Why should we feel envy of the 'social and pecuniary' class immediately above our own but not of one 'considerably in advance'?

8. On what grounds does Veblen assert that 'all canons of reputability' and 'decency' are ultimately determined by 'the wealthy leisure class'?

9. Make a précis of the passage in not more than 150 words (one-quarter), and supply a title.

Punctuation

Punctuation is often blamed by bad communicators for their bad communication. It seems that people are not ashamed to admit they cannot punctuate, but are ashamed to admit they cannot construct a sentence or use words clearly.

Faulty punctuation always slows up reading, and may lead to misinterpretation of meaning. Sound punctuation helps the Rx to grasp the structure and logic of a sentence quickly. But punctuation cannot compensate for misuse of words or faulty sentence structure.

The notes that follow are not intended to be comprehensive. All that is attempted is (1) to list the most common applications of our punctuation marks, with examples, and (2) to draw attention to a few applications where there is widespread uncertainty or difference of opinion.

A. Full stops

The full stop marks the end of a sentence. One of the most widespread misuses of punctuation in business writing is to substitute a comma:

NOT *These units may be installed with the minimum of trouble and expense, they are silent and odourless in operation.*

This is clearly two sentences and there must be a full stop after *expense,* or a conjunction to join the sentences.

The opposite fault is to open with a capital letter, and close with a full stop, a unit of language which is not a sentence:

NOT *Their easy-clean finish and attractive design are outstanding features. Harmonise with modern kitchen surroundings.*

Although there is a finite verb in the second part of this, there is no subject and it cannot stand as an independent sentence. A very common version of this error is to start a letter:

NOT *With reference to your order of 10th May.*

In literary writing there has been much experimentation over the last half century with fragmented sentences in which either the subject or the finite verb has been omitted; but where such 'sentences' occur in business writing other than advertising it is the result of carelessness or ignorance, not experimentation.

B. Commas

Commas are essentially separators. (*Comma* is derived from a Greek word that means 'that which is cut off'.)

1. Single commas separate words, phrases, or clauses, in series:

a. In this shop he bought newspapers, magazines, cigarettes, and matches.

b. He ran down the stairs, along the corridor, through the doorway, and down the road.

c. He dug the garden, planted some seedlings, and then went for a drink.

Many writers systematically omit the comma before the *and* that links on the last item of a series. This is a matter about which the student must make up his own mind and then be consistent. The argument in favour of retaining this comma is that it allows the writer to differentiate between two items joined by *and* simply because they are the last two of a series (*cigarettes, and matches*) and two items joined by *and* because they are thought of as belonging together (*fish and chips*).

As commas are separators we expect to find one comma fewer than there are items to separate:

d. You will find this a clean, silent, and odourless appliance.

NOTE No comma after *odourless*.

Where only two adjectives precede the noun, no comma is used, except where there is some disparity between the two adjectives. Thus *his short satisfactory reply* but *his immediate, inadequate reply*. It will be found that where the sense can be improved by inserting an *and* between the two adjectives, a similar effect is produced by inserting a comma.

The commas separating more than two adjectives preceding a noun are nowadays usually omitted also, unless it is felt that the adjectives build up in importance (as in example *d.* above).

e. Tomkinsons, Allpress Ltd, and Bowlings have submitted their tenders.

NOTE: Some writers would put a comma after *Bowlings*. This seems undesirable by the argument of 'one comma fewer', and it also introduces a comma between subject and verb.

Since some writers would not use the comma after *Allpress Ltd* (because in front of *and*), there are four 'correct' punctuations possible, for this short sentence; nevertheless the punctuation above is strongly recommended.

2. An introductory word or phrase is nowadays marked off from the main body of the sentence only where failure to do so would produce initial doubt how to read the sentence:

   a. However we look at this matter we can see no excuse for him.

   b. However, we look at this matter in a rather different light.

   c. In spite of this improvement we are unable to increase the dividend.

   d. In spite of this, improvement has been steady throughout the year.

NOTE: The modern tendency is towards reduction of commas and those marking off brief introductory matter are rapidly disappearing. Until quite recently it would have been considered obligatory to place commas after *matter* in *a.* above and *improvement* in *c.*

3. Two commas are used to mark off:

   a. words in apposition

   b. the person/s addressed

   c. a parenthesis

   d. a participial phrase

   e. the non-defining relative clause.

NOTE: Where the item to be marked off starts the sentence, only one comma is needed (at the end of the item) and similarly where it ends the sentence (one comma at the start of the item).

EXAMPLES:

Of *a. Our regional manager, Mr J. F. Jones, will deal with this matter.*

Of *b. It is our opinion, gentlemen, that these figures compare favourably with any that could be supplied by any other company in the kingdom.*

Of *c. These units, silent and odourless in operation, offer the minimum inconvenience in the kitchen.*

Of *d. Referring to your letter, I find you quote the 1970 figures.*

Of *e. Commas, which are frequently omitted, are probably the most useful punctuation marks.*

BUT NOTE: *Commas which are frequently omitted are those indicating a parenthesis.* Here *which are frequently omitted* is a defining relative clause – it defines which type of comma is referred to – and therefore must not be enclosed between commas. On the other hand, omission of the commas round *which are frequently omitted* in example *e.* would make nonsense of the sentence – the most useful punctuation marks would seem to be omitted commas.

It will be observed that it is a characteristic of material enclosed between a pair of commas that it can be omitted without complete loss of sense.

C. Semicolons

The semicolon is a heavier stop than a comma but less heavy than a full stop. In certain circumstances it can be used as a superior substitute for either.

1. Where two or more sentences are felt to be more closely connected in meaning than others in the paragraph, this connection can be indicated by linking the sentences together by means of semicolons:

> *The situation since he has taken over the area can hardly be described as satisfactory; sales have dropped by nearly half, and complaints about service have trebled.*

Of course, such sentences can be linked by other devices, such as conjunctions. There is, however, a crispness about this sentence that would be lost if, for example, the conjunction *for* were substituted for the semicolon. On other occasions the semicolon is too dramatic, too staccato, for the effect required.

2. Since semicolons are to some extent alternatives to conjunctions, it might be thought that the two would never be used together. This is true of the subordinating conjunctions (*because, as, since, if* etc.) but a semicolon can be used immediately before the coordinating conjunctions (*and, but, or, yet* etc.) where the effect of the more usual comma at that point would be reduced because the sentence already includes several commas.

3. To separate phrases or clauses in series, semicolons may be preferred to commas where the phrases or clauses are rather long and include commas of their own. However, the type of long literary sentence for which such punctuation is necessary is inappropriate to business communication.

Items in a list, especially if these include their own commas, are often more clearly separated by semicolons than by commas (see also first example under *Colons* below).

D. Colons

In business writing the colon can be said to have only one function – 'that of delivering the goods that have been invoiced in the preceding words' (Fowler).

In other words, it separates a clause introducing a list, quotation, or summary, from that which it introduces.

> *a. Accessories available through your local distributor include: wing*

> *mirrors; seat belts; roof racks; auxiliary lamps; anti-mist panels; hand tools; exhaust trims.*

> *b. This then is the present position: he has caused a reduction in sales, alienated several old customers, and substantially damaged the firm's reputation for rapid and efficient servicing.*

NOTE in *a.* above an alternative punctuation would be no colon after *include*, and commas to separate items. The decision which to use is based upon the length and complexity of the list. Where a list is punctuated with semicolons it is usual not to add an *and* before the last item.

Where the material that follows starts on a fresh line the introductory colon is replaced by some writers (and most typists) by colon-and-dash (: –) This is quite unnecessary.

E. Dashes

1. The habit of allowing dashes to usurp the roles of the four punctuation points already dealt with has nothing to commend it; but this is not to say that dashes have no functions of their own in punctuation.

2. Their most valuable use is as a pair to mark a parenthesis where commas would be inadequate either because there are other commas present that disguise the bracketing effect required, or because the material in parenthesis is rather abruptly inserted into the sentence (or both):

> *The rubber-insulated sub-frames, front and rear, serve to reduce road noise and in conjunction with other sound-insulating devices – the use of emulsion felt, for example – help to combat driving fatigue on long runs.*

3. Single dashes may be used:

> *a.* to gather together the various elements of a compound subject, or list of items or series of clauses, preceding it:

> *The suspension, the steering, the transmission, the method of mounting the engine – all these incorporate new design principles.*

> *b.* to attach a comment or afterthought to a sentence:

> *They are prepared to offer £5 000 – more than I had expected.*

> *c.* to indicate a surprising ending to the sentence, for the purposes of 'pointing' humour or drama.

> *They are prepared to offer £5 000 – in cash.*

This last application (*c.*) should be very sparingly employed. Since it signals so clearly to the Rx, 'This is going to be a shock or a joke', the expectation aroused has to be fully satisfied or the Rx feels frustrated.

F. Brackets

Where heavier insulation of a parenthesis is required than even dashes provide, brackets are used. References and glosses (or other types of brief explanation or expansion) are the most usual material thus marked off. The previous sentence provides an example of this use of brackets, and many others will be found in this appendix.

Such bracketed material is inserted into the sentence without alteration of the punctuation that would have been correct before its insertion. Occasionally a complete sentence is inserted in brackets at the end of a complete sentence. In such a case the preceding sentence takes its full stop and the material in brackets has its own capital letter and full stop. The first sentences of Section B of this appendix provide an example.

G. Question marks

Question marks are added to every direct question. This ruling includes commands couched in the form of a question:

Will you send me a copy of your current price list?

They must not be used after indirect questions:

NOT *He asked me why our tender was late?*
Direct questions use the actual questioning words, not a reported form of them.

H. Exclamation marks

Since these should be reserved for genuine interjections and exclamations it is unlikely they will be employed in any form of business communication except advertising (where, in some of its manifestations, *Hurrah! Wham! New!* etc. are only too plentiful).

I. Apostrophes

1. Apostrophes are used to indicate missing letters as in *one o'clock*, for *one of the clock*, and the colloquial *can't, they're* etc.

2. To show that nouns are possessive, we have a choice between *of* and *'s*. There is a marked tendency to prefer the *of* form for the inanimate nouns and *'s* for the animate. Thus although *the river's bank* is sometimes written, *the bank of the river* sounds more natural; *the hat of John* is only theoretically possible – *John's hat* is what we really say. The *'s* should be used only to show possession; it is an unexpectedly common practice to place an apostrophe either before or after the 's' that ends most plural nouns, whether possessive or not.

The rule is that possession may be shown by adding *'s* – except with plural nouns ending in 's', when only the apostrophe is added.

Thus *one boy's cap*, but *ten boys' caps* and NOTE *ten children's caps*.

Singular nouns ending in 's' normally take the full *'s* ending. The most usual examples are personal names:

Keats's poems   *Delius's music*   *St James's Park*

Appendix II

Direct and reported speech

A. When we wish to record what people have said (or reproduce what they once wrote) we can either quote their actual words (direct speech) or employ our own words to give the gist of what they said (indirect or 'reported' speech).

B. Direct quotation is normally indicated by enclosing the quoted words between single or double inverted commas (which, is a matter of taste). Quotations within a quotation are indicated by the use of single inverted commas where double are the standard choice, or vice versa. Only the actual words of the speaker may be enclosed between inverted commas, never an indirect version.

In factual material of the kind dealt with in this book the words that indicate who is the speaker invariably precede the words spoken, and are linked to them by a comma:

> *Immediately after the breakdown Tomkins said, 'I am to blame. I have not been carrying out the monthly maintenance.'*

A colon may replace this comma for quotations from written material or when the introduction is more elaborate than a plain verb of saying.

Writers of fiction, who make extensive use of direct speech, introduce variety by such devices as indicating the speaker at the end of what is said or in the middle. During the last half century an increasing number of novelists have experimented with such devices as omitting the inverted commas, usually (but not always) using italic type to mark out the words purporting to be quoted, or omitting the linking comma. Such variants are not recommended for business use.

When it is necessary to record a number of short verbatim statements by various speakers, or a discussion, it is convenient to use the playwright's method – the name of the speaker (usually in capitals) followed by a colon directly introducing what is said with no inverted commas:

TOMKINS: *I am to blame etc.*

C. The following are the principal ways in which a reported speech version differs from the words originally spoken.

1. First and second person pronouns are replaced by third person equivalents.

2. If the leading verb (i.e the verb of saying introducing the reported speech) is past tense, all finite verbs change as follows:

> Present becomes past (*he is* becomes *he was*)
> Past becomes pluperfect (*he was* becomes *he had been*)
> Future becomes secondary future – equivalent in form to the conditional (*he will* becomes *he would*)

3*a*. Adjectives and adverbs of place become more rem.te in place (*here* becomes *there*)

  b. Adjectives and adverbs of time become more remote in time (*now* becomes *then*).

The following sentence illustrates these differences:

Direct speech: *The speaker said, 'Ladies and gentlemen, I^1 am^2 very happy to be here^{3a} today^{3b}*
Reported speech: *The speaker said he^1 was^2 very happy to be there^{2a} that day.^{3b}*

NOTES

1. Expressions such as *Ladies and gentlemen* which are characteristic of direct speech and make no contribution to meaning are ignored.

2. Some writers add a *that* after the leading verb – this sometimes aids clarity, but often serves no purpose.

3. It is often preferable to substitute a more specific word for the general one called for by the 'rules'. Thus a person's name may be substituted for *he*, a place name for *there*, a date for *that day*.

4. When the leading verb is in the present tense, the verbs of reported speech retain the tenses of the original.

Since a report of what has been said (or written) always follows the saying or writing, it might be expected that all reference to what was said would be past tense, but in fact leading verbs in the present tense are not uncommon:

> *Have you heard? Tomkins says he is to blame.*
> *The Prime Minister says there is no cause for alarm.*
> *Shakespeare tells us that it is Time's glory to stamp the seal of time on aged things.* (Samuel Butler)

It would seem that we feel justified in using the present tense where the original Tx has said something and *continues to 'say'* it. Thus Tomkins and the Prime Minister have not changed their stories – as far as we know, if asked they would say the same thing again. As for Shakespeare – every time his works are read he speaks again. This justification of the present tense can always be made for written material. Spoken material – except of the kind represented by the statements of Tomkins and the Prime Minister above – does seem to belong more clearly to the past, and is best introduced by a past tense leading verb.

5. First person pronouns are retained in reported speech when the person making the report is either the original Tx or the original Rx.

Thus one of the speaker's audience may report:

The speaker told us he was very happy to be there that day.

Tomkins, reporting his own outburst, at the inquiry might say:

I said I was to blame. I had not been carrying out the monthly maintenance.

D. Although reported speech is usually preferred to direct speech for reports (presumably because of its freedom from inverted commas) it has two disadvantages which should be borne in mind when deciding which to use.

1. Reported speech with its pile-up of third person pronouns tends to ambiguity, necessitating clumsy repetitions if the sentence is to be clear:

The sales manager reminded the area representative that he (the representative) had suggested an autumn selling campaign and the sales manager had expressed doubts as to its advisability.

2. Word-for-word transcriptions of direct speech into reported speech often sound rather unnatural; but freer versions introduce an element of distortion.

Thus a straightforward reported speech version of Tomkins's statement would be:

Immediately after the breakdown Tomkins said he was to blame and that he had not been carrying out the monthly maintenance.

A more polished version would be:

Immediately after the breakdown Tomkins admitted responsibility, revealing that he had not been carrying out the monthly maintenance.

If this version is now compared with the direct speech version on page 261 it will be seen to be subtly more damaging to Tomkins. Slight distortions and shifts of emphasis are very likely in reported speech as additional stages of decoding and coding are inserted into the communication process:

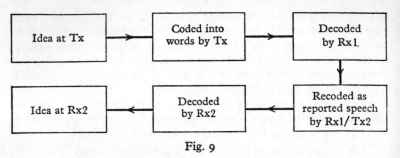

Fig. 9

Where circumstances demand extremely accurate reporting of what a man said (if his words are to be used as evidence, for example) only direct speech is satisfactory. With written material too, verbatim quotation is often the only fair representation of the original writer's meaning.

Postal Coding

The Post Office has been gradually introducing a system of *postcodes* (public postal address codes) that will eventually cover all, or almost all, of the country. The postcode is a condensed form of the address information needed for sorting a letter at each stage of its journey to the postman who is going to deliver it. By encoding the information it is possible to convert it into a pattern of dots that can be 'read' by sorting machines.

The postcode is in two halves. The first (or 'outward') half consists of letters (or a single letter) followed by a number. The letters identify the 'post town'; the number may indicate a smaller town within the area of the post town, or a district of the post town. The second (or 'inward') half of the postcode consists of a figure from 0 to 9 followed by two letters. This may identify a street, part of a street, even an individual address if it is one where more than twenty letters are normally received by the first delivery.

In the example CF6 2PR, *CF6* is the outward half, *2PR* the inward half. *CF* identifies the post town (Cardiff), *6* a small town (Barry), *2PR* a specific very small area of Barry, where the letter is to be delivered.

For efficient working of automatic sorting, and to avoid delay in delivery of letters, it is necessary to show postcodes as part of the address on envelopes. To ensure that letters sent to them are correctly postcoded, firms and local and central government departments have to incorporate their postcodes into their letter headings. Similarly people writing from private addresses have to remember to include their postcodes with their addresses. It is also necessary to include the postcode with the inside address of a business letter.

For all these applications the following rules, based on Post Office suggestions, should be observed:

1. Make the postcode the last item of the address. Preferably it should be on a separate line; if it has to share a line with other information it should be separated from this by at least the width of two characters in handwriting or two spaces on a typewriter.
2. If you consider that placing the postcode on a line by itself will make the address take up too much space, put the county on the same line as the post town.

3. Separate the two halves of the postcode by a space the width of one character in handwriting or one space on a typewriter.
4. In handwriting, use block capitals for the letters of the postcode. On a typewriter use upper case.
5. Do not join the characters of the postcode in any way.
6. Do not use full stops or other punctuation marks with the postcode.
7. Do not underline the postcode.

Appendix IV

Metrication Guide

	Unit	Symbol	Comment
1. LENGTH	metre	m	
	millimetre	mm	0·001 m
	kilometre	km	1 000 m
2. AREA	square metre	m² or sq m	
	hectare	ha	100 m × 100 m
3. VOLUME	cubic metre	m³ or cu m	
	cubic millimetre	mm³	
4. CAPACITY	litre	l	
5. WEIGHT	gramme	g	
	kilogramme	kg	
	tonne	t	
6. TIME	second	s	
7. VELOCITY	metre per second	m/s	
8. TEMPERATURE	degree Celsius	⁰C	approved name for 'Centigrade'
9. ELECTRICITY			
(current)	ampere	A	
(potential)	volt	V	
10. POWER	watt	W	
	kilowatt	kW	
11. PREFIXES	mega	M	1 000 000
	kilo	k	1 000
	hecto	h	100
	deca	da	10
	deci	d	0·1
	centi	c	0·01
	milli	m	0·001
	micro	μ	0·000 000 1

NOTES

1. Do not put a full stop after a symbol (except to mark the end of a sentence).

2. The same symbol is used for both singular and plural.

3. The type case of the symbol (i.e. capital letter or not) must be as above – particularly important in distinguishing *mega* (M) from *milli* (m).

4. Do not hyphenate units based on a prefix (NOT *milli-metre*).

5. Do not use a comma to mark off thousands. A space is preferred.

6. Always use o before the decimal point when the quantity is less than one.

7. Whole numbers should be given without a following decimal point.

8. Do not mix units (20·75 *kg* NOT 20 *kg* 75 *g*).

9. Always write the unit in full if there is the slightest chance that use of the symbol will cause misunderstanding.